DISCARD

Shelley in America in the Nineteenth Century

His Relation to American Critical
Thought and His Influence

BY JULIA POWER

GORDIAN PRESS
New York
1969

Originally Published 1940
Reprinted 1969

Library of Congress Catalog Card Number: 70-90370

To the Memory
of
My Mother
and
My Father

PREFACE

The subject, *Shelley in America in the Nineteenth Century*, is of necessity a survey subject. Although it has been limited to *His Relation to American Critical Thought and His Influence*, the field covered is still very extensive. Since Shelley was not generally known before the publication of his complete works, 1839–1840, every mention of him previous to that time becomes important and should be made use of in determining his position in the critical thought of the time. Because of the diversity of ideas in the different sections in America in the first half of the century, it has been necessary to consider Shelley's position in each of these sections. In the third quarter of the century such literary activity as existed centered in the Middle Atlantic Section, and in the last quarter both literature and criticism became national. During the latter half of the century, therefore, no division has been made as to place. I have chosen to give to the years connecting the Romantic and the Realistic Periods the title of the Transition Period.

The extent to which research work on this subject could be carried on is without limits. The amount of material has far exceeded what I had hoped to find. I had already written a doctorate dissertation on Shelley criticism in England in the nineteenth century, only to find that the subject had been used by Willis Pratt of Cornell University. Although I believe that I have secured most of the material on the subject, I am sure that there are many items of interest which will come to light later. I was not able to obtain copies of a few periodicals that should contain some mention of Shelley. And it was not possible to go through the files of notes and correspondence of many of the people I have mentioned who may have manifested further interest in the poet. I feel justified, however, in publishing this work at this time because I believe that it will open for discussion many questions which either have not been considered or have lain dormant for years.

I have attempted to give quotations from periodicals and books in their original form, without changing the punctuation or spelling, and without apology except when necessary.

The research work for this discussion was done in the libraries of the Universities of Nebraska, Minnesota, and Chicago; the Newberry Library, Chicago; the Congressional Library; the public libraries of Boston and New York. To the librarians in all these institutions, I express my appreciation for courtesies extended.

I should like to take this opportunity to acknowledge my indebtedness to Dr. Louise Pound for encouraging me to proceed with my doctorate in English and for her criticism of this work. I should also like to express my apprection to the other members of the English faculty of the University of Nebraska, especially to Dr. H. A. White for his kindly interest, and to Dr. F. W. Upson, formerly Dean of the Graduate School, for his encouragement and help.

University of Nebraska

Julia Power

CONTENTS

SHELLEY IN AMERICA IN THE NINETEENTH CENTURY

INTRODUCTION

PERCY BYSSHE SHELLEY is so closely associated with America that it would seem as though his wandering spirit, "mingling with the elements" for almost a century, had at last found a haven in a land where he is appreciated not by "the few" but by the many. Time, to which he was willing to consign his fate, has removed all barriers to recognition of the poet and acceptance of the man. He has taken his place as a poet of all time. The number and the quality of the articles and treatises on Shelley in the America of the twentieth century bear ample testimony to the place he holds in the hearts of American critics and lovers of literature.

Shelley was born on August 4, 1702, a day of importance in the national affairs of France, marked by the exodus of large numbers of nobles and by the decree of the National Assembly that all religious houses should be sold for the benefit of the nation. Nineteenth century writers, recognizing Shelley's indebtedness to the Revolution for certain tendencies in his thinking, have been inclined to look upon him as a "child of the Revolution." He is so termed by Alfred E. Hancock[1] and George E. Woodberry[2] and by Edmund Gosse, who refers to him as a certain type of revolutionist born out of due time and directed to the bloodless field of literature. Gosse believes that Shelley might be considered the incarnation of the hopes of Lafayette: "Like LaFayette, Shelley was intoxicated with virtue and glory; he was chivalrous, inflammable, and sentimental."[3] Shelley seems to have inherited not only the spirit of revolution but that of universality as well. Although born on English soil, of English parents, he does not belong so much to England as to the world at large. He himself felt no kinship with any country. There is not in his poems a single regret for leaving his native land. His poems to England are in the same universal spirit as are those to France, Spain, or any other country. It is only the oppressed among mankind, regardless of country, who appealed

---

[1] References are to Notes, p. 196.

1

to Shelley. Nor were his affections for family or friends, except as they needed him, strong. He did not interpret filial devotion in terms of family love. He at no time shows any sense of affection towards even the mother who bore him. His feeling of love and kinship embraces all mankind. Nor would he have it otherwise. His interests were in the events of the world, in man as a part of the universe. His own wish that his thoughts be scattered over the whole world is expressed in the closing lines of his *Ode to the West Wind*:

> Drive my dead thoughts over the universe
> Like withered leaves to quicken a new birth!
> And, by the incantation of this verse,
> Scatter, as from an unextinguished hearth
> Ashes and sparks, my words among mankind!

Three countries, however, may justly lay more claim to Shelley than may others: England, the land of his birth; Italy, the land of his adoption; and America, the home of his paternal great-grandmother and the country where his grandfather, Sir Bysshe Shelley, was born and spent his early years. For Timothy Shelley, the great-grandfather of the poet, had migrated to America in the early part of the eighteenth century.

The Shelley estate in England probably did not yield much income at that time. Two hundred pounds a year was not a sufficient sum to induce a young man to remain in England while waiting for the inheritance of the ancestral estate, particularly when letters from across the ocean told of fabulous sums that might be acquired in a short time. It was but natural, then, that Timothy Shelley should join the other young men who were migrating to America. His father may have seen thereby an opportunity to replenish the coffers of a country gentleman. Or he may have felt that a few years in a new country would furnish valuable training for the future lord of an English estate. Timothy Shelley may have been an adventurer, a wayward son. At least he does not seem to have been successful in acquiring money readily, for, in 1735, in order to establish himself in the mercantile business, he gave a note for 200 pounds, stating therein that he would be the possessor of an estate yielding 200 pounds sterling and now in the possession of his father, John Shelley of Fenn Place in Great Britain. That he either was unable to pay the note or neglected to pay it seems probable in that although he inherited the estate in 1739 and returned to England, the note was not paid in 1743 when it was placed on record.[4]

While in America, Timothy Shelley married a widow, Johanna Plum, a member of a prosperous Newark family. Malone states that the Plum family was large and widely connected and worthy of being united with the Shelleys. Two sons were born of this union, John and Bysshe, the latter being the grandfather of the poet. When Timothy returned to England at the death of his father, he was accompanied by his two sons, but not by his wife. What became of Johanna Plum is not known. There may have been an earlier separation, or she may have decided to remain in the colonies with her own people. There is a record of a Johanna Plum who died March 9, 1760, but it is difficult to decide, says Malone, whether she was spinster, wife, or widow. Samuel Plum, who had come from New England, was one of the original settlers of Newark. It may have been from this sturdy New Englander that Shelley inherited some of his ideas of freedom and equality.[5]

Shelley seems not to have been interested in his close association with America. Only occasionally did he mention America in his writings, as in The Revolt of Islam [6] and in A Philosophic View of Reform,[7] and rarely did he refer to his American ancestry. Shelley's earliest association with America is through the novels of Charles Brockden Brown. Writers of the nineteenth century early noticed the influence of Brown on Shelley. Peacock lists Brown among Shelley's favorite writers and among those who had most influence in molding his character. In giving Shelley's reaction to the novels of Brown, he states that the summer-house in Wieland made a great impression on Shelley, and that Constantia Dudley, the heroine of Ormond, held one of the highest places in Shelley's "ideality of human character." He declares that Shelley was captivated by the grave-digging scene in Edgar Huntley and was interested in Arthur Mervyn, but disapproved of the ending.[8] Dowden calls attention to Peacock's discussion of Brown's attraction for Shelley and refers to Brown as "Godwin's disciple in romance." [9] Thus he believes that both writers were influenced to some extent by Godwin. It was, however, for critics of the twentieth century, M. T. Solve and Eleanor Sickels, to determine the exact indebtedness of Shelley to Brown. In "Shelley and the Novels of Charles Brockden Brown," Solve discusses the similarities and the differences in the mental textures of Brown and Shelley.[10] He believes that they had charteristics in common, such as an intense and alert mind housed in a body that was inadequate, a habit of romantic and visionary speculation, and a morbid and vigorous personality. He states that both were hypersensitive to the defects of the social system and strove to ameliorate the condition of the ignorant and deluded masses, and that the minds of both were formed upon the same reading, the sensibility group, the necessitarians and materialists, and the transcendentalists. The chief difference, he believes, is that Brown was more mature in his thinking, as is revealed in his *Jane Talbot* in which he criticises Godwin's doctrines. Solve's conclusions regarding Shelley's thinking, however, seem to be based on the immature Shelley, the author of *Queen Mab* and the *Revolt of Islam*. Miss Sickels discusses at length the similarities in the writings of Brown and Shelley.[11] She finds parallels between *Zastrozzi* and *Edgar Huntley; or the Sleep-Walker* and between *St. Irvyn* and *Wieland*. She believes, however, that more definite influences are revealed in Shelley's poetry. There are parallels to both *Arthur Mervyn* and *Ormond* in the *Revolt of Islam,* and to *Ormond* and *Wieland* in *Rosalind and Helen*. She states that the name "Constantia" in the poem "To Constantia" was suggested by the name of the heroine of *Ormond*.

Shelley was little known in America during his lifetime. An occasional notice or brief article, a passage from a poem, or an excerpt from an article taken from an English magazine constituted the only information on Shelley that was given in the American periodicals. The very first mention of Shelley in any work published in America seems to have been in 1818, in the American edition of Leigh Hunt's *Foliage*, which contained two sonnets on the poet and was dedicated to him.[12] The very earliest notice of any of Shelley's works, however, was in the *Belles-Lettres Repository and Monthly Magazine*, published in New York, for March 1, 1820. In the column "Literary Intelligence" appeared the notice, "*Prometheus Unbound,* a Poem," by Percy Bysshe Shelley.[13] The second notice, also of *Prometheus Unbound,* was given in *The Literary and Scientific Repository and Critical Review* for July, 1820.[14] In the same issue were published extracts from reviews of Shelley's works in English periodicals. These excerpts, from the *Quarterly Review's* criticism of the *Revolt of Islam, Blackwood's* review of *Alastor,* and the *New Monthly's* review of *The Cenci,* were so selected and arranged as to present Shelley in a somewhat favorable light. In January, 1821, the same magazine reprinted a brief but favorable criticism of Shelley from the *Retrospective Review*.[15] In the *American Atheneum* for September 1, 1821, under "Paragraphs," was published the first American criticism of Shelley.[16]

The publisher of Shelley's *Queen Mab* has been indicted by the Society for the Suppression of Vice. It is dreadful to think that for the chance for a miserable pecuniary profit, any man would become the active agent to disseminate principles so subversive of the happiness of society.

This criticism refers to the English pirated edition of *Queen Mab*; no mention is made of the American edition. Several notices of Shelley are given in the *Literary Gazette or Journal of Criticism*, published at Philadelphia, for the year 1821. Under "Selected Poetry," in the number for May 5, occurs a selection of 40 lines from "The Sensitive Plant," by Percy Byshe *(sic)* Shelley.[17] In the issue for August 4, in the same column, is given a selection, "From Mr. Shelley's new poem *Queen Mab*,"[18] the application of the term "new poem" being an indication that Shelley and his work were not well known to the editors of the magazine. The *Saturday Magazine*, in part a compilation from the British periodicals, published in New York, likewise noticed Shelley a number of times during the years 1821 and 1822. In the number for October 20, 1821, under "Literature," was published a brief notice from the *London Literary Gazette* regarding Shelley's *Adonais*.[19] Shelley is mentioned in the issue for April 13, 1822, in a fictional article on "Southey and Byron," in which he is made to come to the defense of Byron.[20] Further reference is made to Shelley's association with Byron in Switzerland and to the Shelley and Byron party as one that was shunned like pestilence by every respectable person in Switzerland.[21] All the mentions of Shelley in the *Saturday Magazine* are unfavorable. Except for knowledge gained from these few notices and from the English reprints in the American magazines, American readers during Shelley's lifetime were compelled to rely for their information about the poet solely on the English periodicals.

Shelley was noticed a number of times in American periodicals between 1825 and 1830, during those years when Mary Shelley and the friends of Shelley were attempting to keep his name and poetry before the public.[22] Most important of these friends was Leigh Hunt, who was well known in America where he exercised considerable authority in literary and non-literary circles. As always, it was to those who were interested in literature that Shelley appealed, the best indication being the article in the *New York Literary Gazette and Phi Beta Kappa Repository*.[23] A third, but minor, force for Shelley recognition in these early years was the pirated editions, particularly of *Queen Mab*, some of which found their way into America.[24] All these forces combined to increase the knowledge of Shelley in America during the late twenties and to prepare the way for the more rapid development of his popularity in the thirties, so that Mary Shelley dared to risk an American edition of his prose works in 1840.

THE ROMANTIC PERIOD
(1830-1850)

CHAPTER I

NEW ENGLAND

Romanticism and Renaissance

THE ROMANTIC PERIOD in New England developed slowly. It might be said to have come in with the poetry of Wordsworth, which influenced Bryant and, to some extent, Freneau. Bryant's indebtedness to Wordsworth was first revealed in his poems published in 1821, among these being the revised *Thanatopsis*, in which the Wordsworthian influence is easily recognizable. Although Wordsworth continued during the next decade to be the favorite contemporary English poet among the New England conservatives and Byron became even more popular with the general reading public, romanticism did not make any great progress until the thirties. New England was stolid and conservative. Its literature was classical; Latin and Greek were the languages taught in its schools. Its religion was Calvinistic or Unitarian. Its politics remained wholly Federalist. Not until the advent of the industrial revolution was New England fully awakened. With the building of the Erie Canal and the consequent rise of New York as a shipping point, there was a change of occupation in New England. Shipping, no longer very profitable, gave place to manufacturing. The establishment of factories meant not only the rise of the commercial class but a general influx of laborers. The whole system of life must be changed. No longer would neighbor meet neighbor on equal footing in the town meeting. The capitalist and the foreigner would have a voice. New measures must be taken against this usurping capitalist as well as against the mob, regarding whom there was ever a dread in the mind of the native New Englander. The whole life, moral, intellectual, and spiritual, was affected. And, most of all, the dignity of labor was lowered. It was on this principle, the dignity of labor, that the life of the people of this section had been based. New England democracy had suffered a severe shock. But New England arose to the occasion. From the smoldering intellectualism came a renaissance of learning that was vigorous and far reaching in its effects. Merging with the slowly developing romanticism, this renaissance contributed to the strength and permanency of the Romantic revival.

Although there were traces of the renaissance early in the century, not until the fourth decade did the movement manifest itself in its entirety. The renaissance in scholarship had begun about 1820, soon after Edward Everett and George Ticknor returned from Europe with German standards of scholarship which they introduced into Harvard where they accepted positions as professors. About the same time came the final separation of the Unitarians from the Calvinists. The renaissance was, in reality, the awakening of a people proud of their heritage, of their English tradition, and of their American independence, but most of all of the fact that they were New Englanders. In the pediod of activity that followed, the Unitarians were the leaders. In freeing themselves from the dogmatic ideas of the Calvinists, they had already prepared the way for the acceptance of German philosophy and romanticism. They were aided in this preparation by the conscious German movement which had already made such great progress that a German department was established at Harvard in 1825. The works of Coleridge and Carlyle had likewise contributed their share to the revival of learning, and the poetry of Wordsworth, with its transcendental philosophy, had long been popular.

The years between 1830 and 1836 witnessed a rapid development of the spiritual aspect of that part of the renaissance that became known as transcendentalism. Its cultural aspects were of slower growth. With the organization of the Transcendental Club in the fall of 1836, the movement to adopt the metaphysical idealism of Germany and to absorb German culture was fully launched. That the influx of German and French literature and its increasing popularity would meet with a great deal of opposition in New England was to be expected. Some of the strongest opposition was among the Unitarians, what might be termed the right wing of the group. The conservative group was led by the Reverend Andrews Norton, whose Puritan principles caused him to oppose a great deal of the foreign literature on moral grounds and to establish in 1833 the *Select Journal of Foreign Periodical Literature*. He was opposed to the whole German school of philosophy and to the French and English followers of that school. The influence on New England, however, was not limited to the contemporary thinkers of western Europe but included philosophers ancient and modern, even those of the Orient. Emerson, Alcott, and Thoreau were intensely interested in the philosophy of India, but not as were the English Romanticists for whom it did not represent truth but rather poetic license.

It is but natural to expect that in a section in which there were so many conflicting forces the only type of writer who would be accepted would be one whose views would agree with those of one of the various groups, or a writer who, like Byron, would appeal to the popular tastes. Shelley belongs to that group of writers who cannot be classed as adhering to any one system of philosophy or to any one school of thought. He was not a follower of Plato nor of the neo-Platonists, although he borrowed freely of the ideas of both. If one reads Shelley's poetry for the theories contained therein and then attempts to make the poet conform to any one system of philosophy, he finds that he is faced with a number of irreconcilable doctrines. Shelley read widely and often indiscriminately. And he made use of only those ideas that appealed to him and which he found useful in the various poems. His readiness to take from each writer the ideas that he found satisfactory for his own use, to adapt them, and to discard others, and his inclination to reject these theories after having used them are best exemplified by the use he made of Godwin's *Political Justice*. He used Godwin's theories quite freely in *Queen Mab*, but when the work was published in 1821, he repudiated the views expressed in his early work as the result of youth and inexperience. It is to be expected, therefore, that the poetry of Shelley would not be generally popular in New England. His views did not contain anything tangible to assist a people recently awakened to the fact that they must formulate their own ideas in intellectual as well as in theological and political matters in order to meet the needs of a fast-changing world.

Because of the variety of opinion in New England, it seems best, in attempting to determine Shelley's place in the Romantic Period, to make the following divisions: Shelley and the New England Transcendentalists; the New England Poets and Shelley; Some New England Shelleyans; Shelley and the New England Periodicals; the Emerson–Andrews Norton Controversy.

Shelley and the New England Transcendentalists

An attempt to determine Shelley's place in the entry of romanticism into America may well begin with an examination of the interest manifested in him, or the lack of it, by the New England Transcendentalists. The Transcendental Club was organized on September 19, 1836, when R. W. Emerson, R. H. Hedge, Convers Francis, J. F. Clarke, and A. B. Alcott met at the home of George Ripley and organized a club for the discussion of contemporary views on philosophy, theology, and literature. Among those who joined later were Margaret Fuller, Elizabeth and Sophia Peabody, Theodore Parker, Orestes Brownson, H. D. Thoreau, N. Hawthorne, W. H. Channing, George Bancroft, A. A. Bartol, J. S. Dwight, Jones Very, and C. P. Cranch.

The most important work of the club within the next few years was the publication of *Specimens of Foreign Literature* in 1839, edited by George Ripley, the establishing of *The Dial* in 1840, as the mouthpiece of the organization, and the founding of the Brook Farm Association by Ripley and his associates in 1841. Its most important results were to broaden and popularize the spirit of inquiry, to extend culture to include music and the arts, and to liberalize religious views. The whole of the intellectual, aesthetic, and spiritual life of New England was affected directly or indirectly by this group. Whether or not its influence affected strongly matters political and social is still a question.

The lack of permanency of the activities of the Transcendental Club has been the cause of much comment. *The Dial*, which never made a strong impression, was fairly active for two years, languished for two, and met a premature death in 1844. Brook Farm served as a center for ultra-intellectuals and as a meeting place or a source of curiosity for the intellectuals of the surrounding region. Most of the members of the club were not in sympathy with the movement. It became virtually one of the Fourier phalanxes in 1845, and the buildings were consumed by fire in 1847. As to the nature of Transcendentalism, it may be defined in the words of Emerson: "What is popularly called Transcendentalism among us, is idealism; idealism as it appears in 1842." As will be seen later, this idealism took various forms. Since the Transcendental Club included most of the active leaders of the renaissance in New England, their opinions regarding Shelley are of the utmost importance. Before examining these opinions, however, it will be necessary to note something of the views of various members and their relation to the so-called Transcendental movement.

Transcendentalism in New England was not in reality a movement; it was a state of mind. It was not a philosophy, even though it had inherited a transcendental philosophy from Germany. It was not a "gospel," although the Club numbered among its members several preachers. It could be none of these because it was too individualistic. In fact, Transcendentalism is but a term applied variously to a great awakening in New England. It is the expression of a number of individuals from a people finally awakened from its lethargy by the quickly changing conditions of the time. These individuals, all idealists, seek alleviation from their dissatisfaction with the practical as well as with the intellectual and spiritual. They discard what they deem unessential or outworn in the old institutions, whether it be in politics, in education, in economics, or in religion. Each seeks an outlet for his particular dissatisfaction. If he is possessed with the missionary zeal, he enlists a number of followers; if not, he retires to his own quiet abode and lives as much like a hermit as it is possible to do in a progressive nineteenth century. The missionary spirit takes various forms, depending on the reason for the particular dissatisfaction. If the adherent had imbibed too freely from the fountains of French Utopianism, he would be prone to resign all, even to his furniture and library, as did George Ripley, in order to carry out his ideal, Ripley's being Brook Farm. And if, like Ripley's, his reform instincts were strong, he would not only enlist the interest of others, as in Brook Farm, but would devote his life and energies to "advancing the cause" as did Ripley even after he went to New York as literary critic for the *Tribune*. Or if, like Theodore Parker's, his dissatisfaction took the form of religion, he would break with the established church and, even at the risk of complete isolation from his brother clergymen, would spread the gospel as he saw it. To Thoreau, discontent with the existing state of things meant retirement to Waldon Pond. Adopting Rousseau's "Back to Nature" theory, except for a few seemingly necessary material comforts, Thoreau retired to Waldon Pond to lead the simple life. But Thoreau's retirement necessitated a visit to his Concord home every day, and he kept an expense account, a device not thus far discovered among primitive men. In the Bronson Alcotts of the period, the discontent might take almost any form, from establishing a school to establishing a community. Alcott's theories would depend on his latest reading and would vary from the vegetarianism of Pythagoras to the theory of teaching children by the conversational method. For Emerson the change was both intellectual and spiritual. Emerson was not only a preacher but also that unusual combination of student of the library and outdoor nature in one person. The position of preacher he resigned early, when he discovered that his ideas were not in accord with those of the religious denomination he served. His spiritual growth, therefore, was modified by his studies as a preacher, as a student of books, and as an observer of the great outdoors, where by preference a great deal of his time was spent. And all his ideas were colored by passing through the prism of a mind that was by nature given to reflection and meditation. Perhaps Emerson was a fairly thoroughgoing transcendentalist. Margaret Fuller, the most prominent woman of the group, hovered about its borderlands, sometimes making an excursion inward to visit Brook Farm or to assist with some work such as editing *The Dial*. It is probable that Miss

Fuller seized this opportunity to enter journalistic work. At least it was an outlet for her feelings, for Miss Fuller was the one member among the leaders of the Transcendental Club whose dissatisfaction was entirely personal.

Shelley was known to most of the members of the Transcendental Club. Only two, however, Margaret Fuller and Orestes Brownson, wrote about him at length. Ralph Waldo Emerson and Elizabeth Palmer Peabody mentioned him a number of times. W. H. Channing was an admirer of his poetry and of many of his ideas on social reform. Shelley must have furnished an interesting subject for discussion before the fireplace at Brook Farm, especially on some of those occasions when Margaret Fuller came to *talk*, for Miss Fuller, of all the Transcendentalists, was Shelley's most ardent admirer. It was probably on one of those occasions that the youthful George Curtis received his first inspiration to read Shelley. H. D. Thoreau, C. P. Cranch, and Jones Very, who read Shelley's poetry and attempted to model their own early endeavors on his shorter poems, may have been inspired by Margaret Fuller, or they may have read one of the numerous copies of the Galignani edition of Coleridge, Shelley, and Keats that were so popular in the America of the late thirties. James Freeman Clarke was a youthful admirer of Shelley, even as early as 1830, and Bronson Alcott had read his poetry at Germantown. Theodore Parker exhibited a somewhat tardy interest in the poet. To a few Transcendentalists, however, Shelley was practically unknown. Ripley, Hedge, Bartol, and Francis evidently were not aware that such a poet had ever existed. George Bancroft, who admired Byron and visited him at Mount Nero, May 22, 1822, was not sufficiently interested in Shelley to try to see him, although the poet was only a few miles away at San Terrenzo. Byron cannot be blamed for Bancroft's neglect of Shelley, as Bancroft records in his diary that in his conversation with Byron, they spoke at length of Goethe, and Byron said: "Shelley is translating *Faust*, Shelley of whom you may have heard many foolish stories, of his being a man of no principles and all that: but he is not." Then follows the entry: "Lord Byron related to me the late scrape into which he and his servant got at Pisa." [1] But there is no mention of Shelley, who was a member of Byron's party returning to Pisa.

Theodore Parker furnishes another enigma. He should have been interested in Shelley, if not in his poetry, at least in his reputed atheism. Had he considered Shelley's religious views, he probably would have included him among his *Speculative* atheists. In discussing the reaction to Emerson's address to the

divinity students at Harvard, in a letter to George Ellis, then in
Europe, Parker says: [2]

> Mr. Norton opened the cannonade with a broadside aimed at Emerson,
> Cousin, Carlyle, Schleiermacher, Shelley, and a paper called the *Western
> Messenger*.

But he does not comment on the article in the *Messenger* nor
on Shelley. There is, however, an article in the *Massachusett's
Quarterly Review* on "The Poetry of Keats," undoubtedly suggested by Parker but written by a Unitarian minister,[3] Amory
D. Mayo, which contains a great deal of material on Shelley. In
his list of subjects for articles for this magazine, of which he was
editor, Parker included Coleridge, Southey, Wordsworth, Shelley,
and Landor.[4] The article on Landor appeared in the December,
1848, issue, but no articles were published on the other poets
listed. It seems, however, that Parker and Mayo must have
agreed to combine the articles on the Romantic poets and to add
the name of Keats and give him the honor of the title, in that he
was beginning to be recognized as the outstanding poet of the
group. If the paragraph on Shelley does not represent the opinion
of Parker, it does represent the view given in a magazine of
which he was editor. The comment is of value as the view of the
Transcendentalists of the late forties regarding the poet. Concerning the criticism of several nineteenth-century poets Mayo
writes:

> It is now generally understood that sarcasm directed against the poetry
> of Coleridge, Wordsworth, Shelley, Keats, and Tennyson, is but the ex-
> piring echo of a departed criticism . . . it would now be superflous in a
> critic to waste paper and ink in arguing about the merit of these bards
> as a class. Their empire is secure. They have passed into that empyreal
> region to which the shafts of criticism do not fly.

He pays the following tribute to Shelley as a poet:

> That Shelley was gifted with depth of spiritual insight and power to
> describe the most profound emotions of the soul, and the links binding
> it to the material universe, beyond all other English poets, we had almost
> said beyond Shakespeare himself, we cannot doubt. His plumb and line
> sound those awful depths of consciousness, the secret places where joy
> and terror and love are born, which to some men are unknown. But
> alas! he did not live to give complete utterance; his brain was crazed by
> the woes of humanity, his short life embittered by a persecution, of which
> we have no parallel in the history of Modern Literature! Yet what might
> not that Genius, in the maturity of its power, have accomplished, that
> amid the chaos of a life like his could shape such forms of awful grandeur
> as rise before us in "Prometheus Unbound"; that could sway the passions
> as in "The Cenci"; that could glide into the realm of the spiritual world,
> as in "Adonais" and "Alastor," or revel in the pure sunshine of beauty,
> as in "The Sensitive Plant" and "The Skylark"? It has been truly said

of Shelley, "He was a broken mirror, whose fragments reflected the forms of all things. He was a poet for poets." His writings are to the bard what the Belshazzar's Feast of Allston is to the artist—more precious that their creator left them with all their imperfections, to work their way into the souls of men.

The article contains other occasional comments in praise of the poetry of Shelley.

Bronson Alcott is another transcendentalist who furnishes a paradoxical case. He likewise should have manifested interest in Shelley, for they had much in common. Both were worshippers of ideal truth and purity. Both believed in the rule of love over force. Alcott believed that man was ready for the rule of love; Shelley believed that he would be, at least by the millennium. Alcott, like Shelley, was a believer in universal suffrage, particularly in the emancipation of women. Alcott believed that the soul was older than the body; Shelley was quite willing to test out the theory.[5] Both had original ideas regarding the education of children. Alcott developed his ideas into a system and put them into practice; Shelley threatened to test his.[6] And finally, both were vegetarians. Alcott was a believer in and a consistent follower of the Pythagorean theory, but Shelley fluctuated somewhat. Shelley's refraining from partaking of flesh, however, was consistent with his idea of kinship with the animal world. Other parallels might be drawn between these two idealists, for high idealism they had in common. It would appear, then, that Shelley might have influenced Alcott in some of his ideas. Shelley, however, is not listed among the authors in the library at Fruitlands, but Alcott seems to have read him while at Germantown.[7] Although quoting Wordsworth to his pupils was a habit of the seer, there is no record that he ever quoted Shelley. It is highly probable that Shelley was a subject not mentioned in the Alcott household. He probably was banned because of his reported ideas concerning morality and religion.

Elizabeth Palmer Peabody evidently was not an admirer of Shelley. She tells of a meeting with a young man, Lieutenant Greene, who came to her library[8] one evening for a copy of Goethe's works in some language other than German. From the conversation that ensued, Miss Peabody reports that Lieutenant Greene was a "keen student of the science of war and a reader of military biography," but had "little literary culture, his reading having been largely Lord Byron's and Shelley's poetry. *Queen Mab*, he said had been his gospel, and his theology was also Shelley's,—namely, that God is merely a complex of the laws of Nature."[9] But his life in Florida, he reported, had brought him to deeper truth. Then follows a story of a religious experience in which the Lieutenant "discovered that God was behind the complex of the laws of Nature." This discovery caused him to lose faith in Shelley. According to his version of the story, he was sitting in his tent when the realization of his error came to him. He jumped from his seat, seized his *Queen Mab* and flung it from the door of his tent into the far distance. The whole story of this "conversion" as related by Miss Peabody might lead one to believe either that the Lieutenant was somewhat of a fanatic on religion or that he was attempting to impress Miss Peabody whose penchant for reform caused even Dr. Channing no little concern.[10] Greene, however, seems either to have been given to revelations of this kind or to have been uncertain as to the book he was reading. Later he tells of a similar experience but gives Shakespeare, not Shelley, as the author he was reading.[11] It is likewise possible that he resumed his liking for Shelley or felt by 1871 that it was safe to quote him.[12]

James Freeman Clarke had an early appreciation of Shelley's poetry which he appears to have retained throughout his life. On June 4, 1865, he sends his copy of the Galignani edition of Coleridge, Shelley, and Keats to his daughter with the following letter: [13]

This book I bought in 1830, when I was twenty years old. I had just left college and entered the divinity school. I was poor, and it was a good deal to me to pay $7.50 for a book. But the American edition of this work had not then been published, nor had there been then printed in England, a complete edition of either of these poets. So I imported a copy of this Paris edition, and had a great deal of pleasure out of it. During the winter of 1830-31, I lived with my mother in Ashburton Place, and after keeping school all day at Cambridgeport, I passed the evening with my family in my brother Sam's room, he being confined to bed with rheumatism. After I went to my room at night, at eleven or twelve o'clock, I would read awhile in this book, and I hope that you may have as much pleasure out of it as I had then.

It is possible that Margaret Fuller may have been responsible for Clarke's early interest in Shelley. At least they must have shared in common the appreciation of his poetry as they did the study of German during the early years of the fourth decade.

Margaret Fuller was not only the most outstanding woman of the Transcendental Club, but she was also conceded to be the most intellectual woman in America in the first half of the century. Because of her ability as a literary critic, she was selected to be the editor of *The Dial*. After two years of arduous work in writing for and editing it, she turned the magazine over to Emerson and went to New York to become literary critic on the *Tribune*.

Throughout her life Margaret Fuller retained her admiration for the poetry of Shelley. If, in later years when she joined the Transcendentalists and enthusiasm for Goethe was in the air, she turned from the younger to the older poet, she still retained her admiration for Shelley's poetry. At this stage of her intellectual development, the heavier works of Goethe gave her more food for thought than did the immature works of Shelley. Her delight with Shelley's *Defence of Poetry* in 1840 shows that the trend of her thinking was along more philosophic lines. She expresses her joy on finding that Shelley had taken the matter up very much from the point of view she had been presenting in her conversations. "At last," she exclaims, "I have all the great thoughts, and whatever the world may say, I shall be well received in the Elysian fields." [14] In her essay, "Shelley's Poems," written on the occasion of the publication of the first American edition of his poetry,[15] she hails with delight this recognition of the poet and gives a glowing account of her first acquaintance with Shelley.[16] In accordance with her own experience she feels that Shelley's poetry is for youth:

The qualities of his poetry have often been analysed, and the severe critics, impatient of his exuberance, or unable to use their accustomed spectacles in the golden mist that broods over all he has done, deny him high honors; but the soul of aspiring youth, untrammelled by the canons of taste and untamed by scholarly discipline, swells into rapture at his lyric sweetness, finds ambrosial refreshment from his plenteous fancies, catches fire at his daring thought, and melts into boundless weeping at his tender sadness—the sadness of a soul betrothed to an ideal unattainable in his present sphere.

Miss Fuller then tells what Shelley meant in her own life:

Nearer than the nearest companions of life has Shelley been to us. . . . Shelley seems to us an incarnation of what was sought in the sympathies and desires of instinctive life, a light of dawn, and a foreshadowing of the weather of this day.

Her first acquaintance with Shelley, she says, was during her childhood: "When still in childish years, the *Hymn to Intellectual Beauty* fell in our way." She and a party of young persons, "gayer than, and almost as inventive, as those that told the tales recorded by Boccaccio," acted parts from stories. One day, one of the party, the Libellula (evidently Miss Fuller herself), read aloud the *Hymn to Intellectual Beauty* "torn by chance from the leaf of a foreign magazine." Two or three years later she, the Libellula, received a copy of Shelley's poems for a Christmas gift, "and for three days and three nights she ceased not to extract the sweets." She read *Julian and Maddalo, Alastor, Queen Mab,* and *Prometheus Unbound.* She can still remember, she says, "every object seen from the chair in which she sat enchanted during those three days. Miss Fuller agrees with Mr. G. G. Foster's estimate of Shelley as a man, and quotes from the preface to his work:

> Of Shelley's personal character, it is enough to say that it was pervaded by the same unbounded and unquestioning love for his fellow-man and the same holy and fervid hope in their ultimate happiness—the same scorn of baseness and hatred of oppression—which beam forth in all his writings with a pure and constant light.

That Margaret Fuller continued her childhood admiration for Shelley is revealed by an entry in her diary for the summer of 1833. She seems, at this time, to have absorbed the ideas of Shelley with all the sentimentality of a young girl who has found her spiritual ideal. Her words, "Vouchsafe then thy protection, and I may hold on in courage of soul," Higginson believes are but a reëchoing of the lines,

> O man, hold thee on in courage of soul
> Through the stormy shades of the worldy way . . .

from Shelley's poem "On Death." [17] James Freeman Clarke recognized Miss Fuller's youthful enthusiasm for Shelley when, in the memorial volume,[18] he preceded his discussion of her "Life in Cambridge," 1824-1833, by a quotation from Shelley.

In 1836, when Miss Fuller was beginning to gain recognition as a critic, she wrote to a friend regarding her feeling for Shelley: [19]

> As to what you say of Shelley, it is true that the unhappy influence of early education prevented his ever attaining clear views of God, life, and the soul. At thirty, he was still a seeker,—an experimentalist . . . Had Shelley lived twenty years longer, I have no doubt he would have become a fervent Christian, and thus have attained the mental harmony which was necessary to him. It is true too, as you say, that we always feel a melancholy imperfection in what he writes. But I love to think of those other spheres in which so pure and rich a being shall be perfected; and I cannot allow his faults of opinion and sentiment to mar my enjoyment of the vast capabilities, and exquisite perception of beautiy, displayed everywhere in his poems.

Even at this early date Miss Fuller had emerged from the group of blind Shelley worshippers and had joined those who appreciated Shelley's true worth as a poet.

In the letters of Miss Fuller to James Nathan, during the years 1845 and 1846, are numerous mentions of Shelley. On May 30, 1845, just before Nathan's departure for Germany, she writes: "A small copy of Shelley's poems I wish also to make your companion, but keep that until I give it into your hand and point out some passages." [20] In a letter written to Nathan in Europe, February 28, 1846, she expresses regret for the loss of a rose from Shelley's grave that Nathan had sent her and which seems to have dropped from the letter when she opened it. [21]

The second of Miss Fuller's essays on Shelley appeared in 1846. In a series of papers on "Modern British Poets," [22] she says of Shelley: "I turn to one whom I love still more than I admire; the gentle, the gifted, the ill-fated Shelley." Then she echoes the epithet of "Poor Shelley" which seems to have come in during the forties. As regards Shelley the man, she appears to have joined that long line of sensational admirers whose pity Shelley would abhor and whose epithets would cause him probably to seek seclusion in some safe retreat. That she still had confidence in Shelley as a poet is to her credit as a literary critic. Shelley in two particulars, she believes, surpasses any poet of the day, in "fertility of Fancy" and in "sympathy with Nature." Of the former quality she says, "Parts of his *Adonais, Marianne's Dream,* and *Medusa,* are not to be excelled except in Shakespeare." Shelley, she feels, is truly in accord with nature: "To her lightest tones, his being gives an echo; truly she spoke to him, and it is this which gives unequalled melody to his versification." She believes that Shelley's type of excellence in description can only be reached by one who writes outdoors as Shelley did: "The rush, the flow, the delicacy of vibration, in Shelley's verse can only be paralleled by the waterfall, the rivulet, the notes of the bird and insect world." She compares the poems of Shelley and Wordsworth on the skylark and concludes that Shelley in melody and exuberance of fancy was incalculably superior to Wordsworth. She contends that with Shelley one must not expect to be satisfied, but to be stimulated. "We must surrender ourselves to the magnetic power of genius." This is Margaret Fuller's last notice of Shelley. The extant letters telling of her life in Italy [23] are filled with tales of the revolution and with personal affairs. She does not mention Shelley or other poets. Her attention is too engrossed, first with the political situation and later with her child and her efforts to supply the necessities of life, to give her time for literary pursuits. If she visited the grave of Shelley, there appears to be no record of her impressions.

Emerson was not only the leader of the Transcendental Club, but the voice of the New England renaissance as well. His position became secure after his delivery of the Phi Beta Kappa address at Harvard, August 31, 1837. But it was as a moralist, an ethical stimulator, a lay-preacher that Emerson was pre-eminent. He was less great as a poet or a writer of prose, and he was not a literary critic. But to his contemporaries he seemed great in all things, and he wielded an influence beyond that of any other man of letters of his time. The statement made by W. D. Howells regarding Emerson's influence in the West before 1860 might well be taken to include all America: "I myself had not read much of him, but I knew the essays he was printing in the *Atlantic*, and I knew certain of his poems, though by no means many; yet I had this sense of him, that he was somehow beyond and above my ken, a presence of force and beauty and wisdom, uncompanioned in our literature." [24] As a critic of literature, it is generally conceded that Emerson had a defective sense of literary values, although he had the ability to gauge books and men when he understood them. T. W. Higginson calls Emerson a whimsical critic in his judgment of poetry, in that there were whole classes of writers whom he scarcely recognized at all. He quotes as an example Emerson's statement that "Shelley is never a poet." [25] These characteristics of Emerson as a critic are revealed in his notes on Shelley. For Emerson's opinion of Shelley must be gleaned from his *Journals* and from his comments in his essays. It seems best, therefore, to consider these comments in chronological order.

One of Emerson's earliest observations on Shelley is in his entry in his *Journal* for April 7, 1837, when he states: [26] "The man of genius—Swedenborg, or Carlyle, or Alcott—is ever, as Shelley says of his Skylark,

> Like a Poet hidden
> In the light of thought,
> Singing hymns unbidden
> Till the world is wrought
> To sympathy with hopes and fears it heeded not.

It was on November 28, 1839, while recording some ideas concerning poetry in general that he made his oft-quoted comment on Shelley: [27]

Shelley is never a poet. His mind is uniformly imitative; all his poems composite. A fine English scholar he is, with taste, ear, and memory; but imagination, the original authentic fire of the bard he has not. He is clearly modern, and shares with Wordsworth, and Coleridge, Byron and Hemans, the feeling of the infinite, which so labors for expression in their different genius. But all his lines are arbitrary, not necessary, and therefore, though evidently a devout and brave man, I can never read his verses.

This conclusion regarding Shelley seemed to satisfy Emerson. He used the quotation with slight variation in other instances. In his article "Thoughts on Modern Literature," published in

The Dial,[28] he states that the "Feeling of the Infinite" has deeply colored the poetry of the period. He continues:

> This new love of the vast, always native in Germany, was imported into France by De Stael, appeared in England in Coleridge, Wordsworth, Byron, Shelley, Felicia Hemans, and finds a most congenial climate in the American mind. . . . Nothing certifies the prevalence of this taste in the people more than the circulation of the poems—one would say, most incongruously united by some bookseller,—of Coleridge, Shelley, and Keats. The only unity is in the subjectiveness and the aspiration common to the three writers.

Then follows the quotation from his *Journal*, slightly modified, "Shelley, though a poetic mind, is never a poet," the principal change being that the names Richter, Chateaubriand, and Manzoni are substituted for Coleridge, Byron, and Hemans. There is also a change in the last part of the quotation and a broadening of the idea:

> But all his lines are arbitrary, not necessary. When we read poetry, the mind asks,—Was this verse one of twenty which the author might have written as well; or is this what one man was created to say? But whilst every line of the true poet will be genuine, he is in a boundless power and freedom to say a million things. And the reason why he can say one thing well, is because his vision extends to the sight of all things, and so he describes each as one who knows many and all.

That this is good criticism cannot be denied. But one wonders how Emerson, who evidently admired Shelley's "Skylark," could have applied this criticism arbitrarily to the poetry of Shelley. It would be interesting to know which of Shelley's poems Emerson had in mind. It is probable that he was thinking only of the didactic element in Shelley's poems. For great poetry to Emerson was didactic poetry. In his essay on "Poetry and Imagination," Emerson again gives expression to his dislike for Shelley's poetry: [29]

> When people tell me they do not relish poetry and bring me Shelley, or Aiken's Poems, or I know not what volume of rhymed English, to show that it has no charm, I am quite of their mind.

Judging from this comment, one would infer that Emerson disliked even Shelley's lyrics. This may be taken as an example of his "whimsical criticism" to which Higginson calls attention.

There are indications, however, that Emerson tried to understand Shelley. On October 30, 1841, after he has written a beautiful paragraph on nature, he recalls Shelley, and it seems that he writes the following with a feeling of regret: [30]

> *The Age:* Shelley is wholly unaffecting to me. I was born a little too soon: but his power is so manifest over a large class of the best persons, that he is not to be overlooked.

This entry made just after the publication of Shelley's complete works furnishes proof not only that Shelley must have received a great deal of recognition in America, but also that attempts were made to persuade Emerson to consider the poet favorably. Less than a year later he makes another important entry regarding Shelley.[31] After an observation to the effect that he himself is not in a "sufficiently sacred and holiday health for the task" of reading Plato's *Timaeus*, he recalls Shelley. Many might be the conjectures as to why he associated Shelley with Plato at this time. Was there a secret admiration for the youth who took so readily to Plato? Or perhaps Emerson was applying to Shelley's case his own idea of books: "Books are for the scholar's idle time. When he can read God directly, the hour is too precious to be wasted in other men's transcripts of their readings." At least he records in his *Journal*:

> Elizabeth Hoar says that Shelley is like shining sand; it always looks attractive and valuable, but, try never so many times, you cannot get anything good. And yet the mica glitter remains after all.

One reads this quotation with the feeling that Emerson was sincere in his efforts to appreciate Shelley. Perhaps it is true that he was "born a little too soon." He was brought up on the idea that poetry must be ethical, and he found it impossible to change his views. Or this lack of appreciation of Shelley may be attributed to a difference in Emerson's viewpoint regarding nature descriptions, as seems to be the belief of O. W. Firkins: "That Shelley, who gives us what might be called the vapor of landscape, should have appealed little to a man who saw nature as if etched on steel, is not inexplicable to the discerning." [32] Emerson's failure to appreciate Shelley has always been a subject for comment. W. S. Landor noted this lack of appreciation, and in an open letter to Emerson remarked: "Fifty pages of Shelley contain more of pure poetry than a hundred of Gothe (*sic*), who spent the better part of his time in contriving a puzzle, and in spinning out a yarn for a labyrinth." [33]

Although Emerson did not accept Shelley as a poet, he did include "The Cloud" and "The Skylark" among his nature poems in *Parnassus*.[34] He did not, however, include any of Shelley's works among the poems on "Beauty," "Fancy," or "Music." And what seems even more strange, he did not include *Adonais* among the "Dirges and Pathetic Songs," although he included both "Lycidas" and "Thyrsis." This inconsistency arouses the feeling that Emerson as a critic of poetry was whimsical, particularly when in his essay on "Immortality" [35] he quotes Shelley: "The poet Shelley says of these delicately carved white marble cells, 'They seem not so much hiding places of that which must decay, as voluptuous chambers for immortal spirits.' "

It cannot be said that Emerson was prejudiced against Shelley. If he seems inconsistent in his criticism of Shelley's poetry, it must be remembered that he never really wrote a criticism of it. All we have to judge from are his random jottings, and in such notes anyone might tend to be inconsistent. In keeping with his tolerant attitude in matters pertaining to the individual, Emerson did not criticise Shelley's views. And there is no indication that he gave credence to any of the tales circulated regarding the poet. In fact, his "a fine English scholar he is, with taste, ear, and memory," speaks his approval of Shelley the man. It is highly probable, however, that Emerson was a deterring factor in the acceptance of Shelley in America. His reiterated comment, "Shelley is never a poet," like Arnold's epithet of "the ineffectual angel," was undoubtedly accepted by the multitude. In his own group, there were those who, like Margaret Fuller, did not agree with him. In a letter to Miss Fuller at Rome, June 4, 1847,[36] he says, "*Festus* and Shelley have both this merit in timeliness; that is the only account we can give of their imposing on such good heads." This comment as well as the one that Shelley's power was manifest over a large number of the best people would lead one to believe that Emerson met with some opposition in his own circle regarding the poetry of Shelley, but it is also probable that he found many who agreed with his opinions and did not read Shelley.

At least one poem by Emerson bears a close resemblance to the poetry of Shelley. Some parts of the "The Sphinx" are so Shelleyan that were it not heretical to doubt Emerson's veracity in such matters, the reader might be inclined to believe that Emerson was trying to imitate Shelley. The resemblance is in the following stanzas, and is in the general idea, the use of "Daedalian," the last line of stanza two, "Deep underneath deep," [37] the third line of the fourth stanza, "Play glad with the breezes," [38] and the general references to the elements.[39]

> The fate of the man-child,
>   The meaning of man;
> Known fruit of the unknown;
>   Daedalian plan;
> Out of sleeping a waking,
>   Out of waking a sleep;
> Life death overtaking;
>   Deep underneath deep . . .
>
>   .   .   .   .
>
> The waves, unashamèd,
>   In difference sweet,

Play glad with the breezes,
Old playfellows meet;
The journeying atoms,
Primordial wholes,
Firmly draw, firmly drive,
By their animate poles.

Sea, earth, air, sound, silence
Plant, quadruped, bird,
By one music enchanted,
One deity stirred,—
Each the other adorning,
Accompany still;
Night veileth the morning,
The vapor the hill . . .

That Emerson did not recognize in Shelley's ideas any similarity to his own is not inexplicable in that he probably did not read enough of Shelley's poetry to detect the likeness. Emerson proclaimed that "to study" nature" and "to know thyself" were the same thing in that both are but parts of that "Unity and Over-Soul within which man's particular being is contained and made one with all other." Shelley expresses a similar idea when he says of Keats: [40]

He is made one with Nature

.   .   .   .   .   .

He is a presence to be felt and known
In darkness and in light, from herb and stone,
Spreading itself where'er that power may move
Which has withdrawn its being to its own;
Which wields the world with never-wearied love,
Sustains it from beneath, and kindles it above.

Shelley would agree with Emerson that both man and Nature are a part of the Unity, but he goes further and expresses the pantheistic belief that man is a part of Nature and that after death the soul returns to the elements: [41]

He is a portion of the loveliness
Which once he made more lovely, he doth bear
His part, while the one Spirit's plastic stress
Sweeps through the dull dense world, compelling there,
All new successions to the forms they wear;

Emerson's conception of the "Over-Soul" and Shelley's idea of the Spirit of Intellectual Beauty were perhaps suggested by the same ultimate source, Plato, but in the meditative mind of the New England philosopher and theologian, the suggestion assumed a different form from that in the mind of the young idealist and pantheist. Both Emerson and Shelley were interested in Oriental philosophy and both read Sir William Jones at an early age.[42] As to the amount of influence wielded by Jones, and by Hindu thought in general, there seems to be a difference of opinion. Arthur Christy states that Emerson "took from the Oriental philosophy only that which he could accept and mix successfully with his inhibitions and preconceptions."[43] He believes that Emerson's interest in Jones is revealed in the fact that he included translations from Jones in *Parnassus.*

Shelley's relation to Emerson is probably best stated by Denis Saurat when he says that a common, non-Christian stock of myths and ideas exists among certain poets, including Emerson, Shelley, and Whitman.[44] He accounts for the variations in beliefs as follows: [45]

> We have then before us, not certainly, a coherent, well-constructed doctrine handed on from one poet to another, but a conception of ill defined conceptions which yet all belong, so to speak, to the same family of ideas; and this conception is outside the pale of Christianity.

The Dial, the organ of expression for the *Transcendental Club,* published one article and one poem on Shelley and several poems in the manner of Shelley. The article, which appeared in the April, 1841, number, was written by John M. Mackie. It was occasioned by the publication of Shelley's poetry and prose works in America.[46] Although Mr. Mackie seems to be unusually well acquainted with Shelley's poetry, his discussion is quite in the manner of the time. Shelley's "numerous errors" are referred to and are attributed to "lack of judgment, a common fault of youth—a misguided understanding rather than a corrupt disposition—a too implicit trust—the conclusions of his individual understanding." Mackie praises Shelley's "scholarly attainments" and his sacrifice for principles, particularly the fact that he did not fear public opinion. He does not believe that Shelley ever changed his views regarding the Deity, that the God of Shelley was none other than Shelley himself. This conclusion he bases on the essay on "Life." He gives Shelley credit for reading his Bible but declares that he had a decided repugnance to the teachings of the New Testament. He blames the doctrines of Milton and of Mary Wollstonecraft for Shelley's separation from Harriet. As to Shelley's poetry, he holds the common view that Shelley was best in his lyrics and short poems. "In these he breathed his entire soul," states Mackie. He adds that Shelley exceeded others in his love of the beautiful, but lived too much in the ideal world. He was, according to this writer, a complete master of all poetic measures: "His numbers are smooth, various, and beautiful; his language rich, tasteful, and expressive." This article cannot be said to be representative of the opinion of the Transcendental Club or of any school of thought. It represents the views of a contributor and was acceptable to the editors of the magazine. It might even have been touched up by Miss Fuller, although there is no evidence that it was. As a piece of criticism, it is inferior to several articles of the time. The poem on Shelley is of the usual tpye published in magazines of the day.

The poetry of *The Dial*, on the whole, is undoubtedly of a higher quality than that found in other periodicals of the time because of the influence of the English Romantic poets, particularly Shelley, Wordsworth, and Coleridge. Of the poems in the Shelleyan manner, the first is the "Lyric" by "Z," Caroline S. Tappan, published in the first volume.[47] This poem sounds like an attempt at imitation of lines from several of Shelley's lyrics: [48]

> The stars coldly glimmer—
> And I am alone.
> The pale moon grows dimmer,
> And now it has gone.
> Loud shrieks the owl, night presses round,
> The little flowers lie low on the ground
> And sadly moan . . .
>
> I press my hands upon my heart,—
> 'Tis very cold!
> And swiftly through the forest dart
> With footsteps bold.
> What shall I seek? Where shall I go?
> Earth and ocean shudder with woe!
> Their tale is untold!

The poem "Endymion,"[49] by C. P. Cranch, is slightly Shelleyan in atmosphere and diction, particularly the first stanza:

> Yes, it is the queenly Moon,
> Gliding through her starred saloon,
> Silvering all she looks upon;
> I am her Endymion.
> For by night she comes to me:
> O, I love her wondrously!

The most conspicuous Shelley influence, however, is to be detected in .the poems by "T," H. D. Thoreau, in the third volume of *The Dial*, published in the April, 1843, edition.[50] The first is a ludicrous application of "To a Skylark" in the opening lines of the very humanitarian poem, "To a Stray Fowl."

> Poor bird! destined to lead thy life
> Far in the adventurous west
> And here to be debarred to-night
> From thy accustomed nest;
> Must thou fall back upon old instinct now—

The next poem, "Smoke," [51] by the same writer, is a more worthy echo of the same poem:

> Light-winged smoke, Icarian bird,
> Melting thy pinions in thy upward flight,
> Lark without song, and messenger of dawn,
> Circling above the hamlets as thy nest;
> Or else, departing dream, and shadowy form
> Of midnight vision, gathering up thy skirts,
> By night star-veiling, and by day
> Darkening the light and blotting out the sun;
> Go thou my incense upward from this hearth,
> And ask the Gods to pardon this clear flame.

The poem "Haze," also by Thoreau, and the second in the same series, entitled "Orphics," suggests the Shelleyan atmosphere and diction:

> Woof of the sun, etheral gauze,
> Woven of nature's richest stuffs,
> Visible heat, air-water, and dry sea
> Last conquest of the eyes.

Two other poems might be classed as showing the influence of Shelley. The first of these, "Song," [52] has the Shelleyan simile, movement, and diction.

> Like seas flashing in caves
> Where stalactites gleam (11, 1-2, st. I)
> .   .   .   .
> Deep as the sea,
> As the voice of the night,
>   Lofty and free
> As the vast dome of light (11. 1-4 st. 2)

In the next poem, "The World," by Jones Very,[53] the fifth and sixth lines of stanza two recall lines in a lyric from *Prometheus Unbound*:

> Too many, too many
> For eye or for ear . . .

Shelley's relation to the Transcendental group may be found in his influence on individuals rather than on the group as a whole. That the members of this group, who were so influential in molding opinion during the period from 1836 to 1845, did little to further acquaintance with Shelley's poetry was of serious moment. The reasons for individual neglect or opposition, as has been seen, were various. But there were certain characteristics in the group as a whole that caused them to neglect Shelley. As a club the Transcendentalists were concerned with continental literature, as the discussions in *The Dial* and the publication of the *Specimens of Foreign Standard Literature* bear witness. Among foreign writers, Schiller and Goethe received most attention.[54] Schiller was more popular in America as a whole, but Goethe had more adherents among the Transcendentalists. In fact, many of the members were so engrossed with Goethe that it was difficult for any other writer to have a hearing. In the general acceptance of Goethe lies the reason for much of the neglect of Shelley. For Goethe was, in many of his ideas, a maturer Shelley. Goethe the romanticist and Goethe the lover of science had much in common with Shelley. But the Transcendentalists rejected Goethe the romanticist. It was this Goethe that Emerson refused to recognize for so many years, but he was finally made to accept the mature Goethe, the combination of romanticist and classicist. This was the Goethe that appealed to the Transcendentalists. Had they taken the trouble to investigate Shelley's ideas, particularly his views on science, they would have found many of Goethe's theories intermingled with those of Shelley on socialism, humanitarianism, philosophy, and theology, theories that were the result of Shelley's eclectic reading. But Goethe's views on science were clearer than Shelley's in that they were presented in more concrete form. Goethe not only possessed a less turbulent temperament but was more practical in his thinking. Goethe also had a better opportunity to work out his scientific experiments in the laboratory. But, most of all, he had maturity; the experience of many years lay behind him. It was these particular differences that caused the Transcendentalists to seek in Goethe an answer to their problems and to reject Shelley, regardless of the impression that he made, as Emerson terms it, on a "large number of the best persons." For the Transcendentalists were practical idealists. As a recent writer states it, "The Transcendentalists, a realistic, a practical group, . . . sought the reality behind the facade of institutions, the kernel of truth within the husk of convention."[55] That the poetry of Shelley, except for the lyrics, did not appeal to this group is not surprising.

CHAPTER II

The New England Poets and Shelley

Among Shelley's most ardent admirers in the nineteenth
century were the poets. Wherever the true literati were found,
Shelley was sure to have a hearing. It is not surprising, therefore, to find Shelley supporters among the genteel of New England. But there was much in Shelley's poetry, particularly in
that readily available before 1840, which was not likely to interest the major New England poets. It is not probable that
these conservative and retiring men were interested in the im-
practical theories of *Queen Mab*, in the "bloodless revolution" of
the *Revolt of Islam*, or in the visionary schemes for the future
as expressed in *Prometheus Unbound*. Shelley's lyrics and short
pieces pleased them more. But most of these were not generally
available until after 1840. Each of the major poets, however,
seems to have found something in Shelley's poetry to approve,
and no one, except Whittier, condemned the poet for his youthful
effusions and seemingly visionary theories. It is highly probable
that all these men were more interested in the poet than the
records of their lives and works reveal. The early biographies of
the poets were written and the diaries and journals edited by
relatives who were too often squeamish about including anything that might be a reflection on the family name. They feared
that an acknowledgment of acquaintance with Shelley's poetry
might indicate that the ancestor had been an adherent of Shelleyan ideas, socialism and atheism. For the "Idols of the Tribe"
were still predominant in late nineteenth- and early twentieth-
century America.

The youthful John Greenleaf Whittier, editor of the *Essex
Gazette* in 1830, took occasion to express his views regarding
Shelley's religious beliefs. In an editorial on "Infidelity"[1] Whit-
tier refers to Byron as being among the "master spirits of In-
fidelity," but as one haunted by a fearful doubt, and adds that
Shelley likewise had doubts.

And Shelley too—the intimate friend of Byron—desperate and aban-
doned as he was—could never shake off the thick doubts which contin-
ually gathered around him. As if haunted by a demon, from whom he
would fain escape, he fled from one scene of dissipation to another—
from one country to another—seeking an oblivion for the memory of
his guilt, and finding none. He could not deceive himself. The glorious
gift of intellect with which his God had blessed him, revolted at the
dark and cheerless philosophy which turned its greenness and beauty
into a mental desert.

30

There is much in the history of this man's life to convince a rational mind of the utter worthlessness of intellectual power, and extended knowledge, when united with a depraved heart. With all the glorious feelings of high and beautiful poetry, with an imagination that went upward to the stars,—gifts, which if rightly applied might have placed their possessor among the "tall spirits" to whom the great multitude do homage,—he died, as he had lived, with a cloud upon his soul, and the seal of infamy upon his memory.

In a later article, in reply to a correspondent of the *American Daily Advertiser* [2] who had undertaken to defend Shelley from the attack in the *Gazette*, Whittier criticizes Shelley for his treatment of Harriet. He accuses him of stealing away "the pure affections of an innocent school-girl,— a child, unpractised and uninitiated in the duplicities and hollow-heartedness of the world—to carry her away from her friends—to pervert and poison her mind with those wild sophistries, which, under pretext of elevating the character and establishing the 'rights of women,' degrade her from her high place of purity, and render her a suitable companion for the accursed of Heaven?" In the last paragraph, he again refers to Shelley's ability: "No man can think more highly of Shelley's intellectual powers, than ourself— none can be more enthusiastically fond of his enchanting productions. But mere Genius shall never take the precedence of Virtue, in our estimation." Although Whittier's criticism of Shelley is severe and exceedingly intolerant, it is but the attitude of many people of the time regarding the poet. And it must be borne in mind that Whittier was very inexperienced and very young, of an age when even those with greater opportunities than he had are intolerant. But, as was true of all the maligners of Shelley, he was compelled to acknowledge Shelley's ability as a poet.

Oliver Wendell Holmes mentions Shelley a number of times and seems to have appreciated his poetry. In his *Professor at the Breakfast Table*, he makes the following comment: [3]

Poets are never young, in one sense. Their delicate ear hears the far-off whisper of eternity, which coarser souls must travel towards for scores of years before their dull sense is touched by them. A moment's insight is sometimes worth a life's experience . . . And so many youthful poets have written as if their hearts were old before their time; their pensive morning twilight has been as cool and saddening as that of evening in more common lives. The profound melancholy of those lines of Shelley,

> If I could lie down like a tired child
> And weep away the life of care
> Which I have borne and yet must bear

came from a heart, as he says, "too soon grown old"—at twenty-six years, as dull people count time when they talk of poets.

This beautiful sentiment could be expressed only by one who had a keen insight into human nature and an appreciation of poetry. In the same year, 1853, Holmes gave lectures on Wordsworth, Moore, Keats, and Shelley before the Lowell Institute in Boston. He closed each of these lectures with a poem on the poet whom he had discussed. The following stanzas are from his poem *After a Lecture on Shelley*: [4]

> One broad white sail in Spezzia's treacherous bay;
> 　On comes the blast; too daring bark, beware!
> The cloud has clasped her; lo! it melts away;
> 　The wide, waste waters, but no soul is there.
> Fade, mortal semblance, never to return;
> 　Swift is the change within thy crimson shroud;
> Seal the white ashes in the peaceful urn;
> 　All else has risen in the silvery cloud.
> Breathe for his wandering soul one passing sigh,
> 　O happier Christian, while thine eye grows dim,—
> In all the mansions of the house on high,
> 　Say not that Mercy has not one for him!

The feeling towards Shelley the man, reflected in this poem, is that of the more tolerant persons of the time. It is an attitude of sympathy for one lost because of his failure to believe in orthodox Christianity. The feeling of Holmes for Shelley the poet, however, was very different. Speaking of a floral harp which had been given him as a tribute, he says: "It made melody in my ears as sweet as those hyacinths of Shelley's, the music of whose bells was so

> delicate, soft, and intense,
> It was felt like an odor within the sense." [5]

In his biography of Emerson, Holmes finds occasion several times to compare Emerson with Shelley. In commenting on the ethical quality in poetry, he states, "And, after all, few will dare assert that 'The Vanity of Human Wishes' is greater as a poem than Shelley's 'Ode to the West Wind' or Keats' 'Ode to a Nightingale' because no line of either of these poems is half so often quoted as 'To paint a moral or adorn a tale.' " [6] Emerson's use of the redundant syllable recalls to Holmes a similar characteristic in the poetry of Shelley: "Emerson occasionally crowds a redundant syllable into a line; . . . Shelley employed it freely." [7] But his most extensive comment is on Emerson's "Threnody," a lament over the death of his first-born son. After stating that the poem has the dignity of "Lycidas," Holmes continues: "It may well compare with others of the finest memorial poems in the language—with Shelley's *Adonais* and Matthew Arnold's *Thyrsis*, leaving out of view Tennyson's *In Memoriam* as of wider scope and larger pattern."[8] One of his interesting comparisons is between Emerson's translation "The Flute from Hilali" and Shelley's "Ode to the West Wind." Both, he asserts, possess the same idea of confused personal identity, as in "Hilali,"

> Saying, Sweetheart! the old mystery remains
> If I am I; then thou, or thou art I?

or of transfer of personality, as in Shelley,

> Be thou, Spirit fierce
> My spirit! Be thou me, impetuous one.[10]

This knowledge of and interest in Shelley's poetry on the part of Holmes proves not only that he was well acquainted with the work of Shelley but also that he accepted him as one of the leading poets.

Longfellow, during the time that he was professor of modern languages at Harvard, 1836-1854, seems to have been interested in Shelley, judging from the notes he made in his interleaved copy of the first part of *Faust*. He made a note to the effect that "the Earth-Spirit is Shelley's Nature's vast frame—the web of human things." And the remaining pages contain references to Shelley's translations from the "Walpurgis-Night" and notes on some of the allusions to the "Walpurgis-Night's Dream." [11] Longfellow must have held Shelley's translations from *Faust* in high regard since in his edition of *Poets and Poetry of Europe* he included Shelley's translation of the May Day Night." [12] He had, of course, plenty of authority for recognizing this work, as it received very high praise in most of the reviews. But other indications of Longfellow's feeling for the poetry of Shelley appear at various points in the records. On October 4, 1846, he wrote in his journal: "In the evening our souls panted for the southern landscape, and for song; and we took Shelley, and were wafted on his wings far up and away. There are certain moods which his poetry meets and satisfies more than any other." [13] In his declining years he still had the youthful poet in mind. In a letter to J. T. Fields, from Portland, August 10, 1879, just a few years before his death, Longfellow writes of the noise and bustle in Portland and contrasts it with the preceding quiet Sunday with the Fields at Manchester which he said reminded him of Shelley's verses, "As the moon's soft splendor." In a later letter he enclosed the poem which he said he had preserved in his scrap book and which was rarely found among Shelley's poems.[34] This poem was reprinted by Longfellow in *The Waif*, a thin volume of selections which he had published many years before.[15] That Longfellow was an admirer and lover of Shelley's poetry seems evident from these few facts.

Among the New England poets, however, James Russell Lowell appears to be the one who knew Shelley's work best. Lowell made the acquaintance of Shelley's poetry very early. According to his own statement, he became interested in Shelley in 1834, before he was fifteen years of age. In a lecture on Coleridge, in 1885, he said: "It is just fifty-one years ago that I became the possessor of a reprint of Galignani's edition of Coleridge, Shelley, and Keats in one volume. It was a pirated book, and I trust I may be pardoned for the delight I had in it." [16] As this was the year in which Lowell entered Harvard, he may have procured the book while he was still in the school of Mr. Wells in Cambridge, or after entering Harvard. Whether or not he received any encouragement in his admiration for Shelley's poetry while at college does not appear to be recorded, but his taste for the poet seems to have developed during the next few years. By 1845 he had formed a high opinion of Shelley's poetry as revealed in a letter to Poe,[17] whose early poetry he compares to that of Shelley. He writes:

Your early poems display a maturity which astonishes me & I recollect no individual (& I believe I have all the poetry that was ever written) whose early poems were anything like as good. Shelley is nearest perhaps.

In view of the above quotation it is difficult to understand Lowell's comment in his essay on Poe in 1845. After stating that no augury can be drawn from a poet's lispings, he gives a number of illustrations, among them being the following concerning Shelley: [18]

The earliest specimens of Shelley's mind already, also, give tokens of that ethereal sublimation in which the spirit seems to soar above the region of words, but leaves its body, the verse, to be entombed, without hope of resurrection, in a mass of them.

This criticism, coming so soon after the letter to Poe, is surprising. Possibly it was made to flatter Poe whose favor the youthful Lowell was anxious to gain.[19] Four years later, however, he shows his early admiration for Shelley's poetry. In a conversation with Stoddard on the difference between imagination and fancy, when Stoddard objects to the use of fancy without imagination, Lowell replies that all fancy is not open to this objection and quotes the opening stanzas of Shelley's "Skylark" to illustrate "wherein fancy is so closely allied to imagination as to be inseparable from it." [20]

Lowell was appointed to the chair of modern languages and belles-lettres at Harvard University in 1855, to succeed Longfellow. By this time he had reached a stage of development wherein he felt qualified to attempt criticism of a technical nature. In his lecture entitled "The Imagination," [21] he refers to Shelley's use of imagination in *The Cenci* which he believes is second only to Shakespear's use of it in the parting of the lovers in *Romeo and Juliet*. Shakespeare, he states, "has so mingled his own consciousness with that of the lovers, that all nature is infected, too, and is full of partings."

> Look, love, what envious streaks
> Do lace the severing clouds in yonder east.

"In Shelley's *Cenci*, on the other hand," he continues, "we have an instance of the poet's imagination giving away its own consciousness to the object contemplated, in this case an inanimate one."

> Two miles on this side of the fort, the road
> Crosses a deep ravine; 'tis rough and narrow,
> And winds with short turns down the precipice;
> And in its depth there is a mighty rock,
> Which has, from unimaginable years,
> Sustained itself with terror and with toil
> Over a gulf, and with the agony
> With which it clings seems slowly coming down;
> Even as a wretched soul hour after hour,
> Clings to the mass of life; yet clinging, leans;
> And leaning, makes more dark the dread abyss
> In which it fears to fall: beneath this crag
> Huge as despair, as if in weariness,
> The melancholy mountain yawns.   (III, i, 244-257)

He then quotes the lines from Calderon's *Purgatorio de San Patricio*, from which Shelley took the hint for his description, as an example of sentimentalism, that is, of a passage in which the poet substitutes his own impression of the thing for the thing itself, forces his own consciousness upon it. This, he says, is an example of the subjective tendency whose excess is so lamented by Goethe and Schiller and which, when it becomes a habit, is a token of disease. This is discriminating criticism, and could not be objected to by the most radical opponent of Lowell's method of criticism.

When writing on Lessing, Lowell states that Lessing is best remembered as a nobly original man. Like that of Dr. Johnson, a great deal of his thought has a direct bearing on the immediate life of man. "His genius was not a St. Elmo's fire, as it so often is with mere poets—as it was in Shelley, for example, playing in ineffectual flame about the points of his thoughts." [22] Lowell had evidently been reading Matthew Arnold's recently published essay and had in mind Arnold's comment that Shelley was an "ineffectual angel." In 1867, in a discussion on the poetry of James Percival, he states: "Shelley and Wordsworth are both stilted, though in different ways. Shelley wreathes his stilts with flowers." [23] Lowell means that Wordsworth and Shelley are on stilts and that Percival tried to use a taller pair which makes his commonplaces more conspicuous. He implies that Shelley and Wordsworth can afford to be on stilts when he remarks: "Shelley has his gleams of unearthly wildfire, Wordsworth is by fits the most deeply inspired man of his generation; but Percival has no lucid interval." In 1874, in a letter to Mrs. Lippit, Lowell attributes to Shelley the ability to accomplish the virtually impossible: "Shelley almost alone (take his 'Stanzas to an Indian Air,' for example) has trodden with an unfaltering foot the scimitar-edged bridge which leads from physical sensation to the heaven of song." [24] In an essay on Wordsworth, 1875, Lowell states that "we cannot expect in a modern poet the thrush-like improvisation, the bewitchingly impulsive cadences, that charm us in our Elizabethan drama and whose last warble died with Herrick; but Shelley, Tennyson, and Browning have shown that the simple pathos of their music was not irrecoverable, even if the artless poignancy of their phrase be gone beyond recall." And he adds later: "In the great poets, there is an exquisite sensibility, both of soul and sense. . . . Wordsworth shows less of this finer feminine fibre of organization than one or two of his contemporaries, notably than Coleridge or Shelley." [25] In 1877, in a letter to James B. Thayer, Lowell objects to a writer in the *Cornhill Magazine* stating that Keats, Shelley, and Swinburne had restored to the ode its harmony and shapeliness: "He and I have different notions of harmony. He evidently means uniformity of recurrence. It isn't true of Shelley, some of whose odes certainly were written on the Cowley model." [26] This is the last of Lowell's criticisms of Shelley. If Lowell appears vacillating in his judgment of Shelley,[27] his seeming inconsistency may be accounted for in each instance. That included in the article on Poe may be dismissed as the attempt of a youthful writer to gain the favor of an older and much admired critic. The disparaging criticism in the Lessing essay is undoubtedly the result of accepting Matthew Arnold's conclusions regarding Shelley, an error of which many wise minds were guilty. His unfavorable comment regarding Shelley as a writer of odes is at least fair criticism. With the exception of the examples just mentioned, Lowell's criticism of Shelley is, on the whole, favorable.

One of Lowell's early attempts at writing a theory of poetic criticism was in a lecture, *The Function of the Poet,* read before the Lowell Institute in the winter of 1855. Charles Eliot Norton, in a prefatory note to this essay,[28] refers to it as an immature piece of work, but as the expression of a genius. "It is not unworthy," he states, "to stand with Sidney's and with Shelley's *Defense of Poesy.*" He does not mention, however, that Lowell is indebted to either Sidney or Shelley for any of his ideas; and there is no reason that he should, for the indebtedness is very slight. In the first ten paragraphs of the lecture there are indications that Lowell was acquainted with the essays of both Sidney and Shelley and that he might have turned to them for inspiration. Certain terms, such as "seer" and "maker" and references such as Plato's excluding the poets from his Republic perhaps came from Sidney's *Defense.* Lowell's conception of the moral value of imagination acting through poetry for the regeneration of man is a Shelleyan idea, but Lowell expresses this idea negatively while Shelley expresses it positively. Lowell states his idea as follows:

> Whoever learns to love what is beautiful is made incapable of what is low and mean and bad. . . . He who translates the divine into the vulgar, the spiritual into the sensual, is the reverse of a poet.

Shelley, in his discussion as to the manner in which poetry acts to produce the moral improvement of man, expresses the same idea positively:

> Poetry lifts the veil from the hidden beauty of the world, and makes familiar objects be as if they were not familiar; . . . The great secret of morals is Love; or a going out of our nature, and an identification of ourselves with the beautiful which exists in thought, action, or person, not our own.

Lowell believes that the "poet under whatever name, always stands for the same thing—imagination." Shelley says that "A man to be greatly good, must imagine intensely and comprehensively; . . . The great instrument of moral good is the imagination; and poetry administers to the effect by acting upon the cause." [29] Other indications of Shelleyan influence are found in the phrasing, such as references to Beauty, but these are so impalpable that it is difficult to place them. Lowell undoubtedly herein used the ideas of Shelley, as he did those of other critics, as an aid to formulating his own ideas, for the essay shows but few indications of direct borrowing.

To attempt to show that one poet has been influenced by an-

other is a difficult matter. The matter must be approached with
caution. An examination of Lowell's poetry, however, reveals
that the early poems were influenced by Shelley. The resemblance in "To Perdita, Singing" is in the movement, stanza form,
repetition, use of simile, and rhyming of words that do not sound
alike. Some examples of false rhyming are "river" and "never,"
"influence" and "whence," and "fountain" and "mounting." The
Shelleyan similarity in "The Moon" is in ideas and in several
parallel lines. The ideas of the soul "seeking some unknown
thing" and of the "eternal law of love" moving "through life and
death" are Shelleyan:

> A voice of something beautiful
> Whispered a dim foreboding.
> .   .   .   .   .   .
> One strong eternal law of Love . . .

There is also a close resemblance to Shelley in the second stanza
of "Remembered Music." [30]

> Or in low murmurs they began
> Rising and rising momently,
> As o'er a deep Aeolian
> A fitful breeze, until they ran
> Up to a sudden ecstasy.

Other poems that seem to reveal Shelleyan characteristics are
"Summer Storm," "Threnodia," "The Sirens," and "Ode to Happiness." The first of these poems contains a number of lines that
are Shelleyan, the following being examples:

> Now leaps the wind in the sleepy march,
> And tramples the grass with terrified feet,
> The startled river turns leaden and harsh,
> You can hear the quick heart of the tempest beat.
>   (ll. 40-45)

The foregoing lines, in movement, resemble Shelley's "The
Cloud." The following lines are Shelleyan in movement, and the
stanza form, with its variation in rhyme, may represent an
experimenting suggested by early forms used by Shelley in
Prometheus Unbound:

> The blue lightning flashes,
> The rapid hail clashes,
> The white waves are tumbling,
> And, in one baffled roar,
> Like the toothless sea mumbling
> A rock-bristled shore,
> The thunder is rumbling
> And crashing and crumbling,—
> Will silence return nevermore?   (ll. 57-65)

In "Threnodia," the following lines are reminiscent of Shelley's "Skylark:" [31]

> Far, far into the skies,
> Gladding the earth with song,
> And gushing harmonies,
> Had he but tarried with us long.

Although "The Sirens" is obviously influenced by Tennyson's "Ulysses," certain lines show indebtedness to Shelley.

> Our little isle is green and breezy

might recall the first line of the "Euganean Hills," and

> The low west wind creeps panting up the shore,

the "Ode to the West Wind." The "Ode to Happiness" contains the following Shelleyan and Keatsian lines:

> Spirit, that rarely comest now
> And only to contrast my gloom,
> Like rainbow-feathered birds that bloom
> A moment on some autumn bough
> That, with the spurn of their farewell
> Sheds its last leaves,—thou once didst dwell
> With me year-long, and make intense
> To boyhood's wisely vacant days . . .

The first two and the last three lines recall Shelley's "Song," [32] beginning "Rarely, rarely comest thou." Lowell's *Prometheus* was undoubtedly directly inspired by Shelley's *Prometheus Unbound* and probably indirectly by the many other poems on the Promethean myth.

Of the minor poets of New England, Ellery Channing ranks among the first. He was accorded a place among the poets of his day by Emerson, who published one of his poems, "The Flight of the Wild Geese," in his *Parnassus* and sent some of his verses to Carlyle, who pronounced them "worthy indeed of reading." Although Channing is now almost unknown, he deserves a place in an anthology of the period because of the lyrical quality revealed in some of his poems. It is in individual lines rather than in poems as a whole that he shows his ability as a poet, the best known example being the well known line, [33]

> If my bark sinks, 'tis to another sea.

Channing, however, was too much inclined to imitation to develop his own abilities as a poet. He early attempted the lyrical flights of Shelley but later contented himself with the more serene style of Wordsworth and Emerson. His most beautiful poem, "The Earth-Spirit," is filled with Shelleyan lines reminiscent of the "The Cloud." [34]

> I have woven shrouds of air
>   In a loom of hurrying light,
> For the trees which blossoms bear,
>   And gilded them with sheets of bright;
> I fall upon the grass like love's first kiss;
>   I make the golden flies and their fine bliss;
>
>   .   .   .
>
> I laugh aloud in sudden gusts of rain
> To see the ocean lash himself in air,
>
>   .   .   .
>
> I polish the green ice, and gleam the wall
> With the white frost, and leaf the brown trees all.

In the first stanza of "The Flight of the Wild Geese," the line,

> Toiling to lift Time's curtain,

probably was inspired by a similar idea in Shelley's "Hymn to Intellectual Beauty," and lines 9-12,

> Suddenly
> High in the air,
> I heard the travelled geese
> Their overture prepare . . .

by his "Skylark." One of Channing's most ambitious poems, "A Poet's Hope," reveals the Shelley influence in scenes of traveling swiftly through space and soaring into the sky, and in such lines as,

> And weave it in the strands of living light,

and

> O Time! O Death! I clasp you in my arms, . . .

The "Italian Song," a poem from the *Second Series*, shows that Channing was still inclined to attempt a Shelleyan lyric occasionally.

> The old Tower gray
> Bids purple day
> Paint the gray mosses with its Tyrian hue,
>   And fine-toned night
>   Rounds with dim light
> Each crumbling stone into proportion due.
>
>   .   .   .
>
>   My tinkling lute
>   Converts the mute
> And humble silence into golden singing;

> The laden air
> Rich scents doth bear,
> Around the ruin, vase-like odors flinging.

Channing's appreciation of Shelley's poetry is revealed in his "Conversations in Rome," in which he has his artist state that if Shelley and Keats are to live at all, it will be in their verses.[35]

William Wetmore Story, a new England minor poet whose position has never been determined but whose work often appears in anthologies, not only admired Shelley's poetry but also wrote some of his own best poetry under the influence of Shelley.[36] The poem "Sunrise" contains passages reminiscent of Shelley.

> Where the mountain's clear sharp line is drawn,
> The light mounts steadily,
> While below in many a chasm deep,
> The mists of night still lingering creep,
> And the lower slopes are half asleep,
> And dimly dreaming,— (Line 3-8)

> The wild geese drop from the thin clear height,
> Where all night long they have held their flight,
> And settle on lake and mere;
> Up springs the lark, and, lost in the light,
> Carols his rapture—out of sight,
> Thrilling the atmosphere. (Lines 44-49)

The last part of the poem is characteristically Shelleyan in movement, atmosphere, tone, and lightness of coloring and touch.

> To swell the chorus that evermore
> Is shouted from flashing peaks that dare
> The thin cold depths of the breathless air
>
> .   .   .   .
> Where the clear cool stream with a murmurous flow,
> .   .   .   .
>
> All are chanting their song as one,—
> From the base of the thunderous avalanche
> And the cataract's dizzy booming
> To the whisper fine of the quivering breeze
> That hurries through myriad leagues of trees
> And the insects infinite humming.

The poem "Moonrise" as a whole is vaguely reminiscent of Shelley but also shows the influence of Wordsworth as well as that of Longfellow and the German Romanticists, especially of Novalis. The most Shelleyan passages are:

> The riotous day is gone
> With his cymbals clashing, his bright spears flashing,
> His tumult and rout, his Bacchanal's shout,
> His gladness and madness, and laughter and raving;—
> .   .   .   .

> The stars in their blue unfathomable tomb
> Gleam far and bright,—
> They are waiting the coming of the moon,
> The Regent of the night. . . .

Another minor poet who manifested an interest in Shelley was James Gates Percival. That Percival knew and admired his poetry might be inferred from the fact that he included several Shelley selections in his edition of Knox's *Elegant Extracts*.[37] As to Shelley's influence on Percival's own poetry, it is very slight. Some of the "Songs" and "Lays," published in the 1845 edition of his poems, entitled *The Dream of a Day and Other Poems,* affect the Shelleyan manner. Lowell believed that Percival's *Prometheus* was influenced by Shelley. He states: "It is easy to trace the literary influence to which the mind of Percival was in turn subjected. . . . In *Prometheus,* it is Shelley who is paramount for the time, and Shelley at his worst period, before his unwieldy abundance of incoherent words and images, that were merely words and images without any meaning of real experience to give them solidity, had been compressed in the stricter molds of thought and study."[38] Shelley can hardly be held responsible for the vagueness in Percival's poem as it is doubtful if Percival had read Shelley's poetry at this time. Although his *Prometheus* is written in the Spenserian stanza, the same form Shelley used in *The Revolt of Islam,* it does not show any indebtedness to Shelley's poem. It does, however, show the influence of Byron's poetry, which was very popular at this time.[39]

A few names of less importance deserve mention because some attention has been given to the work of these poets in recent years. Washington Allston is better known as a painter than as a poet. "The Angel and the Nightingale" appears to be the only poem in which there is any indebtedness to Shelley. The poem, for the most part, is an imitation of Spenser's *Faerie Queene,* with occasional lines and stanzas that recall Shelley or Wordsworth. The Shelleyan influence is in the sixth, seventh, and eighth stanzas of the second part. These stanzas are reminiscent of *The Revolt of Islam.* Thomas William Parson's "Paradise Gloria"[40] may have been inspired by Shelley's "Euganean Hills," the indications of influence being in the first two lines, in the idea of a secluded city:

> There is a city, builded by no hand,
> And unapproached by sea or shore.

As has been seen from the foregoing pages, however, New England poets as a group owed little to Shelley. Only occasionally, as in the case of Lowell and some of the minor poets, could any

Shelleyan influence be detected in their poetry. That they knew Shelley and recognized him as a poet, the evidence given by Holmes and Longfellow, as well as by Lowell, will bear testimony. It is possible that the two former poets, particularly Longfellow, knew Shelley better than records would indicate, could the written and unwritten opinions of these poets be examined.

Some New England Shelleyans

To the New England Shelleyans we must turn to find the most loyal supporters of Shelley, those individuals who admired without reservation and yet with no maudlin sympathy. Among these men are found such great names as those of Nathaniel Hawthorne, John Lothrop Motley, George William Curtis, and Phillips Brooks. The name of the great William Ellery Channing cannot be listed among the enthusiastic supporters because Channing was not a whole-hearted follower. These men were romanticists, even in their advanced years, and they were romanticists of the finest type.

Nathaniel Hawthorne had more in common with Shelley than is generally recognized. Like Shelley, Hawthorne evidently enjoyed probing into the occult sciences. Just as the youthful Shelley spent many hours in the world of wonder, so Hawthorne spent a great part of his life in the same atmosphere. How delighted Shelley would have been with some of the thoughts set down in Hawthorne's *Note-Books*, such as "A snake taken into a man's stomach and nourished there from fifteen to thirty-five years, tormenting him most horribly. A type of envy or some other evil passion." Even the torments of Prometheus cannot equal this.

Hawthorne was deeply interested in and appreciative of Shelley. He does not fail to include him in his essays of general criticism on the poets. There must have existed a spiritual link between this quiet, humorous man, with his fondness for calling up the ghosts of the past in the "Old Manse" in New England, and the young poet who in his imagination inhabited Field Place with an alchemist and a "Great Old Snake," to the terror and admiration of his small sisters. Hawthorne's attitude, half serious, half playful, but always sympathetic, reveals a sincere feeling for the younger poet. When, in his imagination, he meets the younger romanticists, Byron and Shelley and Keats, in England in 1845, and has Shelley not only reconciled to the Church of England, but with a "small country living" and writing on "the poetico-philosophical proofs of Christianity on the basis of the Thirty-nine Articles," it is done with a touch of sympathetic humor approached by no other writer on Shelley except Pea-cock.[41] The whole discussion of the imaginary meeting with Shelley argues, if not a wide acquaintance with Shelley, at least an understanding of him that could be gained only by a careful reading of the poet. Shelley's putting Hawthorne at his ease, his assuring him that there was "a harmony, an order, a regular procession in the development of his works, from *Queen Mab* to the discourse on the Thirty-nine Articles," is so characteristic of the Shelley at Oxford that one wonders how many times in his quiet study Hawthorne must have smiled over the antics of Shelley as presented by Hogg in the "Oxford Articles" in the *New Monthly*.[42] Hawthorne's discovery of a development to-wards Christianity in Shelley's ideas is but an early interpre-tation of a later nineteenth- and twentieth-century theory as to the poet's views on religion. His criticism of Shelley's early poetry as cold, too unfeeling, too much of the fancy and intellect, "a concrete arrangement of crystallizations, or even of icicles, as cold as they were brilliant," is withal excellent criticism, as is his comment, "I consider the productions of mis maturity super-ior, as poems, to those of his youth. They are warmer with human love, which has served as an interpreter between his mind and the multitude." His appreciation of Shelley the man is revealed in the comment: "In his private character, Shelley can hardly have grown more gentle, kind, and affectionate than his friends always represented him to be. . . ."[43]

Hawthorne's *Marble Faun*, which was partly written in Italy, 1857–1859, is concerned with the Cenci story. There is nothing in the story or in Hawthorne's correspondence or journals to lead one to believe that he was indebted in any way to Shelley, not even for the suggestion of using Beatrice Cenci as the subject or inspiration of a part of the novel. For Hawthorne's best com-ment on Shelley's poetry, the reader must turn to "Earth's Holo-caust," [44] a satire on reform, in which among a variety of articles cast into the bonfire are the works of some of the best authors:

Speaking of the properties of flame, methought Shelley's poetry emitted a purer light than almost any other productions of his day, con-trasting beautifully with the fitful and lurid gleams and gushes of black vapor that flashed and eddied from the volumes of Lord Byron.

Purity and beauty, the two chief characteristics of Shelley's poetry, are appreciated by Hawthorne. For pure poetry and for beauty in poetry, Shelley had no peer in his age save Keats, but for reflecting the pure light of poetry, that airy, filmy, gleaming atmosphere, he had no equal.

It is a historian, however, John Lothrop Motley, to whom credit must be given for being one of the most consistent and confirmed admirers of Shelley. Motley seems to have developed a liking for Shelley in his early school days at Round Hill. It was in Cambridge, after his return from Cogswell's school, that he and Holmes became acquainted. Holmes reports that they took long walks together and quoted poetry, Shelley being then a great favorite of Motley's.[45] And when he was an undergraduate at Harvard, although Goethe was given the preference, Shelley and Byron remained favorite poets.[46] Motley's very interesting letter to Dr. Holmes from Bournemouth, England, in 1873, shows that his enthusiasm for Shelley had increased rather than abated with the passing years and that he had not relinquished his old habit of quoting Shelley's poetry: [47]

Yesterday the sun was shining, and I sat a long time on the cliffs, looking out on the channel.

> The sun was warm, the sky was clear
> The waves were dancing fast and bright,

as if it had been the Bay of Naples, which the dejected Shelley so exquisitely sang.

He then tells of his delight at a visit from Sir Percy Shelley and of his own subsequent visits to the home of the Shelleys, his neighbors, who, he writes, "have a veritabel *cult* for the memory of the poet." Then follows a description of the shrine which Lady Shelley and Sir Percy had erected to the poet:

In one of the rooms is a sort of shrine to Shelley, a cast of the marble monument erected to him in the neighboring church at a place called Christchurch, and tables covered with glass, under which are memorials and relics, locks of his hair and of Byron, Trelawny, Leigh Hunt, and other of his companions, a glove found in the boat in which he was drowned, a soaked little volume of Aeschylus, which he had with him in the last moments, and other things.

He then relates an anecdote regarding a childhood picture of Shelley, and closes with

Perhaps I am boring you with all this about Shelley. Perhaps you think me wrong in my admiration of his poetry. You are a much better judge, being a poet yourself, than such a prosaic animal as I am, but I hope you will sanction my enthusiasm.

It is but natural that the impulsive, warm-hearted imaginative youth, George William Curtis, should have felt the fascination of Shelley. Perhaps his associations at Brook Farm, where he spent the time between the ages of eighteen and twenty, were responsible for this interest. In an autobiographic sketch sent to Rufus Griswold some ten years later, Curtis writes: [48]

> At Brook Farm I made many of my best friends and tried all the asceticisms,—the no meat, the long hair, the loose dress, etc.—but was not a proper member.

He states that while he was at Concord, on a farm, he wrote verse, and lived the simple life, and concludes the letter with, "Voilà tout! and Shelley died when he was no older than I am." Thus Curtis seems to have associated Shelley with his years spent at Brook Farm and Concord. In the conversations on literature at the Farm Shelley must have received some consideration, particularly from Margaret Fuller who was a frequent visitor and who often "talked." It is even probable that John S. Dwight, under whom Curtis studied music at Brook Farm, was a Shelley admirer. He could hardly have been oblivious to the music of Shelley's verse. The many references to Shelley in Curtis's letters to him after leaving Brook Farm are ample evidence that the older and the younger man must have found in Shelley a common bond of sympathy. On a hot June day, Curtis's imagination reverts to the description of the funeral pyre of Shelley, and in a mood of extravagant playfulness, he writes to Dwight,[49] "As Shelley's body when lifeless was caused to disappear in flames and smoke, so may mine before its tenant is departed." He states that he had been inspired by his recollection of Shelley to write verses to him and Keats.

A little more than two years later, November 22, 1846, a visit to the graves of Shelley and Keats at Rome furnishes inspiration for one of those charming, smooth flowing descriptions that were so characteristic of Curtis:[50]

> The roses were in full blossom as Shelley says they used to be in midwinter. It is a green and sequestered spot under the walls of old Rome, where the sunlight lingers long, and where in the sweet society of roses whose bloom does not wither, Shelley and Keats sleep always a summer sleep.

If the comment of Curtis which follows this quotation savors somewhat of the pessimistic, or if it seems sophisticated, it probably was prompted by a deep and sincere love for the poets and is much more acceptable than is the overwrought sentimentalism of many of the Shelley admirers of the time:

> Fate is no less delicate than stern, which here united them after such lives and deaths. And yet here one feels the grimness of the Fate which strikes such lips into Silence.

In his letter from Naples a few months later, he writes Dwight that he plucked roses from the graves of Shelley and Keats and led a Roman life for a winter, "not for myself only, but for you."

In an article "Southern Italy," published in *Sartin's Union Magazine*,[51] for July, 1848, Curtis begins his description of Naples with a quotation from Shelley's "Ode to Naples:"

> Naples! thou heart of men which ever pantest,
>   Naked beneath the lidless eye of Heaven!
> Elysian city, which to calm enchantest
>   The mutinous air and sea—they round thee, even
>   As sleep round Love are driven.

So sang Shelley, and his feeling is invaluable, because his nature was so exquisitely delicate, that it responded truly to the external impression as a harp which is finely strung to every whisper and wail of the wind. The "Stanzas Written in Dejection near Naples" I would willingly quote entire, as a most subtle echo in a poet's thought and melody of the luxurious silence and delight of a southern Italian day. If it is mournful music, it is only because his whole being was then modulated in a minor key; and although he could then appreciate the character of every influence which moved him, he could only express it as he did. Thus through the unselfish sadness of these verses, still breathes the soul-satisfying temper of the day, and feeling the want of accord with its character, not of sadness, but of that sort of sadness, he says:

> Some might lament that I were cold
>   As I, when this sweet day is gone,
> Which my lost heart, too soon grown old,
>   Insults with this untimely moan;
>   They might lament—for I am one
> Whom men love not,—and yet regret,
>   Unlike this day, which, when the sun
>   Shall on its stainless glory set,
> Will linger, though enjoyed, like joy in memory yet.

So in his *Julian and Maddalo,* the passionate tale vaguely realizes the dreary, inexplicable sadness of some days in Venice.

It is in such unconscious impressions of days and things upon men so real as Shelley, that the Italian character is best felt.

After reading this article, one wishes that Curtis had written more about Shelley. And again the comment of William Dean Howells comes to mind. He wrote of Curtis:"[52] It must always be a keen regret with the men of my generation who witnessed with such rapture the early proofs of his talent, that he could not have devoted it wholly to the beautiful and let others look after the true."

Other and later comments on Shelley are found in the letters of Curtis while he is traveling on the continent. In a letter from Vienna to C. P. Cranch in Rome, Curtis, in referring to Jenny Lind's singing in Berlin, comments: [53]

For this is one of the overarching joys of life—this is that morning sky and Shelley's skylark who sang and soared into it. May you one day know what it is, or if not, have faith that the same genius which drew us to Rome does not fail of another expression in our own day. . . .

The remainder of the letter is omitted. One wonders why. It is possible that Cranch was, like several other nineteenth-century writers, an admirer of Shelley in his youth. And, like the others, he may have wished to deny, in later years, any affection for a poet to whose name the appellation of "atheist" was appended. At least on May 7, 1883, he wrote a poem to Curtis in which a visit to the grave of Keats is described but in which no mention is made of Shelley, regardless of the fact that Shelley, not Keats, was the idol of Curtis's youth. The poem, a part of which is given below, is a beautiful tribute to Keats.[54]

> Till by the grave of Keats we stood, and found
>   A rose—a single rose left blooming there,
> Making more sacred still that hallowed ground,
>   And that enchanted air.
>
> A single rose, whose fading petals dropped,
>   And seemed to wait for us to gather them.
> So, kneeling on the humble mound, we stooped
>   And plucked it from its stem.
>
> One rose, and nothing more. We shared its leaves
>   Between us, as we shared the thoughts of one
> Called from the field before his unripe sheaves
>   Could feel the harvest sun.
>
> That rose's fragrance is forever fled
>   For us, dear friend, but not the Poet's lay.
> He is the rose—deathless among the dead,
>   Whose perfume lives today.

The name of Shelley might be substituted for that of Keats and thus add to the appropriateness of the poem as a tribute to Curtis.

After his return from Europe the circumstances of his life did not permit Curtis much longer to indulge in flights of fancy. But he never entirely lost his liking for Shelley, although it is very probable that the conventions of the circle in which he moved deprived him of this joy as well as of others. In later years, in his address on Bryant,[55] he refers to the "aerial fervor of Shelley." And, in 1882, in an essay on Longfellow,[56] he calls Shelley the poet of aspiration. But the heavy responsibilities of business and politics and the demands of social life left Curtis little time in which to enjoy his favorite poets.

When Phillips Brooks was graduated from Harvard in 1855, like many other brilliant young men, he was undecided as to his future profession. Probably to relieve a mind seething with ideas, he formed the habit of recording his thoughts on various subjects, such as history, religion, and literature, but chiefly on the last. To this habit we are indebted for his illuminating discussion on Shelley's poetry [57] with which he seems to have been very familiar. To him, *Queen Mab,* regardless of its faults, was re-markable and worthy of study. Shelley's fault, he says, was that he caught only Nature's half of the dialogue and thought he had heard the whole. He praises Shelley for not being "content in darkness" as so many were. Unlike most people who did not agree with Shelley's views, Brooks finds him stimulating. The religious views expressed in *Queen Mab* bring the following response from this young student: "I must say the blasphemy, for we must use the word, of that strange poem has done more to make me a Christian than many a wise homily." For the *Revolt of Islam* he has only the highest praise. He considers it to be "the purest conception and embodiment of his creed as con-ceived and embodied by the purest soul that ever believed in the power of mere human love and joy and virtue to regenerate the world." The answer to the theory expressed in the poem, he states, was in Shelley's own purity. He avers that Laon and Laone's creed was for them, not for mankind. No other person of the nineteenth century showed such broad and clear under-standing of Shelley's attitude towards religion. The purity in Shelley, he states, is the same as in the religion of Christ. Then follows the discerning observation: "Shelley's error throughout seems to me too low an estimate of man's actual and too high a faith in man's (unaided) possible." He cannot understand how Shelley failed to recognize the divine beneficence that spoke to him in Nature as it spoke to no other living soul, that he could look only to man's own help to work out man's perfection. He says: "If purity of heart and earnestness of purpose, and perfect poetry of life and hopes and universal being *are* things to honor and revere, then we must give to Shelley full honor and esteem." His sonnet to Shelley bears further evidence of his love for the poet.

> "If I were one whom the loud world held wise!"
>   So speak'st thou, Shelley, in thy bitter scorning,
>   And turn'st thy pale, strong face to watch the dawning
> Of wisdom on that world's cold, dull, gray skies.
> A cloud rose-fleecy o'er the horizon lies
>   With angel sounds from Bethlem's blessed morning;
>   O could thy soul but hear the mystic warning
> As the rapt gaze sees its pure beauty rise!
> O man alone claims not man's fullest growth;
>   As in their pledging, lovers break the token,
> Each keeping half in witness of their oath,
>   Till each fulfill the word that each hath spoken.
> So heaven holds pledge of manhood's plighted troth;
>   O kneel and pray God take thy fragment broken.

The attitude of William Ellery Channing towards Shelley furnishes a typical example of the effect that is often produced by a false report, even on the mind of one who is generally recognized as sympathetic and tolerant. Channing seems not to have been able to overcome an early prejudice against Shelley, an impression of him received from Southey, who, according to Elizabeth Palmer Peabody, "did not interpret him profoundly." [58] In 1828, Channing wrote to Miss Ruth P. Olney, evidently a Shelley admirer: [59]

> I received distinctly the impression that Shelley was a noble nature sadly perverted, and that, under happier influences, he might have proved the glory of his race. . . .
> I should like to know something of Shelley from one worthy of belief, and capable of estimating him. I am inclined to think of him as a man lost to religion through the folly, hypocrisy, and intolerance of its "friends." How many noble spirits have been ruined by identifying religion with its loud professors! But I mean not to make excuse for such persons. . . .

The remainder of the letter is in the tone of the last sentence. Channing states that these people, evidently the Shelley type, have access to the teachings of Christ and should, therefore, make them clear to their less gifted brethren. Thus while he states his willingness to be convinced regarding Shelley's merits, he makes clear by his attitude that such is not the case. That he read at least one of Shelley's poems and enjoyed it is reported by Miss Peabody who states that he read the "Skylark" with the keenest delight. But, after dwelling on the incidents of his life, as reported by Southey, he said that "Shelley was a seraph gone astray, who needed friends that he never found in this world." [60] Channing might have defended Shelley and done much to alleviate the wrong impressions had he taken the trouble to make a few investigations for himself. He would have found that he and Shelley had much in common, not only in their ideas regarding humanitarianism, socialism, and pacificism, but in religion as well. While he was a tutor to a family in Virginia, Channing became acquainted with the theories of Rousseau, Godwin, and Mary Wollstonecraft, so that he held in common with Shelley many of the same views. His belief in the goodness of man is not far removed from Shelley's contention that all men could be made good. His idea of pure love as "a self-emptying, absolutely disinterested regard for its object," was the theory of love that Shelley put into practice throughout his life, the most noteworthy example being his care of the sick while he was living at Marlowe. But Channing interpreted this love as God's love in man, while Shelley did not recognize the Divine inspiration. Miss Peabody reports Channing as saying: "If all exercised it [God's love], I see that social existence would be an image of God manifest in divine beauty, in correspondence with, but yet transcending the universe. And finally, because it explains Jesus Christ as a historical fact." [61] Shelley likewise believed that social existence would be improved by the exercise of love, a "Love" emanating from the recognition of "Beauty," not transcending, but permeating the whole universe. The chief difference between many of the ideas of Shelley and Channing was that in Channing they had been subjected to the tests of experience and of faith in a Divine Power.[62]

The names of Henry T. Tuckerman and Frank B. Sanborn must be added to the list of Shelley admirers. Tuckerman, who wrote articles on Shelley for the *Southern Literary Messenger*, shows sympathy for Shelley in his "A Day at Oxford." [63] He states that the conservation of learning is often as great an obstacle to humanity as that of ignorance and uses Shelley's expulsion from Oxford as an illustration. Of lack of tolerance at Oxford, he says: "In our own time, a most pure, lofty, and disinterested youth of genius was ignominiously cast from her bosom and Shelley, the atheistic boy, made to feel the ban of unchristian bigotry, when he most needed the light of wisdom and the shelter of charity." In *The Italian Sketch Book*, published in 1835, Tuckerman has a chapter entitled "Graves of Shelley and Keats." [64] The essay is a discussion of the poets rather than a description of their graves. He praises both poets highly and shows great sympathy for Keats, to whom he devotes most of the discussion. Of Shelley, he says:

The romantic imagination, remarkable mental independence, and extreme sensitiveness of the former of these poets, combined, as they were, with high native and acquired powers, and associated with a fate so deeply melancholy, give a truly practical colouring to our recollection of him.

At the beginning of the chapter on "Naples" are two quotations from Shelley's "Ode to Naples," but there is no mention of the poet. Tuckerman's interest in Shelley is best revealed in his articles published in the *Southern Literary Messenger*.[65] Of Sanborn, the friend of poets, Miss Ariana Smith Walker writes:

I have met F. S., the young poet. . . . It seemed strange that Shelley should be the favorite poet of an uncultivated, I should say, self-cultivated boy; but so it is, and he talked of him and of the poems as I never heard anyone talk, after his own fashion.

Sanborn says that he and Miss Walker were in the habit of discussing not only Shelley, but Plato and Emerson of whom they were both eager readers. In later years, Miss Walker expressed her delight with Leigh Hunt's *Autobiography*, because it abounded with gossip of literary men, particularly of Shelley.[66]

W. W. Story, whose *Conversations in a Studio* was not published until 1890, belongs with the New England group of Shelley admirers. Although the conversation on Shelley takes place between two fictional characters, it represents Story's opinion of the poet. He says that the lines of the "Indian Serenade" were written to a long, languid air. He lauds Shelley in a somewhat sentimental manner and regrets that he was not appreciated while he lived, that his perfect verses were cast aside while the almost trivial verses of Byron were cherished and applauded and went sounding through the world. He states that Shelley was too refined and spiritual in his poems for the age in which he lived. He says that "his muse had only wings and not feet. It could soar into ideal heights, but it could not walk on earth." Story must have had more than a passing interest in Shelley's poems in that he examined the manuscripts and found them "almost illegible from corrections."

Of the journalists of the middle of the century, George Stillman Hillard was deeply interested in Shelley. Although he errs in his statement that Shelley did not know Italian, his criticism of the poet in *Six Months in Italy* is discriminating and appreciative. He states that Shelley found the climate and scenery of Italy inspirational: "The clear sky of Italy, its bright and richly colored atmosphere, its sparkling seas, and the azure depth of its clear sky seem to have inspired the lavish and gorgeous descriptions of *Prometheus Unbound*" and the other poems written in this country. In praise of Shelley's descriptive powers he says: "In pure description—such as is not warmed by passion or deepened by philosophic reflection—he is a great master. His sense of color is particularly fine, and he paints the hues of a landscape or a garden as Titian would paint a purple mantle embroidered with gold." He favors the *Cenci*, which he says is the most finished and carefully constructed of Shelley's "poems." Hillard was one of the first critics to praise the style of Shelley's letters which he calls easy and graceful. He detects Shelley's failure to appreciate art as revealed in his letters. His feeling, he states, was fine and true, but his knowledge was superficial.

Perhaps no finer tribute could be paid to Shelley than to say that he was admired throughout the years of the nineteenth century by so varied a group of men as these Shelleyans, by a novelist, a historian, an essayist, a minister, a teacher, an artist, and a journalist. All were men who ranked high in their respective professions.

CHAPTER III

Shelley and the New England Periodicals

The chief organ of New England opinion for the first half of the nineteenth century was the *North American Review*. It was founded in 1815 by William Tudor, a young Harvard graduate, and its editors for many years were chiefly teachers in Harvard. According to Mott,[1] Tudor soon enlisted the aid of a group of Boston and Harvard scholars, partly recruited from the former Anthology Club, which had been maturing a plan for a New England review. The magazine was local until 1824, when Jared Sparks became its editor and met with some success in making it a national magazine; but it remained chiefly a New England periodical until 1850. During the first half of the century, however, it enlisted the support of some of the best literary critics of the country. Among these critics was E. P. Whipple, who was well known in England as well as in America. Whipple, who contributed a number of articles to the magazine during the fourth and fifth decades, was particularly interested in Shelley and other poets of the Romantic period.

Although the *North American Review* contained a great deal of material on Shelley, he does not furnish the subject for a single article in the first 125 volumes. The habit of digression, however, was indulged in to such an extent among writers of the early nineteenth century that an article on one author or his work invariably led to a discussion of the works of many of his contemporaries. Thus many of the articles on Byron contain comments on Shelley. The first mention of Shelley was made in this magazine in 1825 in an article on "Lord Byron's Character and Writings,"[2] in which Shelley is referred to as being "almost domesticated with Lord Byron." The author then quotes from Medwin's *Journal of the Conversations of Lord Byron* an account of Shelley's funeral and Byron's reaction as an example of bad taste in writing. A few years later William Browne Oliver Peabody, a minister and a frequent contributor to the *North American Review,* in a review of Leigh Hunt's *Lord Byron and Some of His Contemporaries,* refers to Shelley, Barry Cornwall, and Keats as poets whose "talents" were eclipsed by an unnatural style. "They might have shone bright in their several stations," declares this critic, "but they chose to strike out new paths for themselves, and the world has shown no disposition to follow them. They seem to the uninitiated, employed as unprofitably as they would be in painting the colors that float before us when our eyes are shut, or setting to music the ringing in their ears; and each by his particular Terrors, has done something to injure the cause of poetry in the world." [3] In a review of Lord Byron's "Conversations on Religion" in the same magazine in 1833, Peabody speaks of Shelley as "the Atheist." [4] Peabody's reaction to Shelley's religious views is that of many people of the time. The only other mention of Shelley in this periodical during the fourth decade is that by H. T. Tuckerman in his review of *Italy: with Sketches of Spain and Portugal*, by the author of *Vathek*.[5] Tuckerman, even at this time an admirer of Shelley, states that Shelley's "romantic imagination, remarkable mental independence, and extreme sensitiveness" combined with "high native and acquired powers, and associated with a fate so melancholy,— give a truly poetic coloring to our recollection of him."

Several other New England periodicals of the thirties seem to have been more interested in Shelley than was the *North American Review*. *The Literary Journal and Weekly Register of Science and the Arts*,[6] an ephemeral journal of Providence, Rhode Island, contains a great deal of information on Shelley.[7] The most important of these articles, "Character and Writing of Shelley," signed "Egeria," was written expecially for the *Literary Journal* and published in the issue for January 11, 1834.[8] This is a very appreciative criticism that contains a great deal of originality but depends for facts regarding Shelley on the statements of Leigh Hunt and Mary Shelley. The writer begins: "The poetry of Shelley has been but little read in this country, and is, indeed, of a nature too abstract and spiritual to become popular with the majority of readers in any country. Yet, Bulwer, in his late work on England, has attributed to it a higher and more powerful influence than to that of any other poet of the present age, Wordsworth alone excepted." He adds that this fact is not surprising since Shelley's poetry produces an impression on minds of a certain class. "His phraseology is remarkably rich, varied, and beautiful; and his imagination luxuriant and inventive; but the principal charm of his writings consists in that liberality of thought and feeling, and in that enlarged philanthropy which inspires every line, and makes us deeply regret that with so much that is excellent and true, much also is blended that is pernicious and false." He says that Shelley's ardor for truth, contempt for prejudice, and indifference to popular opinion drew upon him much censure and involved him in embarrassment. His hatred of oppression and hypocrisy led him to the opposite extremes of infidel and revolutionary principles. He states that although expelled from Oxford, Shelley still pursued his love of truth with undiminished ardor and refers to his study of the Bible:

> The Bible was studied by him with deep interest and attention, and character and precepts of the Saviour were held by him in high veneration. . . . It appears, however, that the Scripture, considered as a divine revelation, presented obstacles to his subtle and speculative reason, which his faith was unhappily incapable of surmounting.

This writer believes that it is not surprising that a mind so peculiarly constituted as that of Shelley, "in its first eager survey of life, was betrayed into inconsequent reasoning and arrived at false deductions. His mind was evidently often exercised in speculation on the origin and existence of Evil, a question over which every reflecting being has at some period mused." He is of the opinion that Shelley might have renounced his views on religion in that he had a mind open to conviction.

In appreciation of Shelley's poetry, this critic writes:

> He has clothed some of the beautiful speculations of the Grecian philosophers in most exquisite verse; and has woven from their fine-drawn theories, a woof so brilliant and so beautiful, that its dazzling splendor almost blinds us to its fragility. His glowing fancies were richly nourished by the pure naptha of a true poetic inspiration; and his keen relish for the charm of nature, enabled him to discover many remote analogies and latent sources of beauty in objects that would have passed unnoticed by common observers.

After a discussion of Shelley's ideas, this writer concludes: "Almost all his poems appear to have had for their object the illustration of some moral or philosophic truth." He states that Shelley's intellectual history is a striking exemplification of the fact that "the tree of knowledge is not that of life." He attributes Shelley's separation from Harriet to dissimilarity of tastes, and comments on his good fortune in marrying Mary, who had kindness of heart and a happy disposition.

The *American Monthly Magazine* finds occasion to mention Shelley several times during this period.[9] In a review of the poems of Mrs. L. H. Sigourney, January 1, 1835, the poet is commended for not affiliating with the "Satanic School." This critic believes that this school has arisen as a result of the idea that madness is a necessary ingredient of a poet. "The evil that has been occasioned by the sanction thus given in jest but received in earnest, is the establishment of a school of poetry, which has been termed, absurdly enough, the *Satanic* or *demoniacal*;— a school, which—founded upon the basis, and following the example laid down in the works of certain authors of undoubted genius, but unfortunately for themselves and for their imitators, of no less undoubted eccentricity—has expressed its admiration of Byron and Shelley by copying, not their beauties, but their extravagances; thus extending the fallacy from its original form, and assuming that because every poet is a madman, therefore every madman is a poet." This article is of interest in view of the fact that the Shelley imitators in America before 1835 were few.

The *Yale Literary Magazine,* conducted by the students of Yale College, for 1839-1840,[10] contains an extensive article entitled "Shelley." This article is important as reflecting the opinions of the students in one of the conservative colleges regarding Shelley. It is one of the most discerning criticisms of the poet written during the first half of the century. The writer begins:

> There are men so blinded by bigotry, as to be unable to see any good beyond the limits of their peculiar creed. What falls not within these, be it ever so lovely and fair, appears distorted in the mists of prejudice. They measure all things, how various, so ever their natures, by one standard, and make a man's genius and talents of no account, if his life be not regulated by their rules. . . . There are others who take an opposite course, and consider genius as almost a palliation for vice and crime. . . . Both these classes have pronounced their judgment upon Shelley; and while the one has covered him with blackness and cast him out, the other has loaded him with indiscriminate praise, and raised him to an elevation undeserved.

This critic formed his opinion of Shelley's character from his writings and from the comments of his friends. He states that Shelley wrote romances under the influence of the German romanticists. He says that Shelley's early manifestation of hatred for tyranny marked his whole career. "Hence his atheism and infidelity; hence his scorn of the customs and proprieties of society; hence his continued struggle against opinions without a real, distinct defense of any plan or principle; and hence the indistinctness and obscurity which prevail in so much of his poetry." He believes that Shelley should have been punished, but less severely, for his conduct at Oxford. He regrets that the good of *Queen Mab* is overbalanced by the evil, but adds that it is not fair to judge him by this work which he later regretted. He states that he is surprised and pained to find the same sentiment, the lack of reverence for Christianity, even in his minor poems.

This writer devotes but one paragraph to Shelley's marital relations. He calls his first marriage "a hasty and ill-judged marriage" which was followed by a separation "which sadly issued in the death of his unfortunate wife, with anguish to himself." In another paragraph, however, he reviews Shelley's opinions on tyranny of custom, marriage, equality, distribution of property, and oppression in government. Then follows a very interesting sketch of Shelley's character:

He was a man of superior talent, one of the few that each age distinguishes from the multitude; a good scholar, especially fond of the Greek writers, and, as has been the case with more than one infidel scholar, of the poetry of the Bible; of a disposition generous and amiable, unless when sometimes made fretful by disease; in his conduct, so far as we have been able to learn, excepting his illicit connexion with her who afterwards became his wife, of irreproachable purity and temperance; an enemy to oppression; and withal possessed of a spirit of vain self-confidence. . . .

He does not regard Shelley as a dangerous writer. He is interested in the poetic qualities of his poetry. Concerning Shelley as a poet, he states that his genius was great, his imagination powerful, his fancy lively, but that his conceptions of subject matter were not always clear. He accounts for this lack of clearness by stating that "there appears to have been in the mind of Shelley a sort of confused and dreamy philosophy, an ill-assorted compound made up from the elements of French infidelity and radicalism, Godwin's *Political Justice*, and the speculations of Plato." This conclusion sounds like that of the twentieth-century critics of Shelley. The figures and symbols used by Shelley, he believes, are often far-fetched, overstrained, and indistinct, and his metaphysical turn of mind is always making itself manifest. He adds, however, that the poems have elegance combined with energy, softness with sublimity. The opening stanza of *Queen Mab*, he believes, is enough to entitle Shelley to a poet's fame, and the description of night in the fourth canto has rarely, if ever, been equalled. He states that while Shelley's poetry has exquisite symmetry and intellect, it has a coldness, a sort of Platonic, passionless affection. He concludes with the statement that Shelley will find a place in the library of the scholar. The criticism of the poetry is a good general criticism, but the fact that *Queen Mab* is the only poem referred to directly would lead one to believe that the writer had but a cursory acquaintance with the other poems.

In the fifth decade Shelley received more attention in the New England periodicals than he had previously. The increase in the number of articles was due, of course, to the publication of his complete works in 1839-1840. He is noticed several times in the *North American Review* and commented on at length by E. P. Whipple and by Francis Bowen, editor of the magazine from 1845 to 1854. In a review of Talfourd's *Critical and Miscellaneous*

Writings,[11] Whipple compares Wordsworth's power of imagination with that of Shelley to the advantage of the latter:

> From a single page of Shelley's writings, there can be selected as many examples of the true power of imagination, as defined by Talfourd, as animate, we had almost said, a whole book of the *Excursion*; and it is equally as true, that the images are as likely to be the embodiment of restlessness, discontent, pantheistic abstractions, and other "spiritualisms" of our nature as of ideas, feelings, and sentiments springing from a harmonized heart and brain.

In his review of Griswold's *Poets and Poetry of America,*[12] Whipple refers to Shelley's superiority to Longfellow in his feeling for beauty. Longfellow, he declares, "feels and loves and creates what is beautiful; but he hymns no reverence, he pays no adoration to the spirit of Beauty. He would never exclaim with Shelley, 'O awful Loveliness!'" Whipple regrets that William Pitt Palmer, who writes occasionally for the magazines, was not mentioned by Griswold. Palmer, he says, "has written a poem on 'Light' in the stanza of Shelley's 'Cloud,' far superior in diction and imagery to a large part of our miscellaneous poetry."

In his review of Wordsworth's *Poetical Works,*[13] Whipple gives some attention to each of the four poets whom he considers to be the great exponents of the imaginative literature of the age: Wordsworth, Byron, Shelley, and Scott. These poets are considered only in association with Wordsworth. Thus Shelley is included in a group of poets whose work is "deeply infected with the spirit of transcendental speculation," a quality which furnishes the inspiration, according to Whipple, for the most popular verse produced in America. All these romantic poets, he believes, display "a prevailing intensity of feeling," but Wordsworth he recognizes as the dominant influence of the period. "He gave, or largely assisted in giving, that tendency to the poetic mind, which produced, at a later period, the magnificent creations of Byron and Shelley" He criticizes both Wordsworth and Shelley, however, for portraying pains the world should feel rather than those it does feel. And it must have chagrined the Wordsworth worshippers of the time when Whipple associated these two poets in his statement that both possessed Christian feeling. He commends both poets further in his "Characteristics of Lord Byron"[14] when he states that Byron's dependence on the world is in marked contrast with the self-reliance of Wordsworth and Shelley. In the same year, in an article on "British Critics,"[15] occasioned by a review of Jeffrey, Hazlitt, and Hunt, Whipple mentions Shelley several times. Referring to the political prejudices of critics, he says of the *Edinburgh Review:* "The same journal which could see nothing but blasphemy and licentiousness in the poetry of Shelley, could find matter for inexpressible delight in the poetry of John Wilson Croker." To show Shelley's attitude towards Gifford and the *Quarterly Review,* he quotes the stanzas from the *Adonais* that refer to Gifford, and adds that Shelley "has, in a strain of invective hot from his heart, fixed a brand on Gifford's brow, which may keep it above the waters of oblivion for some time to come." In his enthusiasm for Shelley, Whipple even attacks Hunt. He disapproves of what he terms Hunt's "billing and cooing," especially if it is employed in some passage which the reader desires to keep sacred from handling. And he seems to be rather sensitive regarding Hunt's attitude towards Shelley: "We cannot see him approaching a writer like Shelley without a gesture of impatience; but generally it is far from unpleasant." By 1845 Shelley was well known in America, but this recognition of him by Whipple, who was best known as a Wordsworth critic, must have aided in establishing Shelley's reputation as an outstanding poet of the period.

Francis Bowen, who was qualified as an educator and as a critic to speak of the German influence on the poetry of the first half of the century, states:[6] . . . for much of the poetry of our own day bears decisive tokens of the study of German models. The effects of this study are sometimes visible in direct imitation, as in many of the poems of Coleridge and Shelley; but more frequently in the prevailing sentiment, and the general coloring imparted to the thought." The German influence, he believes, explains "some of the strange mutations which English poetry has undergone since the opening of the present century. It has ceased to be narrative, epic, vigorous, clear, or equable; it has become philosophic, elaborate, mystical, meditative, and tender. . . . Like a landscape seen by moonlight, it abounds with indistinct outlines and shadowy forms, with figures fantastically blended together, and colors faintly seen and melting into each other in the distance." Bowen probably had in mind the poetry of Novalis as well as that of Coleridge and Shelley. As a critic, however, Bowen is truly American in his tendency to stress the moral influence of the poet rather than his art, as revealed in his review of Lowell's *Poems.*:[7] He praises Crabbe and Rogers, Scott and Southey, Campbell and Moore, as being "more than poets." He says that "they were sensible, high-minded, wholehearted men," and regrets that it was far different with their contemporaries, with Byron, Coleridge, Shelley, Keats, and even Wordsworth," not to mention a crowd of coxcombs who have imitated them." He accuses the romantic poets of egotism and criticizes what he terms their theatrical exposure of private feelings. Then follows a comment that in general tone is characteristic of much of the criticism of the period: "We sadly believe that Burns, Byron, and Shelley have done more harm by their lives, by throwing a mantle of genius over waywardness and wickedness, than they accomplished of good by their writings." One reads this second article by Bowen with regret that the powers of this very able critic were wasted because of his belief in the ethical purpose of poetry and his inability to appreciate the poet regardless of his views.

A review in which a very discriminating critic, probably Orestes Brownson himself, enlists his sympathies in a defense of Shelley is found in the *Boston Quarterly Review* for October, 1841.:[8] Inspired by reading the recently published edition of Shelley's complete poems, this writer gives a very thorough review of Shelley and his work. He regards Shelley as a persecuted spirit, a prey to the reviewers of his time: "From the publication of his first poem, he was considered a prey, upon whom reviewers might expend the utmost rancor of their malignity; and every petty scribbler, who could heap together a few terms of bitter execration, laid an offering on the altar of Cant, and sought to propitiate public favor by abusing Shelley." He regrets that there is no American edition of this complete and final collection of Shelley's poems. He believes that Shelley is beginning to receive the notice and appreciation he deserves. He regrets that English domination in America has made it impossible for Shelley to receive just criticism:

In letters as in costume, we are the merest fools of fashion and slaves of foreign influence, afraid to award deserved praise even to native merit, without the imprimatur of English criticism. Hence we adopted the notions of Shelley expressed by foreign reviewers, without examination or reflection, and united in denouncing him as agrarian, atheist, blasphemer, until his name became a sound of horror, and to read his works was considered an evidence of unsoundness in religion and political faith.

He explains, however, that his object is to consider the genius of Shelley. He is of the opinion that Shelley, enthusiastic, imaginative, and philanthropic, adopted the ultra-democratic doctrines of his day with his whole heart. The *Revolt of Islam,* he believes, is the work that reflects Shelley's feelings at the time. As to Shelley and Harriet, he states that both erred, both suffered, and both are to be pitied. The lack of knowledge of Shelley's writings he attributes in part to certain peculiarities of style and subject, but principally to Shelley's bold avowal of his religious opinions. He contends, however, that Shelley was preëminently religious and had a firm belief in the existence of a Deity, high respect for Christ, but not for Christianity as he knew it. The questionable tendency of his theological opinions, he asserts, would be counterbalanced by the purity of his moral teachings. The last part of the article is devoted to a discussion of Shelley's poetry, which the writer declares is remarkable for the character and the quantity of the imagery. He believes that Shelley should be appreciated for his imagery and for his figures, which he does not regard as over-fanciful and extravagant. Shelley's verse he criticizes as not always of the smoothest, but states that in some parts, as in the choruses in *Prometheus Unbound* and *Hellas* and in some minor poems, it flows in a stream of continuous melody. *Queen Mab*, he says, has the most readers, and the *Cenci* is regarded by many as Shelley's masterpiece. He believes, however, that *Prometheus Unbound*, in both its conception and its execution, is superior to all the rest of Shelley's works.:[9]

If the *North American Review* were to be held as representative of the general attitude of the New England intellectuals towards Shelley, the conclusion would be that he was not considered sufficiently important to devote an article to him. But Byron and Coleridge were the only writers of the Romantic period who received much consideration in this magazine. The articles on poetry were of a general character, and in these Shelley received a fair amount of attention. The fact that other periodicals, such as the *Yale Literary Magazine*, the *Boston Quarterly Review*, *The Dial*, and the *Literary Journal*, published articles on him is an indication that he was receiving recognition. He was criticized in the *North American Review* by W. B. O. Peabody for his religious views and by Francis Bowen for his immoral influence. In the other periodicals, however, he received only the highest praise. The criticism by E. P. Whipple of the *North American Review*, was very favorable. Both Whipple and the anonymous writer in the *Boston Quarterly* regard Shelley as a "persecuted Spirit," both show some appreciation of his poetry, and both consider him to have been a Christian. The critic in the *Yale Literary Magazine*, as would be expected of a writer in a college journal, is concerned chiefly with the poetry, which he says shows elegance and energy, softness and sublimity. He believes that Shelley's genius and imaginative power entitle him to a high rank among the poets. The writer of the article in the *Literary Journal* is interested in Shelley's poetry principally for its philosophic and social theories, but he likewise shows appreciation for the beauty of the poetry.

The Emerson–Andrews Norton Controversy

The attitude towards Shelley in the New England of the late thirties and early forties is best exemplified by the now almost forgotten Emerson–Andrews Norton controversy, a verbal battle that grew out of Emerson's address to the graduates of the Divinity School at Harvard. This address, however, but marked the crisis in a long war between the liberal believers in Christianity, as represented by the followers of Emerson, and the orthodox, as represented by Andrews Norton and his group.[20] In his attack on Emerson's *Address,* Norton gives vent to his pent-up feelings against the whole group of liberals. It was too much for this worthy upholder of the orthodox when Emerson propounded his belief on an occasion when only the most orthodox of views should have been given expression. The feeling regarding the acceptance of Shelley and his doctrines, however, must have been smoldering for more than a year in the mind of Andrews Norton, for the article that aroused his ire was published in the February, 1837, issue of the *Western Messeger.*[21] Perhaps a feeling of sympathy for the benevolent James Freeman Clarke, the editor of the *Messenger, prevailed* with Andrews Norton and deterred any attack on a periodical established on the frontier chiefly for religious purposes. Even in his attack on Emerson and his followers, whom he terms "The New School in Literature and Religion," Norton refers to Shelley only as one of the writers accepted by this school.[22] The article opens with:

There is a strange state of things existing about us in the literary and religious world, of which none of our larger periodicals has as yet taken notice. It is the result of that restless craving for notoriety and excitement, which, in one way or another, is keeping our community in a perpetual stir.

This condition, Norton continues, has been more noticeable since Miss Martineau was among us, but it owes its origin to blundering through the "crabbed and disgusting obscurity of some of the worst of the worst German speculatists," most of the ideas being received at second hand through an interpreter. He then continues with the following reference to Shelley:

The atheist Shelley has been quoted and commended in a professedly religious work, called the *Western Messenger,* but he is not, we conceive, to be reckoned among the patriarchs of the sect.

Norton gives this honor to Cousin and Carlyle, and criticizes these writers and Schleiermacher for seemingly being worshipped in America. This somewhat casual inclusion of Shelley called forth a reply from Clarke, the editor of the *Messenger,*[23] not in defense of Shelley but, according to his own statement, through fear that Norton's article would injure the interests of the *Messenger*. The reply, which is in the form of a letter and published in the *Boston Daily Advertiser* for September 28, 1838, is somewhat of an apology for publishing this article on Shelley. The part of Clarke's letter which concerns the discussion follows:

Louisville (Ky.) Sept. 8

To the Editor of the Boston Daily Advertiser:

The main object of this article appears to be to invoke public indignation against those who venture to approve the writings of Mr. Carlyle and Mr. Cousin, and especially to pour forth a most extraordinary invective against a late address by Mr. R. W. Emerson. With all this I have nothing to do. . . . All I have to say relates to the *Western Messenger*. In attempting to describe what the writer calls "The crabbed and disgusting obscurity of some of the worst German speculatists," he illustrates his remark by saying—"The Atheist Shelley, has been quoted and commended in a professedly religious work, called the *Western Messenger*, but he is not, we conceive, to be reckoned among the patriarchs of the sect." The natural impression on the minds of your readers, from the paragraph referred to, would be, that the *Western Messenger* had either praised Shelley *as an Atheist*, or without discriminating between his Atheistic sentiment and his correctness. Whether we have done this may be learned from the following passage from the article in the *Western Messenger*: —

"Shelley was an unbeliever. For this, we mourn, and must condemn him for not making better use of his power and intellect, which would have taught him the truth of Christianity, and of his feeling heart, which could have revealed to him the unearthly beauty of Jesus. But we must keep one thing in mind, in passing judgment on Shelley for his avowed opinions. His opinions in regard to God and Christ were formed and declared in reference and indignant opposition to the prevailing ideas of bigots on those subjects. He denies God; but it is rather a God, whom bigotry had created, than the God of Nature and Father of Christ. He rejects the doctrine of Christianity, but it is chiefly in view of the dogmas which his creeds have amended to Christian faith—such dogmas for instance, as that God is a God of Love, and yet has predestined, from all eternity, a great part of his creatures to Endless Hell. But much as we condemn Shelley's extravagances, and mourn his proud, rebellious spirit, we must say, that he often exhibits more true Christian feeling, and even Christian Faith, than many who scoff at him as an Atheist and an Outlaw."

Clarke then refers to the statement of the writer in the *Messenger* that Shelley, in many of his sentiments, is more of a Christian than Pollok, and adds: "Perhaps your correspondent means to object to this. Perhaps he thinks a *professed* Atheist cannot have any faith, and that a *professed* Christian must needs be what he professes to be. So did not the Apostle James." He then defends the seeming good in those with whom one does not agree and concludes his letter with: "But while God gives me strength, no such prejudices shall prevent me from giving credit where it is due, even to those from whose sentiments on most points I wholly differ."

In an article entitled "Shelley and the Western Messenger," published in the *Boston Daily Advertiser* [24] for October 5, 1838, Norton replies to Clarke's letter. This article is of interest because it is the only article in which Norton has really given expression to his views regarding Shelley. After acknowledging his responsibility for the article of August twenty-seventh, he quotes from Clarke's letter the sentence in which he reveals his fear of the effect that Norton's attack will have on the *Messenger*, and replies:

> I cannot believe, however, that anyone who cooly reads the words will imagine himself justified in drawing either inference, or suppose me to convey so extraordinary a proposition, as that in a professedly relgious work Shelley was praised for being an atheist, or that he was even commended without some qualifications. That he was *improperly* commended is doubtless implied.

He states that Clarke in refutation refers to a paragraph from the article in the *Messenger* in which Shelley is excused rather than commended. But Norton adds that there is something stronger in another paragraph, and quotes from the article in the *Messenger:*

> Where shall we find a purer love of liberty, than in the *Revolt of Islam*—where a purer friendship than in *Adonais*—where a more glowing love for man than in his *Prometheus* and *Queen Mab*— where a stronger faith in man's capacity for goodness and the goodness of the Supreme Power than in his *Hellas*? Compare him with many of his revilers, and he takes the palm in point of moral elevation, and Christian faith and feeling.

Norton then states that he will pass over the other passages of this article and give only the conclusion:

> Shelley says in the Preface to his *Prometheus*: "I had rather be damned with Plato and Lord Bacon than go to heaven with Paley and Malthus." Begging pardon for using the expression, we say in similar terms: We had rather be damned with Percy Bysshe Shelley than go to heaven with John Calvin and Robert Pollok. Their heaven must indeed be a hell to one who feels a single thrill of love for universal man, or feels a single spark of the divinity stirring within.

In reply to these points, Norton gives his view of Shelley and his poetry:

> Of Shelley, perhaps, many readers have heard but little; for his works are not popular, and never can become so till religion and morality are empty names. He was an atheist and bitter infidel, and his conduct answered to his principles. We are aware of the enthusiastic and senti-

mental tone in which his admirers (for even he, as we have seen, has admirers) are accustomed to speak of him; but we know something also of the revolting history of his life. He was an "outcast" and deservedly so. Our present concern, however, is with his works.

Norton objects to *Prometheus Unbound* and *Queen Mab,* both of which he says were recommended by the *Messenger.* The latter he considers "as openly and *schockingly* blasphemous as any to which the most perverted state of heart and mind ever gave birth—a work, it is said, which Shelley himself repented and endeavored to suppress." He then gives several quotations from *Queen Mab* which he characterizes as "hard, fearless, brazen exposition." He likewise objects to *Prometheus Unbound* as being a symbolical drama in which Prometheus is a personification of that spirit which is to deliver men from the tyranny of religion, and Jupiter is the type of whatever man has worshipped as God. He says that there is much in Shelley's poetry corresponding to the sentiment he utters of preferring "Hell's freedom to the servitude of Heaven," and much that expresses a tone of defiance toward the Supreme Being, with feelings wavering, as it would seem, between the denial and the dread of existence. He objects to Shelley's views on marriage, which he says Shelley represents as an odious institution, thus striking at the root of the decencies of life, of our best affections, and of human civilization. He compares Shelley's idea of liberty with that of a fanatic Jacobite of the French Revolution. He concludes with the statement that he will forbear to discuss further the question of Shelley's praise in the *Messenger.*

This battle is brought to a close a month later when James Freeman Clarke publishes in the November, 1838, issue of the *Messenger* [25] an article, "The New School in Literature and Religion," in reply to the first article by Andrews Norton and bearing the same title. Clarke's letter was published in order to explain his position further and to conciliate his readers, some of whom must have been affected by the convincing argument of Norton. Clarke quotes Norton's comment regarding the "atheistic Shelley," and then proceeds to explain his own position:

When, in our simplicity, we inserted an article upon Shelley in the *Western Messenger,* we were not aware that because a man was an Atheist, he might not be commended for writing good poetry. We lamented the nature of his opinions, we mourned over his want of faith, and expressly stated our aversion to his general views. We did not expect, therefore, to be accused of commending him, as though we had been praising him for his Atheism—least of all did we expect that we were to become members of "a new school" through the medium of that article.

This half-apologetic letter must have aroused sympathy for Clarke and his periodical. And Clarke was probably convinced from that time on that he should not allow his personal feelings to intrude too far into his business affairs. At least, the battle between Clarke and Norton was closed.

The original article "Shelley and Pollok," [56] which brought Shelley into the conflict between the Emerson and Andrews Norton groups, was a cleverly written article by one who signed it with the initials "D. L." The writer, who held socialistic views, evidently wrote the article with the purpose not only of defending Shelley against his enemies but of attacking the orthodox believers in Christianity, particularly the Presbyterians, whom he specifically mentions. This part of the article is tactfully avoided by both Norton and Clarke:

> Compare him with many of his revilers, and he takes the palm in point of moral elevation and Christian faith and feeling. Even what is called his atheism is better than the theism of some of his bigoted condemners. His "Spirit of Nature" is more like the God and Father of our Lord Jesus, than is the terrific Jehovah, whom we hear thundered out in such savage terms from some of our Presbyterian pulpits. In proof of this compare an extract from Shelley's *Queen Mab* with a passage from that paragon of Calvinistic poets, Robert Pollok. Look on the two and say which is the most Christian.

This is undoubtedly the passage that aroused Norton's ire against the *Western Messenger*. And he can hardly be blamed for resenting this somewhat personal attack. Whether or not Clarke had any part in composing the article is not known, but it is possible that this part may have escaped his attention, or it may have been published without his knowledge. His interest in the article was in defending Shelley, not in attacking anyone. For Clarke had sympathy for Shelley as a man and admiration for him as a poet.

Echoes of this controversy that was aroused by Emerson's address to the divinity students, however, were heard throughout the succeeding years. In January, 1839, Albert Baldwin and James Waddell Alexander published their joint article "Transcendentalism," [27] occasioned by the publication of Emerson's *Address before the Divinity College* and two books by Victor Cousin. In criticizing the belief that the world was created out of nothing, these authors comment on Shelley:

> This doctrine was early carried into Greece, and adopted by many of their philosophers. . . . It seems to have special affinities for poetry: In modern times it has made its reappearance in the polished periods of Pope's "Essay on Man," and it runs through the wild and impious imaginations of Shelley.

In the same year the *Boston Quarterly Review* [28] published an article entitled, "Norton on the Evidences of Christianity," prompted by the publication of *The Evidences of the Genuineness of the Four Gospels,* by Andrews Norton, 1837. The writer, probably Brownson, states that the charges that Norton has brought against some of his former pupils could be brought against him, in that Norton was once severely criticized for praising an infidel. The writer then adds: "He would do well, then, not to fill the newspapers of this city with too many denunciations of a young man who chances to say a good word for the poet Shelley."

In July, 1840, the *Boston Quarterly Review* [89] again comes to the defense of Shelley with an ironic article, "Chat in Boston Bookstores," signed "Dahlia." This amusing conversation regarding literature takes place in a Boston bookstore between two fictitious characters, Professor Partridge and the Reverend Mr. Nightshade, probably a pseudonym for Andrews Norton. It is the minister, however, who defends Shelley. The part of the dialogue which concerns Shelley follows:

Rev. Mr. N.—Here I see new volumes about a favorite of mine.

Prof. P.—Shelley—is he a favorite of yours—, why so?

Rev. Mr. N.—Do you ask? For the inspired music of his verse, for his tenderness, his purity, his high ambition to educate his own soul and redeem the souls of others.

Prof. P.—Yet only the other day I read of the "wild and impious ravings of Shelley."

Rev. Mr. N.—Those who denounce him, do so from reading single passages in his works. If they entered into the spirit of them, such harsh judgment would be impossible. They would see that, if he rebelled against God, it was against the God of the Jews, not the God of the world or the heart. That the spirit of Christ animated all his struggle against Christianity, in the corrupt form under which he saw it, and that it was his need of pure and spiritual relations, which led to the violations of the social contract. I feel confidence that none will read him enough to know him, who will not say, even if grieved or repelled by his errors, that his was a noble, aye, and a most religious nature. Had he lived longer, he would have explained himself to the satisfaction of opinion as well as sentiment.

I have read somewhere that he was on the point of becoming a Christian when he died.

Prof. P.—That is not true, nor should he be so defended. He had learned to venerate the character of Christ, but he was no more reconciled to the idea of a special revelation than at first. This should be admitted by his friends, and defence rested on his love of man, his reverence for the soul, and his constant aspiration to the destiny which befits an immortal spirit. If his words blasphemed the opinions of his religious contemporaries, his thoughts worshipped at the same altar, and the difference was one of phraseology. This will be easily under-

> stood by any who look with unprejudiced minds into his history.
>
> But the clock strikes two,—good morning, I will see you again before you leave town.

The Emerson–Norton controversy with its results is an excellent illustration not only of the feeling towards Shelley at this time, but of the trend of critical thought during this period.

The attitude towards Shelley in the whole of New England during the second quarter of the century may be considered as fairly representative of the views of this section regarding the literature and the social ideas of the time. The strict religionists did not accept Shelley or any other writer whose ideas or morals did not appear to be in accord with their beliefs. They rejected Goethe even more strenuously than they did Shelley. They were opposed in their attacks on Shelley by many of the more liberal minded, particularly by those with socialistic views, who seem to have considered Shelley as one of their group. The New England major poets recognized in Shelley a poet of ability, but their interest in him was individual. Longfellow admired his lyrical poetry and was interested in his translations from *Faust*. Lowell, as a critic, was concerned with his style of writing. Holmes had sufficient interest in him and other English Romantic poets to use them as subjects for lectures. Whittier admired Shelley the poet, but he could not condone his religious views and his reputed morals. As has been noted, the periodicals were somewhat divided in opinion. Shelley was defended a number of times by Orestes Brownson in the *Boston Quarterly Review,* but he was neglected in the *North American Review,* the most representative of the New England journals, whose contributors were concerned with the eighteenth-century writers and Shakespeare, and with certain aspects of German literature.

The one group which might have promoted Shelley, the Transcendentalists, were too absorbed with German culture and French socialistic ideas to give Shelley much attention. They failed to see that the work of this young English poet contained, if not a developed system of thought, at least the germ of much that they were seeking. They cast him aside with a cursory reading or rejected him after a short period of enthusiasm and turned their attention to other writers who fitted in better with their immediate interests. The philosophic ideas of the mature Goethe and the eclectic philosophy of Cousin suited them better. Margaret Fuller long retained her loyalty for Shelley as a poet, but she replaced him as the chief object of her study with Goethe. Various members of the Transcendental group seem to have found in Shelley a model for their poetry. Among these aspirants to write in the style of Shelley were the poets Ellery Channing, H. D. Thoreau, Jones Very, and C. P. Cranch. It is highly probable that George W. Curtis and Nathaniel Hawthorne gained their first appreciation of Shelley from association with the Transcendentalists at Brook Farm. With J. L. Motley, Shelley was always a favorite poet. But, like Margaret Fuller, Motley turned to Goethe for intellectual refreshment. Phillips Brooks likewise found in Shelley a poet whose ideas appealed to his youth. Brooks, however, was interested chiefly in Shelley's ideas on religion, and he readily recognized in the poet a man with advanced views on Christianity.

New England was a region in which ideas and ideals were undergoing rapid transformation, and it was chiefly to the youth, who were fast rejecting the outworn creeds and seeking new ones, that Shelley seems to have appealed. And it was those who were poets or who were unprejudiced critics of poetry who were the most ardent admirers of his verse. Emerson remains the most noteworthy exception. Shelley's failure, therefore, to make much progress in New England by the middle of the nineteenth century may be found in the following reasons: He was rejected by most of his admirers after their period of youth was over; he was superseded by Goethe; he was banned as an atheist and an immoral character.

CHAPTER IV

THE MIDDLE ATLANTIC SECTION

Shelley in Philadelphia

Romanticism in the Middle Atlantic Section assumed a very different form from that in New England or the southern states. Here was no uniform group with like traditions or interests, but, instead, a heterogeneous population made up of the people from various countries in Europe. Settlers from Germany, Sweden, and the Netherlands formed colonies in which they preserved the language, religion, and customs of the mother countries. They had no common ideals such as united the people in the North and the South. Nor was diversity in nationality and social customs the only distinguishing feature of this section. Located between the Federalist North and the Democratic South, the people of the central section were of both parties. Their political views might be those of New England or of Virginia, or they might be modified by ideas brought from the Old World. Diversity of opinion in politics as well as in other matters developed. The tendency towards variety in politics, however, found its greatest exponents in the metropolitan cities, Philadelphia and New York, cities that differed widely in manner of development and in character.

Philadelphia had early felt the pressure of foreign influence. This influence dates back to the last decade of the eighteenth century, when Philadelphia was the capital of the new republic, or even earlier, when it harbored foreign military officers within its borders. With this influx of foreigners of distinction, it developed a culture unsurpassed by that of any other American city of the time. The success of its merchants made it the most prosperous of cities and a leader in fashions. The founding of publishing houses made it a center not only for the dissemination of culture, but likewise for the dissemination of new ideas. The presses of Philadelphia reprinted English books, among which were the works of Mary Wollstonecraft. Radicalism was early welcomed in this section by the liberal group, especially by Charles Brockden Brown. Brown's novels revealed, in the last decade of the eighteenth century, many of the doctrines of Mary Wollstonecraft and William Godwin. After the capital was moved, Philadelphia suffered an economic decline and a general loss of prestige. But it did not lose its place as a general educational center. It continued for many years to be the home of some of the

70

best publishing houses of the country and a center for periodicals.

Shelley received notice in a number of these periodicals during the fourth and fifth decades. Even as early as 1828, the *Philadelphia Monthly Magazine: Devoted to Literature and the Fine Arts* contained an article, "Percy Bysshe Shelley," signed with the initials "P. P." [1] This writer gives what was probably the popular view regarding Shelley among those who knew him vaguely. He begins, "There are few men of genius who have so misused their powers as did Shelley. There are few whose character is so little understood this side of the Atlantic, as is that of this extraordinary poet." He says that Shelley is considered to be an unbeliever, a man without principle, and a poet without merit. He contends however, that Shelley's intentions were good, that he believed he was doing what was right, and so he pities the poet for his errors and regrets that powers of so high an order were lost to the world. He states that Shelley was an amiable man whose motives were always pure. Shelley's poems, he declares, will never be popular. He prophesies that they will be read for a time by scholars, but that even they will eventually neglect them. He acknowledges that there are splendid and sublime passages in the poems but complains of too much obscurity and intricacy. He believes that *Alastor* is the best of the long poems. But Shelley, he says, is best in his short poems. He aimed at too much in the long poems; he was ambitious to awe and startle the reader. He states that Shelley is a striking example of the mischief that misdirected genius can cause to its possessor. "In his heart, everything was pure and gentle and generous. In his mind, everything was wild, extravagant, and diseased."

Godey's Lady's Book, as early as May, 1831, accorded Shelley a place within its pages by publishing a literary effusion of twenty-eight lines, entitled "Sonnet to Shelley," [2] the number of lines for the sonnet being in proportion to the gushing sentiments of "N. P.—Genessee," who wrote it "expressly" for the *Lady's Book.* In March, 1834, this same magazine published a copy of Shelley's poem "Good Night," [3] with music "composed and respectfully dedicated to Mrs. Shelley by Mrs. Townshend Stith." In 1836 were published sketches of lives of the English poets, with their photographs. The February number contains a sketch of Shelley, with a photograph on the opposite page.[4] A short biographical sketch of his life is given, with a brief comment on his poetry. His first marriage is referred to as "an ill-assorted marriage" the result of which was very unfortunate. His second marriage meets with approval. "On the decease of his first wife, he married Miss Godwin, daughter of the celebrated author of *Political Justice* by Mary Wollstonecraft." In the *North American*

Magazine, May, 1833, also were published sketches of English poets under the title "Poetical Portraits." [5] This writer presents Shelley as a notorious character who defied the "gray-haired theologians at Oxford" and his father as well, eloped with a "boarding-school beauty," and wrote atheistic works for radical presses in order to obtain money.

The first mention of Shelley in the *American Quarterly Review,* the leading Philadelphia magazine of the period, was in a review of *Philip von Artevelde.*[6] Shelley is called a follower of the "fantastic school," and his poetry is characterized as "vague and shadowy and unreal." The reviewer, evidently an advocate of eighteenth-century criticism, agrees with Taylor's statement that Shelley "seems to have written under the notion that no phenomena can be perfectly poetical, till they shall be decomposed from their natural order and coherency." He then gives his own opinion of Shelley:

> We have often been delighted with the genius of Shelley. We have been charmed with his imagery, his diction, his melody of versification. We have wandered with him in ideal regions of majesty and beauty . . . and have been entranced into forgetfulness of the world, . . .

He adds that while he appreciates these "magnificent illusions and would not part with a single charm of the modern school, it produces a relish for indifference for the more enduring kind of poetry." He believes, however, that elevation and expansion of the intellect are more important than gratification of the senses.

The anonymous article called "The Shelley Papers," which appears in the June, 1836,[7] number of the same magazine, is in an entirely different vein. It begins: "The three greatest poets of this century are, we think, Shelley, Wordsworth, and Byron. We place them in what seems to us their order of merit." Then follows a long discussion of Byron as the inferior poet and a discussion of poetry in which the writer gives three principles which he says are at work, "the enquiring and doubting, the conservative, and the revolutionary." These principles, he avers, belong to Shelley, Wordsworth, and Byron respectively. The writer then makes a statement (unusual at that time) that the poetry of Byron demoralizes youth, while that of Shelley and Wordsworth creates an admiration for a higher standard of morals and purer sources of poetry. He says that in Byron's ascendency and the confusion it created, Shelley and Wordsworth were for the time nearly overwhelmed, but were forming a strong though tranquil undercurrent, deeper and more powerful though less observed. He prophesies that in a few years they will be read more than any poets of their time. He includes Shelley with

Dante and Milton as a group of poets whose work was not understood because they gave rein to the imagination. Shelley's treatment by the reviewers he attributes to illiberality in politics and literature, but adds that "The refined, antique Toryism that enchained literature and morals . . . is rapidly passing to a shadow," the last strongholds being at Oxford and Cambridge. Then follows a criticism of the Oxford system for lack of appreciation and understanding of the genius of Shelley.

That this writer's views are unusual is clear from his statement that he is aware that in taking this attitude towards Shelley he will stir strong prejudice, but he believes that Shelley should be excused because of his youth and inexperience and his deep love for truth. To this writer, Shelley was a poet of intellect and feeling, "purely a creature of imagination—a being so spiritual that he and the world had nothing in common. Their only bond was in the higher powers of the mind." He sympathizes with Shelley in his spirit of inquiry regarding religion. Shelley's atheism, he says, was of an ideal nature; he felt that there was a power pervading all things. He quotes from Shelley's poems to show his mind and character. He believes that Shelley, like Milton, will be appreciated by only the select few. In a third article in the same magazine, a discussion called "Modern English Tragedy," [8] prompted by a review of Thomas Noon Talfourd's *Ion*, the writer refers to Shelley's *Prometheus Unbound* and *Cenci*. He believes that in the former drama Shelley approached Aeschylus in the high power of the imagination, but was unable to present the abstractions of the great theme with an interest higher than human. He says that Shelley knew so little of the world that in all his beautiful poetry the mind scarcely recognizes a familiar association. This fault, he avers, is fatal to dramatic poetry.

The first American edition of Shelley's complete poetical works was published in Philadelphia in 1845.[9] G. G. Foster, a member of the Fourierite group and an ardent admirer of Shelley, was the editor. He states that to express his thoughts of Shelley has always been his desire.[10] His unbounded enthusiasm for the poet and his ideas is revealed in the following quotation from his preface to the poems:

From earliest youth, Shelley has been one of my idols; his burning genius it was that first flamed for me over the world of the sublime and the beautiful—that world where the soul of man walks uncumbered of its chains, and holds converse face to face with its immortal Source.

Foster, who always encountered financial difficulties, seems to have appealed to Horace Greeley for assistance in securing a publisher for his work on Shelley. At least, Greeley wrote to Rufus W. Griswold as follows:[11]

New York, May 13, 1845

Rufus W. Griswold, Old Friend:

Our friend Foster has got up Shelley's Poems in the best style, with appropriate introductions, etc. There is not a copy of them to be had here, and I presume not in the Country. You know they ought to be published, and yet there is no house here that is fit to do it. Won't you speak to Carey and Hart about it? There is no risk, and Foster don't (sic) stand on terms, unless they ask pay from him, and that you know is inadmissible. Just have them brought out, or write me about the matter anyhow.

Yours,

HORACE GREELEY

Greeley was mistaken in his statement that there was not a copy of Shelley's poems to be had in New York and presumably in the country, as may be seen from the number of reviews in American periodicals of Mary Shelley's edition of the poems, published by Moxon in 1839. Foster's first edition of the poems proved to be popular in that it was exhausted in less than eighteen months.[12] Several new editions appeared under the names of different publishers within the succeeding fifteen years.[13] The first review of the work in a Philadelphia periodical appeared in *Graham's Magazine* for February, 1846.[14] It is described as a very elegant edition with typography and paper such as is not usually found in books of this size. The reviewer refers to Foster's preface on Shelley as one of the most glowing that he has ever read. He agrees with many of Foster's ideas regarding Shelley but fears that his introducing Fourierite theories into the preface will prevent the sale of the book, in that these theories will prejudice the reader against both the editor and the poet. He approves of Foster's high regard for the vocation of the poet but does not believe that Shelley is a fair representative of what a true poet should be. "His speculative belief did irreparable mischief; and not all the kindness of his nature, nor the comparative purity of his conduct can remove the evil which his doctrines taught, and a few inconsiderate acts of his life upheld. In a word, Shelley was a freethinker." He joins Foster in his admiration for Shelley's poetry which, he says, is just beginning to be appreciated. "His glowing language—his exhuberant fancy —his lofty ideality—and the graphic power of description he wields, have had no superior, in many points no equal, during the nineteenth century." He praises the "Sensitive Plant," says that the "Lines to an Indian Air" have never been surpassed, calls the *Cenci* a masterpiece, finds gleams of superior genius in *Prometheus Unbound,* and refers to the *Revolt of Islam* as a noble poem.

He objects, however, to the poetry in general because he considers it obscure. Thus, he believes, it will always be a sealed book to the masses.

Rufus W. Griswold, who had more than a passing interest in Shelley as a poet, included a number of his poems in his *Poets and Poetry of England*. In his prefatory essay on Shelley, Griswold makes the following criticism:[15]

> Shelley's predominating faculty was his imagination. Fantasy prevails to such an extent in his long poems that they are too abstract for the "daily food" of any but ideal minds. No modern poet has created such an amount of mere imagery. There is a want of simplicity and human interest in his productions which render him "caviare to the general." He has been well designated the poet for poets. Two or three of his short pieces are models of lyric beauty. His classic dramas abound in rich metaphors. The *Cenci* is unquestionably the most remarkable of modern plays. Greek literature modified his taste, and a life of singular vicissitude disturbed the healthful current of a soul cast in a gentle but heroic mold. His aspirations were elevated, and his genius of the first order.

Griswold believes that Shelley might have been a Christian had he suffered less from man's inhumanity. Regardless of the poet's religious belief, however, this critic considers him one of the world's noblest natures. He concludes with the comment:

> In our own country more justice has been done to Shelley's genius, motives, and actions than they have received at home.

Shelley in New York

From the beginning of the century Philadelphia was gradually giving way to the rapidly growing New York. With the opening of the Erie Canal in 1833, the commercial supremacy of New York over the older city was complete. And the interests of New York were those of a commercial city. There was no intellectual awakening such as was arousing the New Englanders to activity. Culture as it existed in Boston and Philadelphia or in the cities of the South had never been a part of New York life. New York was more literary in the first quarter of the century than in the second. The first quarter had produced the three recognized men of letters, Irving, Cooper, and Bryant. These writers, however, were national, not local. And only one, Irving, really belonged to the city of New York. In this growing city the heterogeneous population that always monopolizes a commercial center was fast replacing the descendants of the old Dutch settlers. These people were interested in competition and trade and in developing their own ideas. They were more concerned with politics than with current European liberalisms. The diversity of nationalities and the variety of interests gave sufficient impetus for discussion. In the second quarter of the century, therefore, prose was the form of literature that flourished. The periodical gave opportunity for expression of diverse views through editorials and articles. As the periodical developed, it was called upon to serve another purpose, that of recreation. Thus the short story, the light essay, and other forms of entertainment found a place in its pages. And New York, with its cosmopolitan spirit, its lack of literary tradition, was ready to serve the American public, to give what the public seemed to demand, popular fiction, particularly that of a sentimental kind, and other light entertainment. It contributed the *New York Mirror and Ladies' Gazette,* a successful family journal, founded in 1823. The periodical of a general nature likewise flourished in New York as in no other city. The *New York Sun,* as a daily, was established in 1833, the *Evening Post* in 1834, the *Morning Herald* in 1835, and the *Tribune* in 1841. The book review, popular with all classes of people, found a ready reception in the periodical. Of poetry there was but little; most of it was occasional verse. The New York poets of the period were not romantic poets, but a motley crew of versifiers—columnists, writers of patriotic songs, of vers-de-societé, of light lyrics. There was no imitation of Shelley here. For any manifestation of interest in Shelley, it will be necessary to turn to the literary critics and the social reformers.

With the establishment of the *Knickerbocker Magazine* in 1833, the more serious literary group in New York came into prominence. Under the editorship of Lewis Gaylord Clark this magazine secured as contributors not only the leading literati of New York but many writers from New England, Philadelphia, and the West. The editors of the *Knickerbocker* immediately expressed a desire for a national American literature. In 1835 the magazine again objected to the "absolute sway" of English criticism "over our tastes and opinions" and added: "There would be some comfort . . . had we a competent or competent tribunals of our own, possessing independence of mind sufficient to venture occasionally an opinion of their own in opposition to that of the *Edinburgh* and *Quarterly,* or even the *London Literary Gazette.*"[16] Later in the same decade the *Democratic Review* exclaims, "Why cannot our literati . . . cease bending the knee to foreign idolatry, false tastes, false doctrines, false principles?" These quotations reveal the general attitude of New York periodicals towards the reviews of English writers and critics. It is to be expected, therefore, that in view of the independence of thought contained in the articles in these magazines, together with the breadth of view in this new cosmopolitan city, the writers in these magazines would be more tolerant in their criticism. The effect this spirit of criticism had on the acceptance or rejection of Shelley will be determined from an examination of the reviews.

In the New York of the fourth and fifth decades Shelley received a fair amount of attention, regardless of the fact that the interest of the periodicals was in popularizing and Americanizing literature. The members of the circle in which Poe was lionized when he came to New York, however, were bent on developing their own talents and were willing to accept Poe as their leader. As has been seen, the tendency was to escape from the influence of foreign, particularly English writers. New York literary influence in this period was American, and the leader in New York letters was N. P. Willis. Barrett Wendell calls him the most characteristic man of letters of his time but believes that his popularity was also an indication of a decline in literature: "A school of letters in which a man of Willis' quality could attain the eminence which for years made him conspicuous was certainly declining." [17] Willis was a hundred percent American. When he went abroad, he took his Americanism with him, and when he returned, he brought it back unchanged. European life had made no impression upon his dazzling butterfly spirit. He fitted about Europe, in and out of homes of nobility, secured letters of introduction of doubtful means, cultivated one person in order to meet another—in fact, he proved to be the journalist supreme. As a traveller, he was the typical American tourist abroad. He was interested chiefly in the spectacular. To secure information about Byron seems to have been one of his chief motives in visiting England. He managed to ingratiate himself into the circle of Lady Blessington, to win her friendship, and through her to meet the Countess Guiccioli, from whom he received the gift of an autographed note from Shelley. This note and his account of his visit to Shelley's grave probably represent the extent of his interest in the poet. In *Pencillings by the Way*,[18] he describes the graves of Shelley and Keats. Writing of his visit to the Protestant cemetery in Rome, he says:

I have been there today, to see the graves of Keats and Shelley. With cloudless sky and the most delicious air ever breathed, we sat down upon the marble slab laid over the ashes of poor Shelley, and read his own lament over Keats, who sleeps just below, at the foot of the hill. The cemetery is rudely formed into three terraces, with walks between; and Shelley's grave occupies a small nook above, made by the projection of a moldering wall-tower, and crowded with ivy and shrubs, and a peculiarly yellow flower, which perfumes the air around for several feet. The avenue by which you ascend from the gate is lined with high bushes of the marsh-rose in the most luxuriant bloom, and all over the cemetery, the grass is thickly mingled with flowers of every die. . . .

He concludes with the statement that Shelley has left no poet behind who could write so touchingly of his burial place in turn as he did of that of Keats. "He was, indeed, as they have graven in his tombstone, 'cor cordium'—the heart of hearts." Willis's interest in Shelley, however, was that of the journalist, not of the literary critic.

It was a New York periodical that contained the very earliest American criticism devoted entirely to Shelley. The *New York Literary Gazette and Phi Beta Kappa Repository*, in 1825–26, published an article "Criticism. Percy Bysshe Shelley" in its first volume.[19] The opening sentnce, "Mr. Shelley was one of those unfortunate beings in whom the imagination had been exalted and developed at the expense of the reasoning faculty," is misleading in that the article as a whole is favorable. The writer continues:

He naturally encountered the fate which even the highest talent cannot avert, when it sets itself systematically in array against opinions which men have been thought to believe and venerate, and principally with which the majority of mankind are persuaded the safeguard of society is connected.

This writer believes that Shelley's errors should be buried with him and that the good should be appreciated. His life, he says, contradicted the opinions he hazarded. He declares that, as a poet, Shelley was superior to all the poets of his age. "In no other writer of the age is the distinction between poetry and prose so strongly marked: deprive his verses of the rhyme, and still the exquisite beauty of the language, the harmony of the pauses, the arrangement of the sentences, is perceptible." Extreme vagueness and obscurity this critic declares to be the besetting sins of Shelley's poetry. He says that Shelley hovers on the confines of the grave, prying into the secrets of immortality, and adds:

But, when abandoning these darker themes, he yields himself to the description of the softer emotions of the heart, and the more smiling scenes of Nature, we know no poet who has felt more intensely, or described with more glowing colours the enthusiasm of love and liberty, or the varied aspects of Nature. His descriptions have a force and clearness of painting which are quite admirable; and his imagery, which he accumulates and pours forth with the prodigality of genius, is, in general, equally appropriate and original.

Except for a brief excerpt from Leigh Hunt's *Contemporaries of Lord Byron,* entitled "The Poet Shelley," published in the *Atlas*[20] for August 4, 1832, the *Knickerbocker Magazine* is the first of the New York periodicals to notice Shelley in the thirties. In the February number, 1833, in the article "Horae Germanica,"[21] the writer criticizes Lord Gower's translation of *Faust* and compares it with Shelley's translation of the "May-Day Night," which he considers to be superior. The third number of the *Knicker-bocker* [22] contains a criticism in dialogue, a form of criticism in vogue in England a few years earlier. In this article, "A Peep at the Pow-Wow," the members of the "Pow-Wow" discuss the poets. The idea that poetry is often unintelligible and yet poetic is expressed, and that of Shelley is given as an example. Both Shelley and Keats are accused of writing much nonsense. Dashington, one of the members, expostulates at some length on poetry:

> Poetry is a voice half lost in the clouds that bound the horizon of human knowledge. It is an adventurous discoverer, journeying with the meteors of fancy beyond the lights of reason; and its language and accents partake of the indistinctness of its perceptions; yet they come home to us with a consciousness of truth . . . they fill us with a belief, with a longing desire for the better inspiration of the day . . . and toward this goal our fantasy is straining . . . some gifted minds have effected glorious things; and Shelley is among them. His fulness and depth and sublimity and beauty are at times poured forth with an excess that makes one gasp for epithets to praise his worth, and yet there is but one— the one word poetry.

Rifflemore, another member, contends, however, that Shelley's translation is an illustration of the fact that all these characteristics might be preserved and the poetry nearly lost. To this argument Dashington replies that Shelley as a translator is "an eagle with clipt wings, dancing in a pas-de-deux,—to the music of the spheres it may be," but "a camel could do better,—a fag, a drudge, a son of patient industry." This criticism of Shelley as a translator is somewhat surprising in view of the fact that this is one type of writing in which he had met with only favorable comment, particularly in the English reviews. These articles include the only mention of Shelley in the *Knickerbocker* before 1857, except for a very poor poem, "Funeral of Shelley," published in the September, 1838, number.

The *New York Mirror* contained a brief mention of Shelley in 1834,[23] and a short article, "Byron and Shelley" in the number for August 24, 1839, written by a woman travelling in Switzerland.[24] An excerpt from the article follows:

> We were on the lake today and were rowed by Maurice, the boatman employed by Lord Byron. . . . "Poor Mr. Shelley," resumed Maurice, "ah! we were all sorry for him! He was a different sort of man; so gentle, so affectionate, so generous; he looked as if he loved the sky over his head, and the water on which his boat floated. He would not hurt a fly, nay, he would save everything that had life; so tender and merciful was his nature. He was too good for this world; and yet, lady, would you believe it, some of his countrymen whom I have rowed in this boat, have tried to make me think ill of him; but they never could succeed, for we plain people judge by what we *see,* and not by [what] we hear."

The writer then becomes sentimental over Shelley's influence on Byron.

The *Corsair,* a general publication, mentions Shelley several times in 1839 and 1840.[25] On February 8, 1840, extracts from a review of the two-volume edition of Shelley's works, edited by Mrs. Shelley, are given under the heading "Shelley's Letters, Essays, and Fragments."[26] The writer does not mention the periodical from which the review is taken, but calls it a "very feeling notice of the publication," and adds that a few extracts from this review, "some most touching and exquisite portions of the work itself, cannot fail of being acceptable to our readers." He believes that the *Cenci* and the *Defence of Poetry* were Shelley's greatest works. He discusses the one and quotes from the other. In this same number of the *Corsair*[27] is published "Extracts from Shelley's Letters from Italy." These extracts include his descriptions of the Cathedral of Milan, Raphael's picture of St. Cecilia at Bologna, Rome and the Coliseum, and Vesuvius at Naples. The selection is of interest as revealing the taste of the editor and, to some extent, of the period. All these articles in this magazine, which was devoted to literature, art, and dramatic criticism, indicate an increased interest in Shelley.

Arcturus,[28] an ephemeral publication, contained an article of three pages entitled "Talfourd's Defence of Moxon," the writer's chief interest being in the rights of the publisher. Of Shelley's work, he said: "The very work indicted, the Notes to *Queen Mab,* (chiefly containing the objectionable passages), has long circulated in this country, both as a separate infidel tract and as a portion of the library edition of the works of the distinguished poet. Yet no public prosecution has ever been undertaken." He adds that, in a world of mingled good and evil, the notes are, at worst, the errors of a misguided mind. The writer then reviews the case and Talfourd's appeal. He compares Shelley with Milton, who, he believes, represented the powers of good as being superior to those of evil: "But the object of Shelley was to preach error wilfully or ignorantly, it mattered not, and it was probably evident to the simplest juryman that the case of *Queen Mab* and *Paradise Lost* could not, by any possibility of logic, be rendered alike." He says that Talfourd's remarks on the nature of poetry were of a higher order of philosophy, that the poet's art cannot lie, "for it is *Eternity revealing itself in Time.*"

A poem "Shelley," by Albert Pike, was published in the *Ladies' Companion*[29] in 1841. This poem constitutes Pike's criticism of Shelley. He evidently believes that Shelley erred in his religious belief but that he should have been pitied rather than persecuted, for he says,

> But he was moral, generous, pure of heart
> Gentle and kind as any sainted child; . . .

Of his poetry, Pike states:

> He wove his wild and fiery thoughts into
> Words, strange, beautiful and vivid as
> His own bright soul; . . .
>
> .   .   .   .   .
>
> Like his own "Skylark" up at Heaven's gate,
> He left the earth, and all its meaner things,
> And soared and sang higher than mortal ken.

But occasionally he would come nearer earth, believes Pike, when some "sudden thought" would rush into his soul and he would become enthusiastic over it.

> His wasted form,
> Attenuated, thin, ethereal, shook
> With the vibrations of his spirit; . . .

These lines show the influence of *Alastor* and reveal Pike's sentimental attitude towards Shelley.

In the *New World* for February 5, 1842, was published a sonnet, "Shelley": [30]

> Immortal son of Song! who sitt'st enthroned,
> With God-like spirits, on Fame's sky-kissed steep!
> Wreathed with flowers, crowned with a sun-beam glory!
> Thou, whose spirit's essence was as lightning—
> Whose heart was like the ever fitful wind—
> Strong as desire, or gentle as content.
> Now, breathing with the tempest's loudest notes,
> And now, with voice of evening's sweetest breeze,
> Wooing, with kisses soft the vales of Greece,
> Hallow'd in song. Thee, Shelley, thee I hail!
> Whose heavenly strains were all too pure and deep
> To charm the world's dull ear. Immortal bard!
> Another age shall estimate thy worth,
> And glory in thy name—the future shall be just.

The *Harbinger*, the publication of the Fourier society, 1842–1847, contains a number of mentions of Shelley and some very Shelley-like poetry. There is no mention of Shelley in the first volume. The second volume contains a review of Foster's edition of Shelley and mention of him in a review of Gilfillan's "Literary Portraits." In the review of the *Poetical Works of Percy Bysshe Shelley*,[31] the writer refers to Foster's enthusiasm for Shelley, which he believes is admirable, and to his readiness to overlook all Shelley's faults as trifling. He says: "To him he becomes as grand and beautiful as a god come down to teach mortals the celestial secrets of Love and Wisdom and Beauty."

This reviewer is of the opinion that religious prejudice has blinded some to Shelley's "all-containing love of Humanity, his great sincerity, and his heroic devotion to . . . truth." He fears that Foster has stated Shelley's claims upon our admiration too strongly, has lauded him too highly, which is not just. He declares that Foster also errs in stating that Shelley's system and that of Fourier are identical. He quotes Foster and then quotes Parke Godwin, whose analysis of Shelley, he says, is the best that has yet been written, to the effect that Shelley had not yet settled, to the perfect satisfaction of his mind, the theories of the Universe, Man, and God. He then compares Shelley and Fourier, between whom he says there was, intellectually, no agreement. Both loved Truth and Humanity, and each believed most firmly in a future reconstruction of Society upon the Division Principle of Love. "But Shelley, led astray by his false metaphysics, formed no other idea of a true social order than a community of property, a system just as opposite to that of Fourier as to that of nature." He pays a concluding tribute to Shelley who, he says, will be appreciated when socialism or Fourierism comes.

In a review of George Gilfillian's *Sketches of Modern Literature and Eminent Literary Men* (being a Gallery of Literary Portraits), the critic states regarding the author's attitude towards Shelley:[32]

A nobler tribute has seldom been paid to Shelley's transcendent merits as a poet, as a pure and childlike man, and one in whom the *spirit* of religion dwelt more clearly than in whole calendars of canonized and church-accepted saints; and yet he mourns a long time over his unfortunate "Atheism," as if it *could* be Atheism!—as if one whose deeds were godlike could be "without God in the world!" The saving clause in his condemnation quite outweighs the whole. The world will not long fear such a man, as the Shelley of this portrait.

The *Harbinger* contains three other notices of Shelley, one of these being the publication of his "Ode to the West Wind." [33]

The *Whig Review,* founded in 1845, likewise contains a number of mentions of Shelley. The first of these is by E. P. Whipple, who reviews Griswold's *Poets and Poetry of England in the Nineteenth Century*.[34] He discusses Shelley at some length, both as a man and as a poet. In his discussion of Shelley's character, Whipple is guilty of a great deal of the overwrought sentimentalism that he criticizes in Hunt. Of Shelley's critics he says: "Smooth, practical atheists preached morality and religion to him from quarterly reviews and defamed him with an arrogant stupidity, and a sneaking injustice, unparalleled in the effronteries and fooleries of criticism." His discussion of Shelley as a poet is in a less perturbed vein. He says that Shelley was "endowed by nature with an intellect of great depth and exquisite fineness; an imagination marvelously gifted with the power to give shape and hue to the most shadowy a' ;tractions . . . a fancy quick to discern the most remote analog. s, brilliant, excursive, aerial, affluent, in graceful and delicate images." He believes that the Cenci and Prometheus Unbound show Shelley's maturity and his great possibilities as a poet.

The review in the same periodical of Foster's edition of Shelley's poems is hostile.[35] The reviewer states that Shelley's imagination, although lofty and delicate, is too predominant and overpowers too much his moods of thought. He cannot agree with all Foster's ideas of the poet's ethics. He says that he admires Shelley's beautiful mind and no less beautiful spirit of humanity, but does not approve of what he terms the "impious blasphemous tones of the modern school of rhapsodical reformers—worshippers of the divine in the human." This criticism is aimed at Foster who referred to Mrs. Shelley as the "evangelist of her trans-figured Lord," a comment in keeping with Foster's fanatical ideas. A somewhat severe and rather erratic criticism of Gil-fillan's Literary Portraits is given by R. H. Bacon in the April, 1847, issue of the magazine.[36] The writer begins by stating: "We agree for the most part with Mr. Gilfillan's estimate of Keats and Shelley, but we utterly despise the affectation of sanctity and the pharisaical whine with which he concludes the sketches of both." Then follows an outburst of righteous indignation against Gilfillan for his praise of these poets that must have astounded the Englishman. Bacon then accuses Gilfillan of attempting to rival Jeffrey, but says that there is a difference between honest opinion and deliberate misrepresentation, "the best illustration of the result of which will be the world's estimation of Words-worth and Southey compared with its estimation of Shelley and Keats some half century hence, when its judgment of these poets has been completed." The same magazine, in May, 1847, contains a very well balanced discussion of the "Character of Shelley," by Joseph Hartwell Barrett.[37] Mr. Barrett believes that as a re-former Shelley was a failure, "merely" an agitator, "without aim and without wisdom." He says that Shelley should have con-fined himself to the ideal sphere which is the poet's peculiar province. Shelley failed as a poet, he believes, because he lacked the maturity of experience and because he intruded himself into his poetry too much. He cites Adonais as an example of a poem that possesses "all the characteristic beauties and defects of Shelley and the former in the highest perfection." Shelley, he insists, was too impatient to write; he was not willing to "await his muse's favors." In May, 1849,[38] was published a poem "The Death of Shelley," by H. W. P., with a footnote stating that the poem was founded on the assumption that Shelley was a literal monomaniac on the subject of Christianity.

The *United States Magazine and Democratic Review* was founded in Washington in 1837 and moved to New York in 1841. It numbered among its contributors Hawthorne, Paulding, Bryant, Whittier, Simms, Alexander Everett, W. A. Jones, and many other literati and journalists of the day. "The book reviews were perspicacious," says Mott; "the rising New England school was treated with greater understanding than was common." And he adds, "But less literary articles upon questions of national policy afforded the pièce de résistance of each Democratic meal." [39] Parke Godwin, a regular contributor to the magazine in its early years, wrote both political and literary articles. Although Godwin was interested in transcendentalism and various social movements, he cannot be classed as a radical. In politics, he was first a Free-Soil Democrat and then a Republican. That his interests were literary as well as political, the number and quality of his works on literature will bear testimony. He not only translated the first part of Goethe's *Autobiography*, but edited the same work. He also edited the works of William Cullen Bryant and accompanied them with a biography. His latest literary work, published when he was eighty-four, was *A New Study of the Sonnets of Shakespeare*.

It is as a literary critic, rather than as an advocate of any social creed, that Godwin approaches his subject in his article, "Percy Bysshe Shelley," in the *Democratic Review* for December, 1843.[40] Although his knowledge of the facts is necessarily limited and, in some instances, inaccurate,[41] Parke Godwin gives an interesting and sympathetic account of Shelley's life. His admiration for Shelley's resistance to the fagging system and for his philanthropy is characteristic of an American of the Parke Godwin type and of the period. It is to his credit as a critic that he dismisses Shelley's marital affairs in a single brief paragraph. It is in his estimate of Shelley's poetry, however, that Godwin shows his superiority as a literary critic. *Queen Mab*, "one of the most extraordinary productions of youthful intellect," he says, resembles Southey's *Thalaba* in meter and general form, but is "superior to that poem in wild grandeur and pathos." The spirit of the poem he characterizes as follows:

It has one broad, deep pervading object—a shout of defiance sent up by an unaided stripling against the powers and principalities of a world of wrong. . . . The blasphemy and atheism of it are the tempestuous writhings of a pure and noble spirit torn and tossed between the contending winds and waves of a heart full of Love and a head full of Doubt.

Godwin's socialistic views come to the foreground when he states that the *Revolt of Islam* is the work which will endear Shelley most strongly to sympathetic minds. He calls it Shelley's interpretation of the French Revolution, which, he says, to Shelley was a failure. "What he wished to teach," writes Godwin, "was the lesson, so necessary in that age, . . . that every struggle for the rights of man, . . . was, in the end, worth the effort." Godwin's appreciation of this poem is best revealed in his splendid discussion of it as a whole and in his comment:

> Bold as it is, in many of its sentiments, it is a noble monument to the loftiness of his aims, the brilliancy of his imagination, the wealth of love in his heart, and the breadth and power of his intellect.

In his discussion of *Prometheus Unbound*, Godwin does not consider the poem as a drama, but approves of the presentation of Prometheus and praises the lyrical parts of the poem. The lyrics, he asserts, are surpassed in graceful ease and harmony only by Sophocles.

> They rise upon the ear like strains of sweet melody, ravishing it with delight. . . . For delicacy and beauty, nothing in the range of verse is finer than the description of the flight of the Hours.

He concludes with the following comment upon the poem as a whole:

> The whole leaves the impression of a noble oratorio, expressive of the Life of Humanity in its passage from early darkness through pain and strife, to the overflowing joy and sunshine of its maturer development.

That Parke Godwin was interested in Shelley and in criticism as a whole is apparent from his statement that *The Cenci* has been so often criticized in both England and Germany that he will not dwell on it. He finds in this drama more of human interest than in any other of the author's poems. In the artistic presentation of the moral aim he believes that it resembles Shakespeare. The language used in the portrayal of the feelings of Beatrice, he says, is of "unsurpassed fidelity and force."

In discussing Shelley's claims as a poet, Godwin writes: "It is with difficulty the critic preserves his mind from the influences of common opinion on one side, or the exaggeration of a reactive sympathy on the other." Then follows an excellent discussion of Shelley's faults and strong points. Among the former are vagueness in phraseology, a peculiar language and diction, haziness of atmosphere in description, and, greatest of all, the frequent obscurity, which takes its origin from two peculiarities, exceeding subjectivity and exquisite delicacy of imagination. Some of his strong points are an elevated conception of the true function of the poet, singular command of language and rhythm, skill in the use of verse forms, imaginative power, and a glowing spirit of freedom and love. This analysis needs no other comment than that Godwin must have made a thorough study of Shelley's style in order to arrive at such exact conclusions. I doubt if any twentieth-century critic of Shelley would disagree with his findings.

Godwin concludes his article with a discussion of Shelley's philosophy and religion, in which he shows the breadth of learning, the clear understanding, and the broad sympathy that make him the best Shelley critic of the period and one of the best of the century.

The *Democratic Review* contains but one other article on Shelley in this period. In an article on "Modern English Poets" in the October, 1846, issue, the writer quotes from Margaret Fuller's article on Shelley,[42] with which he is in accord, and adds a few words of appreciation on Shelley's poetry which he believes should be read "in the luxuriance of midsummer amidst the bonteous prodigality of nature." He says that he first made the acquaintance of *Alastor* in a mountain scene which might have inspired the poem. He does not approve of the Shelley imitators. Shelley, he believes, stands alone as a poet. He calls him an acknowledged interpreter of nature, "one of the Druidical priesthood of the poets."

This article brings to a close the periodical criticism of Shelley in the Middle Atlantic Section for this period. The articles and notices, more than thirty in all, are, for the most part, favorable. The prejudices against Shelley's character and views are few. They appear only occasionally and in short articles. He is mentioned favorably in periodicals of such varying purpose as the scholarly *New York Literary Gazette and Phi Beta Kappa Repository*, the socialistic *Harbinger, Godey's Lady's Book,* and such leading magazines as the *Whig Review*, the *American Quarterly*, and the *Democratic Review*. His poetry receives a great deal of attention and brings forth some discriminating criticism, the three leading articles being published in three different decades. These three articles, "Criticism. Percy Bysshe Shelley," in the *New York Literary Gazette,* 1826, "The Shelley Papers," in the *American Quarterly Review,* 1836, and "Percy Bysshe Shelley," by Parke Godwin, in the *Democratic Review,* 1843, may be classed among the best criticism of Shelley in the nineteenth century. The Middle Atlantic Section was not known during this period as a literary section, but owing to its independence of outlook and its lack of prejudice, its contribution to Shelley criticism was favorable and was of a superior quality.

CHAPTER V

THE SOUTH

Southern Shelleyans

The romantic spirit seems not to have reached the South until well along in the twenties. It is probable that the English periodicals were not read to any extent in this section. Confined to the cities, where there were libraries, or to the book shops, they were procured only by the intellectually inclined. When the romantic spirit did appear, Moore was a general favorite, and with Byron furnished the inspiration for most of the early poets as did Scott for the novelists. Conditions in the South were not conducive to the making of great poets or to the advancement of literature. Plantation life was not favorable to the development of the imagination and of philosophic ideas. There were no civic centers where those who were interested in literature or art could meet and exchange views. Francis Lieber, who had come from Germany and, after a short period in the North, had gone to the University of South Carolina as instructor in modern languages, bemoans the fact that he is compelled to dwell in a section in which he is not able to find intellectual companionship and inspiration. In a letter to Privy-Councillor Mittermaier, May 13, 1841, he writes:[1]

I live at the South, it is true, but with respect to culture and intellectual life, and all a man requires who takes part in the stirring movements of our time, I might as well be in Siberia. There is no use in deluding myself, nor have I the disposition to do so. If Herder complained of a disappointed life, oh, how much more reason have I to despond! . . . A little while since, I had some hope that an opportunity might offer for my return to the North. I had several expectations; but at present I have no prospect whatever in view, and so I am drying up, and even losing my energy. . . .

The South was occupied in building up a Greek state. Its life was that of the aristocracy, and its interests were economic and social, not intellectual. Its romanticism was of the spirit, a deeply imbedded love for the beautiful, the strange, the unusual. This feeling for romanticism was revealed in the attitude towards people as well as towards nature. Thus romanticism became romance. Scott, Byron, Moore, and, later, Shelley and Keats appealed to the writers of this section.

To the outdoor instincts of the Southerner, Scott, with his descriptions of the hunt and the life of the country squire living in a great hall, was satisfying. Byron's poetry, with its love element, its peculiar strength and weakness, its masculinity, its use of nature as a refuge, appealed to the romantic instincts of both women and men. And Moore's gallantry satisfied their feeling for chivalry. It was only by the poetically inclined that Shelley was read, and later Keats. It was the lyrical quality of Shelley, reinforced by that of Poe, and strengthened by the objective beauty of Keats, that seized the poetic minds of the South with a grip that only the War could break. The greatest of the Southern poets was Poe, but such men as Henry Timrod, Paul Hamilton Hayne, and Sidney Lanier, and many of lesser note, might have reached great heights had not the Civil War destroyed their lives, sapped their strength, or taken away their inspiration. The work of such writers as Edward Coote Pinkney and Philip Pendleton Cooke was also cut short at its beginning.

One of the important poets of the South recently resuscitated from oblivion is Edward Coote Pinkney. His biographers, Mabbott and Pleadwell, state that he has a strong claim not only to the title of the first of American lyrists but also to the position of one of the four chief poets of the South and one of the dozen bright stars of his native land.[2] Pinkney was interested in the English Romantic poets, and it is generally recognized that his poetry shows indebtedness to Wordsworth, Byron, and Moore. His acquaintance with Shelley's poetry does not seem so certain. His biographers state that he read "the then obscure Shelley" and the novels of Mrs. Shelley. The parody on *Frankenstein* reveals his mature appreciation of his early liking for works of its kind. At least one of his poems shows a slight indebtedness to Shelley. "To Georgiana" seems to have been influenced by the "Euganean Hills."

> 'Twas eve; the broadly shining sun
> Its long celestial course had run;
> The twilight heaven, so soft and blue,
> Met earth in tender interview.
>
> .   .   .
>
> Like happy islands of the sky,
> The gleaming clouds reposed on high,
> Each fixed sublime, deprived of motion,
> A Delos to the airy ocean.
> Upon the stirless shore no breeze
> Shook the green drapery of the trees,
> Or, rebel to tranquillity,
> Awoke a ripple on the sea.
>
> .   .   .   .
>
> All which lay calm as they had been
> Part of the painter's mimic scene.
>
> .   .   .   .

> And fast went by the moment's bright,
> Like waters shooting through the night. (Lines 1-42)

William Gilmore Simms is not usually thought of as a poet. It is for his prose rather than for his poetry that he is known. Most of his verse, written before 1850, belongs to the early period of his writing. His poem "The Slain Eagle" was undoubtedly influenced by Shelley's *Revolt of Islam*. Like the *Revolt*, it is written in the Spenserian stanza, and it contains passages and lines that strongly suggest the Shelley poem:

> The moral of a chosen race wert thou,
> In such proud flight. From out the ranks of men—
> The million moilers, with earth-cumber'ed brow,
> That slink, like coward tigers to their den,
> Each to his hiding-place and corner then—
> One mighty spirit watched thee in that hour,
> Nor turned his lifted heart to earth again;
> Within his soul there sprang a holy power,
> And he grew strong to sway, whom tempests made not cower.
> (St. V)

> Watching, he saw thy rising wing. In vain,
> From his superior dwelling, the fierce sun
> Shot forth his brazen arrows, to restrain
> The audacious pilgrim, who would gaze upon
> The secret splendours of his secret throne;
> Proudly he saw thee to that presence fly,
> And Eblis-like, unaided and alone,
> His dazzling glories seek, his powers defy,
> Raised to thy god's own face, meanwhile thy rebel eye. (St. VI)

The poem "Atlantis; a Story of the Sea," 1832, also was written under the influence of Shelley. Leon resembles the Leon of the *Revolt of Islam*, and much of the description and conversation recalls the same poem. The flight of the sea-demons, singing, in the fourth scene, was probably suggested by the "Song of the Spirits" in *Prometheus Unbound*.[3]

> Fly! fly!
> Through the perilous sky,
> Spirits of terror and tumult on high!
> Even as we go,
> Working the woe
> Of all that is hatefully happy below!
> Speed! our mission, fierce and fatal,
> Is to spoil superior things. . . .

No American poet was more thoroughly imbued with admiration for poetry of Shelley than was Albert Pike.[4] He must have studied Shelley's poetry assiduously and, consciously or unconsciously, absorbed much of the contents. He adopted the Shelley properties for use in his own poems. His descriptions of

nature are Shelleyan, his birds are always like the lark, his seas
and rivers, little boats, the great steed, the eagle, all are Shelleyan.
Even Shelley's most beloved snake becomes the property of Pike
and is revealed in all its beauty, regardless of the fact that even
Shelley could not have felt any love for the snakes in Arkansas.
Pike hears "sweet music in the grass" as did Shelley, and sees
"dewy diamonds of the dawn," a luxury denied even to Shelley.
He uses similes in profusion, a Shelley characteristic, and his
characters take journeys at an impossible speed over great dis-
tances. His "Ariel," the most Shelleyan of his poems, was undoubtedly written to Shelley and influenced by both the *Revolt
of Islam* and *Alastor*. The first ten of the forty-eight stanzas
show the influence of the latter poem and the remainder show
that of the former. The character Ariel, who appears in a dream
and guides the poet through space and reveals to him the evils
of the world, is probably Shelley:

> I had a dream: Methought Ariel came,
>   And bade me follow him; and I arose:
> Lighter my body seemed than subtle fiame,
>   Or than the invisible wind that always blows
> Above the clouds. So upwards did I aim,
>   With quick flight, as the sky-lark sunward goes,—
> Led by the splendour of Ariel's wing,
> Whose snowy light before fled, glittering.   (St. I)

The following quotations from stanzas III–XI indicate the progress of the journey through space, which is very similar to the
journeys in the Shelley poems.

> Awhile we trod along the quivering peaks
>   Of foaming cloud . . .
>
>   .   .   .
>
> And moored within a labyrinthine bay
>
>   .   .
>
> A boat carved out of orange mist, . . .
>
>   .   .   .
>
> And swiftly then our winged bark flew on,
>
>   .   .   .   .
>
> Then rushed we into chasms, deep, wide, and black,—
>
>   .   .   .   .
>
> And then we issued to the open vast
>   Of cloudless air above . . .
>
>   .   .   .   .
>
> Then we descended, till our barque did float
>   Above the peak of one lone mountain: . . .
>
>   .   .   .   .
>
> Then,bending from the helm, Ariel gazed. . . .

And here Ariel points out to the poet a golden palace in which "liveth Tyranny." The division of the Republic is given in stanza XII. Then follows, in stanzas XIII–XXV, a description of the horde that came through the gates of the castle—Ambition, Rashness, Disappointment, Envy, Avarice, Corruption, Fanaticism, Hypocrisy, Treason, and King Anarchy.

> Then did Ariel leave the snowy sail
>   Of our ethereal barque . . .

and they go on another journey (stanzas XXVI–XLVIII) and see all the evil wrought by these characters. They finally return to the poet's home, which he terms his "sad soul's prison," and Ariel, with a brief adieu, wends upward.

In "The Voyage of Life," somewhat Shelleyan in movement and atmosphere, Pike sails in an enchanted boat, but on this journey he takes his family with him, and the journey is to the southland and somewhat enjoyable.

> We and our little children float
>   Dreaming, in an enchanted boat: . . .

Other poems by Pike that are especially Shelleyan are "The Dead Chase: a Legend," which contains practically all the Shelley paraphernalia; "Morning: a Lament," which reveals acquaintance with Shelley's "Sensitive Plant;" and the song "Love Blooms but Once," which refers to the Golden Age. Nearly all the poems written by Pike, except "To the Mocking Bird," 1828, a poem distinctly influenced by Bryant, show indebtedness to Shelley. Bryant seems to have served as Pike's first model but was rejected soon after 1830 for Shelley. Many of the poems reveal a combined influence of these two poets.

William Pitt Palmer was one of the poets whose early work showed promise but whose development was interrupted by the events of the time.[5] E. P. Whipple believed that Palmer should have received recognition in Griswold's *Poets of America*.[6] Two of his early poems, "Light" and "The Clerk's Dream," show Palmer's apprenticeship to Shelley. The first of these poems is a direct imitation of Shelley's "The Cloud," written on a different subject, but a worthy imitation. The following stanzas reveal the similarity:

I

> From the quickened womb of the primal gloom
>   The sun rolled black and bare,
> Till I wove him a vest for his Ethiop breast
>   Of the threads of my golden hair:

And when the broad tent of the firmanent
    Arose on its airy spars,
I pencilled the hue of its matchless blue,
    And spangled it round with stars.

II

I painted the flowers of Eden bowers
    And their leaves of living green,
And mine were the dyes in the sinless eyes
    Of Eden's virgin queen;
And when the Fiend's art on her trustful heart
    Had fastened its mortal spell,
In the silvery sphere of the first-born tear
    To the trembling earth I fell.

IV

Like a pall at rest on a puseless breast,
    Night's funeral shadow slept
Where shepherd swains on the Bethlehem plains
    Their lonely vigils kept;
When I flashed on their sight the herald's bright
    Of heaven's redeeming plan,
As they chanted the morn of a Savior born—
    Joy, joy to the outcast Man!

VI

The desolate Morn, like a mourner forlorn,
    Conceals all the pride of her charms,
Till I bid the bright Hours chase the Night from her bowers,
    And lead the young Day to her arms;
And when the gay rover seeks Eve for his lover,
    And sinks to her balmy repose,
I wrap their soft rest, by the zephyr-fanned west,
    In curtains of amber and rose.

"The Clerk's Dream" contains echoes of both Spenser and Shelley and is written in the Spenserian stanza. The song within the poem, the song of the Naiads, however, is Shelleyan:

    Prisoned long in caverned fountains
        Lost in dungeons ebon,, eerie,
    From the wild New England mountains
        We at last have broke away!
        Ours are feet that never weary—
    See their silvery sandals glancing
    As in moonlight mazes dancing,
        Trip we onward night and day!

        .   .   .   .

    Onward! then, o'er foamy ledges,
    On! through groves of mirrored beeches;
        Linger not to kiss the sedges
        Waving in the scented gale!

Round the headlands, down the reaches,
Dance we on with murmuring motion!
Hark! we hear thee, parent Ocean,
    And rejoicing bid thee hail!

Thomas Holly Chivers, who is now considered to be a "rare curiosity of literature," was best known in the nineteenth century as the friend of Poe and an admirer of Shelley. So great was his admiration for Shelley that he was called "Shelley-mad." The poetry of Chivers, however, was not influenced by that of Shelley, as a careful examination of his verse will show. Although Lowell called the poems of Chivers "the shell of Shelley," Poe comes nearer the truth when he states that Chivers was not influenced by Shelley or by any other poet. He asks, in his criticism of *The Lost Pleiad,* if it is not a miracle that a poet of the age should compose sixty or seventy poems in which there shall be discoverable no taint—absolutely none—of Byron, or Shelley, or Wordsworth, or Coleridge, or Tennyson.[7] Although G. E. Woodberry believes that Chivers was indebted to Poe, he states that the verse of Chivers had a music of its own, and gives "The Lady Alice" as the fairest example of the rhythm which Chivers evolved. He does not, however, mention any influence of Shelley on Chivers, although he does refer to the infatuation Chivers had for the English poet.[8] That Chivers greatly admired Shelley is revealed in his correspondence with Poe, in his lecture on Shelley, and in other instances. The lecture on Shelley, a part of which was published in the *Southern Literary Messenger* for February, 1844, contains a great deal of overwrought sentimentalism intermingled with some fine appreciation.[9] His poem "Mary's Lament for Shelley Lost at Sea" does not have a single Shelley characteristic. It does not deserve the praise Poe gave it, but it does contain a few good lines. The maudlin tone of the poem is uncomplimentary to both Shelley and Mary. The dedication that Chivers wrote for his biography of Poe is characteristic of the extremes to which he was willing to go in his worship of Shelley:

To the Eternal Spirit of the immortal Shelley, this work is solemnly dedicated, by one who longs to enjoy his company in Elysium.

Chivers should be considered an admirer of Shelley and not an imitator. And if he did not succeed as a poet, his failure was not due to the influence of Shelley but to the fact that he lacked poetical ability.

The Southern Literary Messenger

The *Southern Literary Messenger* was the representative periodical of the South in the second quarter of the century.

Although it was not established until 1834, it soon took its place with the more important northern magazines. Contributions came from all parts of the country. The first critic to notice Shelley in this periodical was Edgar Allan Poe, whose review of Drake's *Culprit Fay* and Halleck's *Alnwick Castle* appeared in the April, 1836, issue.[10] He is again mentioned in the January, 1837, and October, 1839, numbers. In 1840 appeared the first of the articles on the poet by Henry T. Tuckerman, a New England Shelleyan.[11] In this article, which was prompted by the publication of Shelley's *Prose Works,* Tuckerman expresses admiration for Shelley and his principles, especially for his rebelling against the fag sytem at Eton and for his marrying Harriet contrary to his belief regarding marriage. He does not believe that Shelley would be considered an atheist by the "reflective student of his writings" any more than would Milton: "The opinions of Shelley are no more to be regarded as an index to his heart than the blind bard's quiet musings as a proof that the fire of devotion did not burn within." *Queen Mab,* he holds, should be regarded as the crude outbreak of juvenile talents anxious to make trial of the new weapons furnished by the logic of Eton. Of Shelley's poetry in general, he says: "He was too fond of looking beyond the obvious and tangible to form a merely descriptive poet and too metaphysical in his taste to be a purely sentimental one." The article concludes with an observation that is very interesting in that it shows the attempt of a sympathetic critic to appeal to the better instincts of a prejudiced public.

Whatever views his countrymen may entertain, there is a kind of living posterity in this young republic, who judge of genius by a calm study of its truths, wholly uninfluenced by the distant murmur of local prejudice and party rage.

Had this idealistic belief seemingly held by Tuckerman been true, Shelley would have been accepted without reservation in America. But the narrow prejudice that dominated the reviewers of the Romantic period in England when considering anything unorthodox also existed in America. The difference was that in England the reviewers expressed the ideas of the people as they interpreted them, and in America the people demanded that the periodicals consider their prejudices, as the response to Tuckerman's article and his letter in reply well illustrate. The first objection came in the form of a super-sentimental article, by Mrs. Seba Smith, wife of the political Satirist, in the November issue of the *Messenger.*[12] In this article that reflects highly perturbed feelings, Mrs. Smith regrets that a writer of Tuckerman's appreciation and genius "should have employed the hybla of his pen in the defense of a cause so unholy." To her, Shelley was not only a pernicious character with ideas very dangerous to respectable institutions but also a misguided person who had wandered and "needed someone to guide his vacillating footsteps." She believes that only his "sense of the beautiful and of the proprieties of things" saved him from utter degradation.

A second article in refutation of Tuckerman's criticism and signed "A Friend of Virtue" appeared in the *Messenger* [13] for December. The writer, as would be expected from the signature, attacks Shelley on moral and religious grounds and expresses surprise that Tuckerman's article has not excited more comment. He feels it his duty to reply to this article in that he fears the evil influence of Tuckerman's defense of Shelley, particularly his defense of Shelley's ideas regarding religion and marriage. In the January, 1841, *Messenger*,[14] in a letter to the editor, T. W. White, Tuckerman replies to the attack made in the December issue. He criticizes "A Friend of Virtue" for repeating and exaggerating the slanders on Shelley and at the same time acknowledging ignorance of Shelley's life and letters. He quotes Hunt and cites Hogg in order to defend Shelley's character and to show that the poet was, at heart, a Christian. His concluding comment on Shelley and his poetry is rather surprising and causes one to wonder whether Tuckerman was not influenced by the best interests of the *Messenger* and his own interests as well to conciliate the feelings of the public:

> I do not subscribe to Shelley's opinions. I regret that he thought as he did upon many subjects, for his own sake as well as for that of society. The great mass of his poetry is not to my taste. . . . I honor Shelley as a rare character—a sincere man.

This was Tuckerman's last article on Shelley.

The publication of Shelley's prose works in 1840 prompted a review in the *Messenger* [15] that is important because of the enthusiasm of the writer for this volume and his promise of a later review after he has had time to peruse it. The reviewer is acquainted with *Queen Mab* and the notes to that work, but apparently with no other work of Shelley's before this volume. His interest in the letters and in the essay *A Defence of Poetry*, published for the first time, leads one to regret that his promised review never appeared. The 1841 volume contains, in addition to the Tuckerman letter already mentioned, two other notices of Shelley. The first of these, in an article on Byron,[16] is a sentimental reference to what the writer terms "Byron's feeling at the loss of his brother bard and the world's loss of 'her Shel-

ley.'" The second, under "Pencillings on Poetry," [17] is a criticism
to the effect that "poetry has too often been wickedly prostrated
to evil purposes," Shelley and Moore being cited as examples of
poets from whose work no real benefit can be derived. Shelley
is called "a star which left its sisters for a world of cloud and
gloom." The *Messenger,* however, had Shelley supporters. In
March, 1842, appeared a review of *Prometheus Unbound* [18] in
which the writer approves the "justice lately awarded Shelley
by British reviewers," and extols Shelley who he says loved his
race and did not seek revenge on his country as did Byron. He
compares the *Prometheus Unbound* with the *Prometheus Vinctus*
of Aeschylus. The Titan of Aeschylus he believes to be inferior
to that of Shelley, the ruling principle of the former being hate
and that of the latter, benevolence. He approves of Shelley's making the Furies work upon the mind and feelings of their victim
rather than to apply physical torture. He finds a parallel in the
lives of the two writers. He states that Aeschylus, like Shelley,
was accused of impiety and was tried before the Areopagus, but
although acquitted, was rendered so obnoxious to his countrymen
that he spent his life in exile. He believes that Aeschylus was
more fortunate than Shelley, who was condemned without trial.
This review, by an anonymous writer, is a good appreciation of a
work that at this time was not well known.

Beginning with the October, 1844, number, Henry C. Lea, son of
Isaac Lea of Lea and Carey, Publishers, Philadelphia, and then
nineteen years of age, published the first of a series of six articles
entitled "Remarks on Various Late Poets." In all six of these
articles Shelley is given some attention. Lea, who appears to be
a critic of discriminating tastes, is content to confine his remarks
on Shelley to his poetry. He criticizes Leigh Hunt as a poet because he did not portray feeling. Shelley, he says, did not show
feeling in the *Revolt of Islam,* but "His unpretending *Rosalind and
Helen* or magnificent *Cenci* moves the deepest recesses of the
spirit." [19]   In his article entitled "Barry Cornwall's Songs" he
criticizes B. W. Proctor for trying to imitate Shelley. He states
that the difference between the poets is that Shelley sometimes
lets his powerful imagination run wild, but that Proctor tries to
spur his on to the same capers. His next comment that it is a
pity an end could not be put to such imitators is one that must
have expressed the feelings of many of his fellow critics. Elizabeth Barrett Browning suffers by comparison with Shelley in the
eyes of this critic. Her ideas "so inadequately" expressed in *The
Vision of Poets* "may be found exquisitely expressed in Shelley's
Defence of Poetry." She fails as a translator of Greek, Lea be-

lieves, because she "manifests her consciousness of the feat on almost every page," while Shelley could translate Plato and Euripides and yet continue magnificently the *Prometheus Vinctus* without showing that he had ever read a line of Greek.[20] The same writer, in discussing the poetry of Miss Landon (Mrs. Maclean), says, "Shelley was himself the ideal of the imaginative, abstracted benevolence which lies at the bottom of all his poetry." [21] Although this is the last article of the series, Lea, in criticizing the poet William Motherwell, concludes with: "We trust and believe that Motherwell will one day receive the honor due him; not indeed as one of the great masters of the heart, the Byron's and the Shelley's [*sic*] of the past splendid age, but in his true and honorable position as one of the minor poets." [22]

The *Southern Literary Messenger* for February, 1844,[23] contained an extract from a lecture entitled "Genius of Shelley," by T. H. Chivers, M.D. Although this very commendatory estimate by an enthusiastic follower of Shelley contains some good criticism, a great deal of it is exaggerated. Chivers compares Shelley's ability to delineate natural objects to that of Claude in delineating landscapes, and the poems of Shelley to the paintings of Titian in that the execution far surpasses the design. Some comments show thoughtful and discriminating criticism. Shelley's poems, he states, "appear to have been written just for the delight which they gave him," and his "poetry is the *artless* expression of Art. It proceeded from the burning fountain of his soul." His discussion of Shelley's ideality and the eulogistic paragraph in which he attempts to characterize Shelley are good examples of the type of praise which caused people to say that he, Chivers, was "Shelley-mad." His comparison of Byron and Shelley, however, is quite in accord with the changing attitude of the time as regards these writers:

> The difference between Byron's poetry and Shelley's consists in this, that the breathings of the former are the melancholy outbreaks of a spirit at war, from disappointmnt, with the world; those of the latter are the pathetic expressions of a soul which panted after an *ideal of intellectual perfection*. Shelley carolled for the listening ears of an enraptured world, while Byron sang its requiem. Byron was like the sun in eclipse. Shelley was like Hesperus, the leader of the starry host of Heaven.

His last paragraph, in which he states that Shelley's poetry was inspired by the Venus Urania, is a very interesting and thoughtful comparison and shows some discernment on the part of the writer.

The next article on Shelley, published in the *Messenger* for December, 1846,[24] is of particular value in view of the criticism typical of that time. The writer states his position in the first paragraph as follows:

> No poet has been more enthusiastically extolled by his admirers than Shelley, and, in unhappy counter-balance, no poet of the true fire has been so much neglected by the world at large. We mean to give some reasons, which we think natural and good ones, for the extreme neglect which has been the lot of so remarkable a mind and its works.

He then distinguishes between genius and talent, the one having "fire and wings" and the other "sticking to the earth." The greatest minds, he holds, have both. Those with talent and appreciation of genius are clever and useful men but not well known. Those with a reasonable amount of talent and no genius become cynical and retire within themselves. Those with a reasonable amount of genius and no talent do nothing of note. Those with the utmost amount of genius and no talent become poets. To this class he assigns Shelley. He criticizes Shelley's poetry in that no one of his poems is without defects, but he cannot understand why Shelley's "brilliant and teeming mind should so often have shown itself an absurd one." He selects, as Shelley's two best poems, "The Sensitive Plant" and "The Skylark."

> It is impossible to read either of them without high admiration of their rhythm, continuity of tone, and crowding beauties of thought. But both are marked by extravagance of phraseology and idea; and the first by absurd rhymes, and, plentifully, by those unhappy suggestions of secondary ridiculous ideas.

He gives stanzas from "The Sensitive Plant" as illustrations of Shelley's faults. He then quotes stanzas from "The Skylark," which he calls the best of Shelley's poems, to prove that it too "is greatly marred by Shelley's constant fault—extravagance of fancy, surpassing the bounds of reason, interrupting and maiming the sweetest and noblest thoughts." The tone of the whole criticism is suggestive of the earlier English reviews. The writer states, however, that he selected "The Sensitive Plant" for criticism because "a northern reviewer has recently gone out of his way to speak well of it." The northern reviewer who gave Shelley such unlimited praise was no other than the *Messenger's* former editor, Edgar Allan Poe.[25] In his "Marginalia" in the *Messenger*, almost three years later, May, 1849,[26] Poe again eulogizes Shelley. It is but fitting that Shelley criticism in the South for the first half of the century should close with praise from his greatest American disciple, Edgar Allan Poe.

CHAPTER VI

The Influence of Shelley on Poe

The similarity between the poetry of Shelley and that of Poe was noted occasionally by writers throughout the nineteenth century. John Neal, E. C. Stedman, and an unknown writer in the *Southern Literary Messenger* mentioned the resemblance,[1] but not until the twentieth century did anyone make an attempt to trace Shelley's influence on Poe. W. B. Cairns called attention to this influence,[2] but it was left for Killis Campbell, in *The Poems of Edgar Allan Poe* (1917), to give examples of Poe's indebtedness to Shelley. Professor Campbell's findings are accurate but somewhat incomplete because he was interested in the subject of general influences on Poe's poetry, and, consequently, was faced with the task of tracing these influences in the work of numerous poets. The influence of Shelley on Poe, however, was greater than is generally believed. Too much attention has been devoted hitherto, when tracing indebtedness, to searching for parallel passages. It is very difficult to find such passages, for Poe was not an imitator but a careful and consistent student of Shelley. The very early writings, particularly those in Poe's 1829 volume, show clearly that he had studied both Shelley's style and his subject matter. Not until 1835, however, as will be seen, did Poe give attention to Shelley's poetic theory as exemplified in the "Hymn to Intellectual Beauty." That he adopted in part the theory of Beauty therein and probably was inspired by this poem to pursue a deeper study of poetic theory the following discussion will show.

The years of Shelleyan influence on Poe may be divided into four periods. The first is the period of early influence, before 1829, in which the indebtedness appears to be chiefly to *Prometheus Unbound*. The second period extends from 1829 to 1831, during which time Poe seems to have secured a copy of the Galignani edition of Coleridge, Shelley, and Keats,[3] the poetry of which influenced his poems in the 1831 edition and his later writing as well. The third period extends from 1833 to 1840, from the publication of Poe's "Coliseum" to the appearance in America of Shelley's prose works. In this period further influence of Shelley's poetry may be noted, but it is also important as the period in which Poe, while attempting to formulate a poetic theory, discovered Shelley's ideas of Beauty and imagination [4] and applied them, to some extent, to his own poetry and to his criticism as well. The fourth and last period begins with Poe's acquaintance with Shelley's *Defence of Poetry* and the application of the theory of Beauty contained therein to his own poetic theory, and concludes with the composition of "The Raven" in 1845.

The first direct evidence that Poe was acquainted with Shelley's poetry is found in the 1829 volume.[5] The poems "Al Aaraaf," "Sonnet—to Science," and "Fairy-Land" show indebtedness to *Prometheus Unbound*.[6] The first of these poems, "Al Aaraaf," was undoubtedly an early poem, as Poe stated, but it was very probably revised for later publication. There are indications that the poem was made up of several earlier poems,[7] and that certain lines were added in accordance with the purpose of the writer to show that earthly beauty fails when it does not take cognizance of divine beauty. The defense of divine beauty, not a new theme with Poe, probably had its inspiration from his early reading of Moore.[8] The theme, however, furnished Poe an opportunity to refute certain ideas of Shelley as given in *Prometheus Unbound*.

In Part I of "Al Aaraaf," lines 94 to 101, is found the first resemblance to Shelley. This passage, probably added to the lyric after Poe had read the *Prometheus*, is very Shelleyan in content.

> To be carriers of fire
> (The red fire of their heart)
> With speed that may not tire
> And with pain that shall not part—
> Who livest—*that* we know—
> In Eternity—we feel—
> But the shadow of whose brow
> What spirit shall reveal?

The general idea of the carriers of fire probably derives from *Prometheus Unbound*, and the line "With speed that may not tire" has parallels in the same poem.

> On the brink of the night and the morning
> My coursers are wont to respire;
> But the Earth has just whispered a warning
> That their flight must be swifter than fire:
> They shall drink the hot speed of desire!
>
> (II, v, 1-5)

The "Pain that shall not part" might have been suggested by the cry of Prometheus, "Pain, pain ever, for ever!"[9] And the last two lines could have been prompted by a similar use of "shadow" in *Prometheus Unbound*.

> See how he lifts his mighty looks, the Heavens
> Darken above.
>
> > (I, 256-257)
>
> This was the shadow of the truth I saw.
>
> > (I, 655)
>
> Beloved and most beautiful, who wearest
> The shadow of that soul by which I live, . . .
>
> > (II, i, 30-31)
>
> > . . . what canst thou see
> But thine own fairest shadow imaged there?
>
> > (II, i, 112-113)

The passage, lines 124 to 132, is very Shelleyan, and seems to have no connection with the earlier part of Poe's poem. Here Poe refutes the Shelleyan idea that the "Voices of Unseen Spirits," or the "music of the sphere," can be heard and answers with the very practical idea that "Ours is a world of words."

> > . . . a voice was there
> How solemnly pervading the calm air!
> A sound of silence on the startled ear
> Which dreamy poets name "the music of the sphere."
> Ours is a world of words . . .

Shelley is probably one of the poets referred to in "dreamy poets," in that he refers a number of times to the music of the spheres.[10]

> 'Tis the deep music of the rolling world . . .
>
> > (IV, 186)
>
> The music of the living grass and air, . . .
>
> > (IV, 257)
>
> Meanwhile thy spirit lifts its pinions
> In music's most serene dominions; . . .
>
> > (II, v, 85-86)

Poe refutes Shelley's theory that "All Nature Speaks," as expressed in lines of *Prometheus Unbound*. The beautiful lines in which Shelley describes all nature in unison,

> And the wild odour of the forest flowers,
> The music of the living grass and air,
> The emerald light of half-entangled beams
> Round its intense yet self-conflicting speed,
> Seem kneaded into one aerial mass
> Which drowns the sense,
>
> > (IV, 256-261)

Poe answers with:

> All nature speaks and even ideal things
> Flap shadowy sounds from visionary wings—
> But ah! not so when, thus, on high
> The eternal voice of God is passing by;
> And the red winds are withering in the sky.
>
> > (I, 128-131)

Poe is here giving voice to his belief in Divine Power, an idea that is in keeping with that of the original poem on divine beauty.

In Part II, the lyric to "Ligeia," lines 100–155, is probably an earlier lyric revised under the influence of the lyrics of the *Prometheus,* or an attempt at imitation. Lines 124–126, which are very Shelleyan,

> The sound of the rain
>> Which leaps down to the flower
> And dances again
>> In the rhythm of the shower—
> The murmur that springs
>> From the growing of grass
> Are the music of things—

and the succeeding line, 127,

> But are modell'd alas!—

(evidently inserted for the sake of the rhyme), with the abruptness of the transition, indicate that the passage might have been inserted after the lyric was written. The idea of speed in lines 219–224 and the nature of the country traversed are Shelleyan, and Ianthe is a Shelleyan name: [11]

> Thence sprang I —as the eagle from his tower,
> And years I left behind me in an hour.
> What time upon her airy bounds I hung,
> One half the garden of her globe was flung,
> Unrolling as a chart unto my view—
> Tenantless cities of the desert too!
> Ianthe, beauty crowded on me then,
> And half I wished to be again of men.

The passage, lines 231–244, is Miltonic in subject matter and Shelleyan in atmosphere, movement, and diction, even to the use of Shelley's "Daedalian," which is misspelled "Daedalion":

> But, list, Ianthe! when the air so soft
> Failed, as my penon'd spirit leapt aloft,
> Perhaps my brain grew dizzy—but the world
> I left so late was into chaos hurl'd—
> Sprang from her station, on the winds apart,
> And roll'd, a flame, the fiery Heaven athwart.
> Methought, my sweet one, then I ceased to soar,
> And fell—not swiftly as I rose before,
> But with a downward, tremulous motion thro'
> Light, brazen rays, this golden star unto!
> Not long the measure of my falling hours,
> For nearest of all stars was thine to ours—
> Dread star! that came, amid a night of mirth,
> A red Daedalion on the timid Earth.

It would seem, then, that the poem "Al Aaraaf" furnishes proof that Poe was acquainted with Shelley's *Prometheus Unbound* when he published the 1829 edition of his poems.

But Poe's "Sonnet—To Science," likewise one of the 1829 poems, also appears to have been composed under the influence of *Prometheus Unbound*. The *Prometheus* is representative of the developing scientific movement of the nineteenth century in its broadest sense, and it is this aspect of science to which Poe refers in the first two lines of the sonnet:

> Science! true daughter of Old Time thou art!
> Who alterest all things with thy peering eyes.

These two lines and the last six of the sonnet might refer to many poets, particularly to those who were interested in either philosophy or ethics,[12] but the intervening lines seem to refer to Shelley:

> Why preyest thou upon the poet's heart,
> Vulture, whose wings are dull realities?
> How should he love thee? or how deem thee wise,
> Who wouldst not leave him in his wandering
> To seek for treasure in the jewelled skies,
> Albeit he soared with an undaunted wing?

Apart from the general application of these lines to Shelley, there is internal evidence that the lines were prompted by Poe's reading of *Prometheus Unbound.* The idea of the vulture preying upon the poet's heart may have been suggested by the vultures or "Furies" in the Shelley poem and their tearing the heart of Prometheus. And the wings of the vultures, which Poe terms "dull realities," may refer to the subjects which Shelley introduced into his poems. It was these didactic subjects to which Poe objected and to which he probably refers as science. Shelley was the poet of all time who "soared with an undaunted wing" and who wandered in the skies seeking treasure there rather than on earth.

I do not believe that Poe objected to Shelley's use of natural science, if he recognized his use of it, and he undoubtedly did.[13] Shelley uses natural science in a figurative sense, for the sake of comparison, which is a poetic not a didactic use and, therefore, would not be objectionable to Poe. That Poe was early opposed to moralizing in poetry is clear from his reference to Wordsworth in his "Letter to B—." Poe's sonnet is a protest against the introduction into poetry of science in any form. It is but an early expression of his later belief in pure poetry.

The poem "Fairy-land," 1829, contains the following lines reminiscent of *Prometheus Unbound*:[14]

> Comes down—still down—and down
> With its centre on the crown
> Of a mountain's eminence,
> While its wide circumference
> In easy drapery falls
> Over hamlets, over halls,
> Wherever they may be—
> O'er the strange woods—o'er the sea—
> Over spirits on the wing—
> Over every drowsy thing—
> And buries them up quite
> In a labyrinth of light—
> And then, how deep! O, deep,
> Is the passion of their sleep!
>
>   (*Fairy-land*, 15-28)

>   To the deep, to the deep,
>   Down, down!
> Through the shade of sleep,
> Through the cloudy strife
> Of Death and Life;
> Through the veil and the bar
> Of things which seem and are
> Even to the steps of the remotest throne,
>   Down, down!
>
>   (*Prometheus Unbound*, II, iii, 54-62)

> By the woodland noontide dew;
> By the forest, lakes, and fountains,
> Through the many-folded mountains;
> To the rents, and gulfs, and chasms,
> Where the Earth reposed from spasms, . . .
>
>   (*Ibid.*, II, i, 199-203)

The rearrangement of these lines, with a few changes, as given in the 1831 text of "Fairy-Land," indicates that Poe was experimenting with this passage. Another poem, "A Dream within a Dream," contains lines which reveal a similar experimentation with Shelleyan verse. The earliest text of this poem, entitled "Imitation," is very Byronic; but the 1829 version, "To——————", is changed a great deal, and the Shelleyan lines,

> And I hold within my hand
> Some particles of sand—
> How few! and how they creep
> Through my fingers to the deep!

are added. The 1829 versions of both "Fairy-Land" and "A Dream within a Dream" would indicate that Poe had become acquainted with *Prometheus Unbound* between 1827 and 1829.

In the poems of the 1831 volume Poe has furthered his acquaintance with Shelley, particularly with some of the minor poems, and has cast off much of the Byronic influence and replaced it with that of Keats, and of Coleridge as well, although it is possible that the Coleridge influence has been overrated. At least two poems in this volume show a distinctly Keatsean influence. "To Helen," in movement, in atmosphere, in subject matter, and in artistic treatment, is so like the poetry of Keats that it might have been written by him. "The Sleeper," as a whole, is not only in the Keatsean manner but is almost an imitation of Keats.[45] This further knowledge of these poets was undoubtedly secured from a copy of the Galignani edition of Coleridge, Shelley, and Keats, published in Paris in 1829.[16] Poe's "The City in the Sea," first published in the 1831 edition, reflects a study of these three English poets. It is in this poem and under the influence of these Romantic poets that Poe first makes use of the ghastly in his poetry.[17] The indebtedness to Shelley is in the rather general resemblance to "Lines Written among the Euganean Hills," as stated by Killis Campbell, [18] and in certain similarities to *Prometheus Unbound*. The reference to the hours as breathing faint and low (49) was probably suggested by the part given the Hours in the fourth act of *Prometheus Unbound*, and the "Down, down" (51) is reminiscent of the refrain in the "Song of Spirits" in the same poem.[19]

"Israfel," also published in 1831, contains that impalpable Shelleyan influence that is so easily felt but so difficult to place. The story of Israfel might well be interpreted as that of Shelley. There is a close resemblance between the stanzas of this lyric and those of the lyrics of *Prometheus Unbound*. Just as Shelley in each lyric of the *Prometheus* fits the movement, the stanza form, and the rhyme to the character and the subject matter, so Poe adapts each stanza of "Israfel" to the thought and possibly to the changing mood of the lyric. This poem is more than a beautiful lyric; it is an experiment in that variety and originality of stanza form and meter in which Poe had but one equal, Shelley.

No poetry seems to have been written by Poe between that of the 1831 volume and the prize poem, "The Coliseum," in 1833. The chief source for this poem was unquestionably Shelley. It was Shelley who furnished not only the inspiration but much of the material as well as the central idea of the poem. In September, 1832, Medwin published Shelley's fragment "The Coliseum" in the *Athenaeum* as one of "The Shelley Papers." It was this selection that furnished the inspiration for Poe's poem and to which he turned for material, even though he made use of an older poem of his own as a basis on which to write the new. This revising earlier poems and publishing them as new seems to have been a habit with Poe. The direct borrowings from Shelley's "Coliseum" are: "Shattered cornices" from "shattered and shapeless cornices," "crumbling frieze" from "crumbling fragments," "sate on bed

of moss" from "seated . . . on a flight of . . . mossy steps,"
"tottering arcades" from "walls hanging totteringly," and the
lizard gliding "spectrelike, unto his marble home" from the figure
"gliding among the galleries of the Coliseum." The poem "To
One in Paradise," likewise written in 1833, bears a resemblance
to Shelley's poetry.[20] The poem, as a whole, in atmosphere and
movement, suggests Shelley's "Stanzas, written in Dejection near
Naples." The third stanza is very much like the third stanza of
Shelley's poem, except that the parallels do not follow the same
order in the two poems.

> For, alas! alas! with me
> The Light of Life is o'er!
> No more—no more—no more—
> (Such language holds the solemn sea
> To the sands upon the shore)
> Shall bloom the thunder-blasted tree,
> Or the stricken eagle soar.
> (*To One in Paradise.*)
>
> Alas! I have nor hope nor health,
> Nor peace within nor calm around,
> Nor that content surpassing wealth
> The sage in meditation found,
> And walked with inward glory crowned—
> Nor fame, nor power, nor love, nor leisure.
> Others I see whom these surround—
> Smiling they live, and call life pleasure;—
> To me that cup has been dealt in another measure.
> (*Ode to Dejection*)

The "Light of Life" was probably suggested by Shelley's "Life
of Life,"[21] and the line "No more—no more—no more" by the
refrain "No more—Oh, never more!" in his "A Lament."

As the years pass and Poe becomes more experienced, his indebtedness to Shelley for either suggestion or inspiration grows
less. During the late thirties and early forties, therefore, his
poems show less of the Shelley influence and more of Poe's own
originality, more of a style made up of genius plus the study of
other poets, chief of whom is Shelley. In fact, only one poem
after 1845 betrays a direct Shelley influence. This is the poem
"For Annie," evidently revised from one written in the early
thirties,[22] about the time of "Israfel," when Poe was making an
intensive study of Shelley and experimenting with his meter and
stanza forms. Of the later poems, "The Haunted Palace," written
in 1839, has a distinctly Shelleyan atmosphere, with a hint of
Keats and possibly of Coleridge in the closing stanza.[23] The lines,

> Spirits moving musically,
> To a lute's well-tuned law,
> Round about a throne . . .

may have been suggested by the Spirits of *Prometheus Unbound*
coming to the aid of Prometheus. The Echoes in the fourth stanza,

> A troop of Echoes, whose sweet duty
> Was but to sing,

are undoubtedly borrowed from the same poem, even though the
application is different from that in the Shelley poem. The "evil
things," in stanza five, that assail the king resemble the Furies
that tormented Prometheus. The early impression made by
Prometheus Unbound seems never to have left Poe. He refers
to this work again and again, directly and indirectly. The "Sonnet
—Silence," 1840, is evidently an attempt to answer theories of
Shelley as expressed in *Prometheus Unbound*.

> For know there are two worlds of life and death:
> One that which thou beholdest; but the other
> Is underneath the grave, where do inhabit
> The shadows of all things that think and live
> Till death write them and they part no more;
> > (*Prometheus Unbound,* I, 195-199)
> There are some qualities—some incorporate things
> That have a double life, which thus is made
> A type of that twin entity which springs
> From matter and light, evinced in solid shade.
> There is a two-fold *Silence*—sea and shore—
> Body and soul. One dwells in lonely places,
> Newly with grass o'ergrown; some solemn graces,
> Some human memories and tearful lore,
> Render him terrorless; his name's "No More."
> He is the corporate Silence: dread him not!
> > No power hath he of evil in himself;
> But should some urgent fate (untimely lot!)
> > Bring thee to his shadow (nameless elf
> That haunteth the lone regions where hath trod
> > No feet of man), commend thyself to God!
> > (*"Sonnet—Silence"*)

It is possible that Poe has Shelley in mind when he speaks of
the "nameless elf," for Shelley attempted to solve the problem
of existence.

The theme for Poe's unusual poem "The Conqueror Worm,"
1848, was probably suggested by the many references in Shelley's
poems to the conquests of worms. This subject seemed to hold
a fascination for Shelley. Again and again he reverts to it in
his discussions on the subject of death. His early poem *Queen
Mab*, and his *Rosalind and Helen* contain the greatest number of
these gruesome lines.

> . . . and on that arm
> The worm has made his meal.
> > (*Queen Mab*, III, 149-150)

> To turn to worms beneath that burning sun, . . .
> > *(Ibid.,* VIII, 184)
> . . . to-morrow, worms
> In silence and in darkness seize their prey.
> > *(Ibid.,* IX, 112-113)
> When he was in the churchyard lying
> Among the worms, . . .
> > *(Rosalind and Helen,* 318-319)
> When she was a thing that did not stir
> And the crawling worms were cradling her . . .
> > *(Ibid.,* 344-345)
> Because they blush not with remorse
> Among their crawling worms.
> > *(Ibid.,* 466-467)

Other poems likewise contain similar references in less number.[24] The atmosphere of the poem is very Shelleyan, particularly that of the second and fourth stanzas. The last two lines of the first stanza, however, are the most Shelleyan of any lines in the poem.[25]

> While the orchestra breathes fitfully
> The music of the spheres.

In the second stanza, the "vast formless things" that shift the scenery and flap their "Condor wings" were probably suggested by the Furies of *Prometheus Unbound.*

> Mimes, in the form of God on high,
> Mutter and mumble low,
> And hither and thither fly—
> Mere puppets they, who come and go
> At bidding of vast formless things
> That shift the scenery to and fro,
> Flapping from out their Condor wings
> Invisible Wo!
> > *(Conqueror Worm)*
> The darkness and the clangour of your wings.
> > *(Prometheus Unbound,* I, 460)
> The shade which is our form invests us round,
> Else we are shapeless as our mother Night.
> > *(Ibid.,* 471-472)

And the expression "Invisible Wo!" recalls Shelley's

> Ah woe!
> Ah, woe! Alas! pain, pain ever, for ever!
> I close my tearless eyes, but see more clear
> Thy works within my woe-illumed mind, . . .
> > *(Prometheus Unbound,* I, 634-636)

In the fourth stanza, which is somewhat in the manner of Shelley, Poe is more gruesome than Shelley in that he is more realistic:

> But see, amid the mimic rout,
> A crawling shape intrude!

> A blood-red thing that writhes from out
>   The scenic solitude!
> It writhes!—it writhes!—with mortal pangs
>   The mimes become its food,
> And seraphs sob at vermin fangs
>   In human gore imbued.

The "crawling shape" which "writhes" out from the "scenic solitude" undoubtedly owes its suggestion originally to Shelley's "The Coliseum."

Poe's "Dream-Land," 1844, which seems to be a rewritten form of earlier poems, is also very Shelleyan. In the first stanza the reference to "an Eidolon, named Night" is probably borrowed from Shelley's idea of death as the brother of night in his poem "To Night" in that "Eidolon" is symbolic of death. The second stanza is vaguely reminiscent of the *Euganean Hills* [26] and the third of *Prometheus Unbound*.[27] The Shelleyan characteristics are now so intermingled with the Poe that it is difficult to separate them. The poem "The Raven," written in 1845, possibly owes the suggestion for its refrain to Shelley's "A Lament." [28] This poem, then, is the last indication of Poe's submission to Shelley. It marks his final breaking away from Shelleyan influence, and all other influences as well, and his complete independence thereafter in the composition of poetry. Poe undoubtedly recognized this independence when he wrote his "Philosophy of Composition." From this time on his work shows that Poe had developed a style that is wholly his own. Such poems as "Ulalume," "The Bells," and "Annabel Lee" prove that he no longer needed a teacher. And although he never attained the heights reached by Shelley, he became master of that artistic finish in poetry in which he so firmly believed and for which he had striven for so many years.

Poe was influenced by Shelley in the development of his poetic theory as well as in the composition of his verse. His theory, first suggested in his "Letter to B—," which served as a preface to the 1831 edition of his poems, was gradually developed until it reached its culmination in "The Philosophy of Composition" and "The Poetic Principle." It is with one phase only of the development of Poe's theory of poetry that this discussion is concerned, his development of the theory of the Beautiful. For it was on this phase that Shelley exerted a strong influence.

In the "Letter to B" there is no indication that Poe is acquainted with Shelley's theory of poetry. He does not mention beauty in any form as an essential quality of poetry,[29] nor does he refer to the place of imagination in poetry. His recognition of these qualities and his weaving of them into his own poetic theory is first noticed in his criticism of Drake and Halleck in the *Southern Literary Messenger* for April, 1836.[30] He here states that imagination is the soul of poetry, and in a footnote explains by way of illustration:

> The consciousness of this truth was possessed by no mortal more fully than by Shelley, although he has only once alluded to it. In his "Hymn to Intellectual Beauty" we find these lines. . . .

He then quotes the fifth and sixth stanzas of the *Hymn* to illustrate his point. He quotes from *Queen Mab* to show the correct use of ideality or the "Poetic Power," in contrast to the method used by Drake in the "Culprit Fay." He objects to the grotesqueness in the description of Drake's fairy, and adds by way of contrast:

> The fairy of Shelley is not a mere compound of incongruous elements . . . unaccompanied by any moral sentiment, but a being of grace, of color, of motion—of the beautiful, of the mystical, of the august—in short, of the ideal.

He refers to Shelley's "Sensitive Plant," Keats's "Nightingale," and Coleridge's "Kubla Khan" as examples of entire poems of purest ideality. In the same review, in complimenting Halleck for the correct use of ideality, Poe takes occasion to express his contempt for the "herd of brainless imitators" of Shelley, Coleridge, and Tennyson. In reviewing Bryant's poems in the same magazine for January, 1837,[31] he expresses the belief that Bryant's work will be valued in a day to come as will that of "the spiritual Shelleys, or Coleridges, or Wordsworths, or with Keats, or even Tennyson, or Wilson." He quotes three lines from Bryant's "To the Evening Wind" as lines "breathing all the spirit of Shelley:"

> Pleasant shall be thy way *where meekly bows*
> *The shutting flower, and darkling waters pass*
> *And twixt the o'ershadowing branches and the grass,* . . .

The greatest progress in Poe's poetic theory, particularly in his theory of the Beautiful, comes after the publication of Shelley's *Defence of Poetry* early in 1840. In his review of Longfellow's *Voices of the Night*, February, 1840, Poe dwells on the use of imagination and on "beauty," not "Beauty." He credits Longfellow with having a vivid imagination but criticizes him for lack of "artistical power." He says that Longfellow's poems "abound in high thoughts" but fail in poetic truth because they lack the right proportion of "beauty and strength." The term "beauty" is used several times in this criticism but always in its generally accepted sense. The nearest approach to the Shelleyan use of the term is in the reference to the "richly ideal beauties" of Longfellow's "Hymn to the Night."

It is in the review of Longfellow's *Ballads and Other Poems* in *Graham's Magazine* for April, 1842, that Poe shows a knowledge of Shelley's *Defence of Poetry*. The first part of the review, that published in the March number, is brief, and judging from the number of references to European writers, it might be inferred that Poe had been delving into the literature and criticism of various countries. Enthusiastic over his new-found knowledge, he promises an article to demonstrate that the poetry of these writers, among whom are English romanticists as well as continental poets,[32] "has fulfilled the legitimate office of the muse." [33] He praises Longfellow's high ideality but objects to his didaticism, a quality which he believes is owing to German influence. He concedes that a didactic moral may be the *"undercurrent of a poetic thesis."* Lowell, he believes, approaches nearer to writing ideal poems because he selects his themes with greater propriety. He gives "Rosalind" as an example. At this stage of his criticism Poe is interested in ideality and in didacticism as it applies to themes. In the second part of this review of Longfellow's *Ballads,* in the April number of *Graham's,* Poe apologizes for his "hasty observations" in the March number. He still objects to Longfellow's didacticism, but he is more concerned with "Beauty" as the central purpose of all poetry. He devotes at least a third of his article, paragraphs five to thirteen, to a discussion of Beauty, which parallels Shelley's *Defence of Poetry,* paragraphs three to fourteen.

In making use of Shelley's material, Poe uses three methods: direct borrowing of ideas, phrases, and statements; modification of material borrowed; refutation of Shelley's ideas. After stating that he divides the "world of the mind" into pure intellect, taste, and the moral sense, Poe proceeds to discuss, in his fifth paragraph, these qualities in their relation to each other:

> Just as conscience, or the moral sense, recognises duty; just as the intellect deals with truth; so is it the part of taste alone to inform us of Beauty.

When he states that it is the part of taste to inform us of Beauty, he is but reproducing Shelley's idea that the sense of approximation to order or rhythm is called taste, but not taste unless it approximates the beautiful.

> For there is a certain *order* or rhythm belonging to each of these classes . . . from which the hearer and the spectator receive . . . pleasure . . . ; the sense of an *approximation* to this *order* has been called *taste* . . . but the diversity is not sufficiently marked . . . except . . . where . . . *approximation* to the *beautiful* . . . . . *is* very great.[34]

Poe continues, "And Poesy is the handmaiden but of Taste," and Shelley, "Those in whom it [taste] exists in excess are called Poets." Poe's next statement, while not borrowed, unless Poe had previously read the preface to *Prometheus Unbound*,[35] may have been modified by his recent reading of the *Defence:*

> This handmaiden is not forbidden to moralize—in her own fashion. She is not forbidden to depict—but to reason and preach, of virtue.

Shelley believes that poetry, working through the imagination, is an indirect means of moral improvement, but that its purpose is not to teach but to give delight:

> The great instrument of moral good is the imagination; and poetry administers to the effect by acting upon the cause. Poetry enlarges the circumference of the imagination by replenishing it with thoughts of ever new delight. . . . Poetry strengthens the faculty which is the organ of the moral nature of man in the same manner as exercise strengthens the limb. A poet therefore would do ill to embody those of his own conceptions of right and wrong, which are usually those of his own place and time, in his poetical creations, which participate in neither. By this assumption of the inferior office of interpreting the effect . . . he would resign a glory in a participation in the cause.[36]

Poe's next paragraph is in part an adaptation and in part a refutation of Shelley's theory of the Beautiful as taken from his theory as exemplified in various works, but chiefly in the *Defence.* Poe states:

> An important condition of man's moral nature is thus, plainly, the sense of the Beautiful. This it is which ministers to his delight in the manifold forms and colors and sounds and sentiments amid which he exists.

The idea of the sense of the Beautiful being a part of man's nature is a Shelleyan idea, but Shelley does not recognize "immortal nature." Poe continues:

> And just as the eyes of Amaryllis are repeated in the mirror, or the living lily in the lake, so is the mere *record* of these forms and colors and sounds and sentiments—so is their mere oral or written repetition a duplicate source of delight. But this repetition is not Poesy.

Poe is here attempting to refute Shelley's contention that poetry and prose are the same. Shelley states that "The distinction between poets and prose writers is a vulgar error," and that "The popular division into prose and verse is inadmissible in accurate philosophy." [37] Poe then refutes Shelley's theory of the moral value of poetry. After stating that poetry "acts in a divine and unapprehended manner," and that only Time can determine a poet's standing, Shelley proceeds:

A poet is a nightingale who sits in darkness and sings to cheer its own solitude with sweet sounds; his auditors are as men entranced by the melody of such an unseen musician, who feel that they are moved and softened, yet know not whence or why.[38]

Homer, he states, was such a poet, a poet who won the admiration of his auditors "until from admiring they imitated, and from imitation they identified themselves with the objects of their admiration." Poe answers Shelley's contention with the argument that it is the "immortal essence of man's nature" that "proves his divine title." This, his striving for immortality is, he indicates, the unsatisfied longing in Shelley's search for eternal Beauty, "the desire of the moth for the star." But Poe makes no reference to Shelley, even when quoting this line from one of his well known poems.[39] Poe's answer to Shelley is:

He who shall merely sing with whatever rapture, in however harmonious strains, or with however vivid a truth of imitation, of the sights and sounds which greet him in common with all mankind—he, we say, has yet failed to prove his divine title. There is still a longing unsatisfied, which he has been impotent to fulfil. There is still a thirst unquenchable, which to allay he has shown us no crystal springs. This burning thirst belongs to the *immortal* essence in man's nature. It is equally a consequence and an indication of his perennial life. It is the desire of the moth for the star.

Shelley contends that lack of moral perfection in a poet or the vices of an age as reflected in poetry do not affect the beauty of poetry:

But a poet considers the vices of his contemporaries as the temporary dress in which his creations must be arrayed, and which cover without concealing the external proportions of their beauty. . . . The beauty of the internal nature cannot be so far concealed by its accidental vesture, but that the spirit of its form shall communicate itself to the very disguise . . . it is doubtful whether the allay of costume, habit, etc., be not necessary to temper this planetary music for mortal ears.[40]

Shelley's contention that the beauty of the inner nature cannot be concealed, Poe answers with the argument that "It is not the mere appreciation of beauty before us" that makes poetry, but the striving "to reach the beauty above," "a forethought of the loveliness to come." And to make clear his idea, he quotes and cites, with slight modifications and without indicating the source, the ideas of Shelley as given in the *Adonais:* "to anticipate some portion of that loveliness whose very elements, perhaps, appertain solely to Eternity."

> He is a portion of the loveliness
> Which once he made more lovely: . . .
> (*Adonais,* 379-380)

> Life, like a dome of many-coloured glass,
> Stains the white radiance of Eternity.
>
> (*Adonais,* 462-463)

In his next paragraph, Poe's condemnation of the fact that whole poems have been accepted as poetry, and have been used as false standards because certain parts were poetical, is good criticism and might well apply to *Prometheus Unbound.* He attempts, in the succeeding paragraph, to formulate the definition of poetry from a number of ideas that he has gleaned from various sources. His next comment, "Its [Posey's] first element is the thirst for supernal BEAUTY—a beauty which is not afforded the soul by an existing collocation of earth's forms— a beauty which, perhaps, *no possible* combination of these forms would fully produce," is based on the fifth and sixth stanzas of the "Hymn to Intellectual Beauty," a work to which, as has already been seen, Poe had recourse earlier. Here he uses for the first time his expression "Supernal Beauty," a phrase to which he was to cling with that intrepid grasp which characterized Poe. Shelley, while musing on the problem of life as regards all nature, saw the solution in a vision of supreme Beauty or "awful Loveliness." To Shelley, appreciation of beauty in all its forms would free the world from "its dark slavery" of evil. Poe calls this beauty "supernal Beauty" because Poe believed in immortality, and supernal Beauty is above mortal power.

Poetry's second element, Poe says, "is the attempt to satisfy this thirst by *novel* combinations, *of those combinations* which our predecessors, toiling in chase of the same phantom, *have already set in order.*" The "thirst" and the "phantom" refer to the "Hymn," but "our predecessors" undoubtedly comes from the *Defence,* in which Shelley states that "every great poet must inevitably innovate upon the example of his predecessors." [41] Poe continues:

> We thus clearly deduce the *novelty,* the *originality,* the *invention,* the *imagination,* or lastly, the *creation* of BEAUTY (for the terms as here employed are synonymous) as the essence of Poesy. Nor is this idea so much at variance with ordinary opinion as, at first sight, it may appear.

In other words, Poe presents this as an original idea, his own deduction. In the early part of the *Defence,* in the third paragraph, Shelley states that primitive man observed in dancing and singing and imitating natural objects, a certain rhythm and order. Thus Poe's "novelty." And in this dancing and singing and imitating, men did not observe the same order. Thus Poe's "originality." According to Shelley, "There is a certain order belonging to each of these classes of mimetic representation. . . ."

Thus Poe's "invention." And "those in whom it [the faculty of approximation to the beautiful] exisits in excess are poets." Thus Poe's "imagination." The expression of this "influence of society or nature upon their own minds" is Poe's "creation." It will be observed, therefore, that Poe not only used Shelley's ideas herein, but arranged them in the same order.

In the next paragraph, the tenth, the parallel between the two essays is even clearer. Poe begins:

> So far we have spoken of Poesy as of an abstraction alone. As such, it is obvious it may be applicable in various moods. The sentiment may develop itself in Sculpture, in Painting, in Music, or otherwise.

Shelley, in almost the same words, states:

> The grammatical forms which express the moods of time . . . are convertible with respect to the highest poetry without injuring it as poetry. . . . The creations of sculpture, painting, and music are illustrations still more decisive.[42]

In his reference to rhythm, Poe states that "the universality of its use in the earliest poetical efforts of mankind would be sufficient to assure us, not merely of its congeniality with the Muse, . . . but of its elementary and indispensable importance." Shelley, in his seventh paragraph, says that "the language of poets has ever affected a certain uniform and harmonious recurrence of sound, . . . which is scarcely less indispensable . . . than the words themselves." Poe now takes up the topic of music: "It is in Music, perhaps, that the soul most nearly attains that end upon which we have commented—the creation of supernal Beauty." Shelley begins his next paragraph with:

> An observation of the regular mode of the recurrence of this harmony in the language of poetical minds, together with its relation to music, produced meter, or a certain system of traditional forms of harmony and language. Yet it is by no means essential that a poet should accomodate (sic) his language to this traditional form.

Poe, earlier in his paragraph, has already answered Shelley's last contention with "We cannot make up our minds to admit (as some have admitted) the inessentiality of rhyme." In the eleventh paragraph Poe defines the poetry of words as "the *Rhythmical Creation of Beauty*." It has no dependence, he avers, unless incidentally, upon either Duty or Truth. Shelley, in his ninth paragraph, declares that "A poem is the very image of life expressed in its eternal truth."

After a short paragraph in which Poe attempts to clear himself on the question of rhythm, probably to make sure that he will not be accused of plagiarism, he adds a paragraph, evidently for the purpose of throwing his readers off guard, for he knows very well that he cannot be accused of plagiarizing Keats:

Of the poets who have appeared most fully instinct with the principles now developed, we may mention *Keats* as the most remarkable. He is the sole British poet who has never erred in his themes. Beauty is always his aim.

One may agree with this statement regarding Keats, but the insertion of this paragraph here with the emphasis on the name of Keats reveals a self-consciousness or feeling of guilt on the part of Poe who knew that he was not voicing the theories of Keats but those of Shelley.

Poe's statement in the next paragraph, together with his use of the word "beauty" in the remainder of the article, is ample proof that in his discussion of "Beauty" he has not been giving expression to his own original views. He concludes: "In the general acceptation of the term *Beauty* we are content to rest; being careful only to suggest that in our peculiar views, it must be understood as inclusive of *the sublime*." His reverting in his discussion of Longfellow's poems to the "general acceptance" of the term "beauty" shows that he had not yet made Shelley's ideas his own. Not until he wrote his lecture on "The Poetic Principle" did Poe feel certain that he had absorbed Shelley's theories sufficiently to inculcate them into his own theory with something of freedom or, perhaps, to build a theory around Shelley's ideas. In "The Poetic Principle" Poe takes over from his review of Longfellow's ballads practically the whole discussion of the theory of the Beautiful and of the ethical value of poetry. He makes but few changes, these changes being, for the most part, a matter of eliminating and condensing in order to secure unity in the subject as a whole. He herein makes it clear that "a sense of the Beautiful" is an "immortal instinct" and that the "thirst unquenchable" belongs to the "Immortality of man." There is no question here as to Poe's position regarding the immortality of the soul. Here he uses the term "supernal Loveliness," a modification of the earlier "supernal Beauty." He has related the idea of the moral aim of poetry to his own classification of the three divisions of the mind: "Just as the intellect concerns itself with Truth, so Taste informs us of the Beautiful, while the moral sense is regardful of Duty." After this recapitulation, he adds, in explanation, further ideas from Shelley:

> *That* pleasure which is at once the most pure, the most elevating, and the most intense, is derived, I maintain, from the contemplation of the Beautiful. In the contemplation of Beauty we alone find it possible to attain that pleasurable elevation, or excitement, *of the soul,* which we recognise as the Poetic Sentiment, and which is so easily distinguished from Truth. . . . I make Beauty the province of the poem, simply because it is an obvious rule of art that effects should be made to spring as directly as possible from their causes.

This passage is Poe's reproduction in terms of "Poetic Sentiment" of Shelley's theory of the Beautiful as exemplified in his "Hymn to Intellectual Beauty" and in his *Defence of Poetry.* Similar ideas and expressions may be found throughout the *Defence.*[43]

Poe's reason for not directly acknowledging his indebtedness to Shelley is a problem for which there might be various solutions. The best solution may be found in the introductory paragraphs to his sketch "The Visionary," as published in *Godey's Lady's Book* in January, 1834, but dropped from all subsequent printings: [44]

There is a name—a sound—which, above all other music, vibrates upon my ear with delicious, yet wild and solemn melody. Devoutly admired by the few who read, and by the very few who think, it is a name not as yet, indeed, blazoned in the escutcheon of immortality; but there, nevertheless, heralded in characters of that Tyrian fire hereafter to be rendered legible by the breath of centuries.

It is a name, morover, which for reasons intrinsically of no weight, yet in fact conclusive, I am determined to conceal. Nor will I, by a fictitious appellation, dishonor the memory of that great dead whose life was so little understood, and the received account of whose melancholy end is a tissue of malevolent blasphemies. . . .

Poe's direct recognition of Shelley as an outstanding poet was first revealed in his review of Elizabeth Barrett's *A Drama of Exile and Other Poems,*[45] in 1845, and was published again, with a few changes, in "Marginalia" in the *Southern Literary Messenger,*[46] 1849. Here Poe not only pays tribute to the genius of Shelley but also recognizes Shelley's influence on Tennyson:

If ever mortal "wreaked his thoughts upon expression," it was Shelley. If ever poet sang—as bird sings—earnestly—impulsively—with utter abandonment— to himself solely—and for the mere joy of his own song— that poet was the author of "The Sensitive Plant."

Thus begins his discussion of "Shelley and Tennyson," in which he states the belief that the early poetry of Tennyson was influenced by Shelley but that Tennyson later investigated this early manner of writing and corrected the faults he had acquired by imitating Shelley, while retaining the better influence, the purity of his poetical style. And here Poe expresses his ideal of poetry, the ideal that he believed Tennyson was striving to attain, and evidently the ideal towards which he himself was working. He expresses it as "that mental and moral combination which shall unite in one person (if ever it shall) the Shelleyan *abandon* and the Tennysonian poetic sense, with the most profound Art (based both in Instinct and Analysis) and the sternest Will properly to blend and rigorously to control all." Thus, he at last, even though indirectly, acknowledges something of his indebtedness to his greatest teacher, Shelley.

THE TRANSITION PERIOD
(1850-1872)

CHAPTER VII

THE PERIOD OF SENTIMENTALISM

IN THE MIDDLE of the nineteenth century interest in literature centered chiefly in the Middle Atlantic Section. In those turbulent years preceding the Civil War, New England writers as a whole were giving their attention to the cause of the abolition of slavery and other reform movements. Such literary activity as existed in this section was represented by the major writers, some of whom, as Lowell, divided their time between national affairs and letters. The general upheaval in the South during the Civil War period was disastrous to its literary development. The romanticism of the thirties and forties had left its impression on this section. Young singers of the South aspired to the lyrical heights reached by Poe, Shelley, and Heine, and desired to write nature poetry in imitation of Keats. But the war destroyed the singers or turned their inspiration into other channels. In the years immediately preceding the war, the energies of the one literary magazine, the *Southern Literary Messenger,* were spent in discussing political questions. No space could be devoted as heretofore to the encouragement of letters. The chief poet of the South at this time was Paul Hamilton Hayne. The lyrics of Hayne, however, do not show any very definite Shelley indebtedness.[1] Hayne's chief association with the English poet is through his sonnet to Shelley: [2]

> Because they thought his doctrines were not just,
> Mankind assumed for him the chastening rod,
> And tyrants reared in pride, and strong in lust,
> Wounded the noblest of the sons of God;
> The heart's most cherished benefactions riven,
> They strove to humble, blacken, and malign,
> A soul whose charities were wide as heaven,
> Whose deeds, if not his doctrines, were divine;
> And in the name of him, whose sunshine warms,
> The evil, as the righteous deemed it good,
> To wreak their bigotries' relentless storms,
> On one whose nature was not understood:
> Ah well! God's ways are wondrous, it may be,
> His seal hath not been set to man's decree.

The late forties and early fifties witnessed the development in the Middle Atlantic Section of two tendencies in the world of letters, a taste for the sentimental and a desire to cultivate art for art's sake. Industry had already gained the ascendency, so that men's minds were occupied with the materialistic and writing was being done with one aim, to satisfy the desires of a public whose tastes had not been cultivated. The devotion to sentimentalism is revealed in most of the periodicals of the time. The *New York Ledger* was a popular magazine, and *Harper's New Monthly*, whose purpose was to serve "the great mass of the people," filled its pages with stories of the sentimental type. The second tendency, the desire to develop art for art's sake, was represented by a small group of writers in New York and Philadelphia.[3] This group is important at this time because it held the view that poetry is not ethical but is an art. But the advocates of this idea failed to reach any perfection in their art, and their work had nothing else to recommend it. It lacked the substance of the New England poetry and the inspiration of that of the South. They must be given consideration, however, because they were devotees of Shelley.

The Periodicals

Although intellectual activity in the fifties and early sixties was at a low ebb, one periodical arose to satisfy the needs of those who desired stimulating and scholarly reading. The *Atlantic Monthly*, established in 1857, answered such a requirement. Practically all the other magazines of the period either devoted their pages to the discussion of national questions or catered to the popular demands in literature. Some magazines, such as *Graham's* and the *American Whig Review*, did not survive the fifties. Shelley probably received his share of attention in the sixth decade. A number of articles were devoted entirely to him and he is mentioned in others. In all he is given almost unlimited praise as a poet. He is credited with introducing originality and melody into verse and with influencing Tennyson in such qualities as vivid imagination, delicate fancy, and pure diction. His immortality as a poet is assured. His ability as a poet is accorded the recognition that had always been given it by leading and fair minded critics, but the language is now couched in more extravagant terms as befitting an age of highly-wrought sentimentalism. It is the attitude towards Shelley the man that has changed. His villifiers and maligners have given place to his apologists and patronizers, types of people against whom Shelley would have rebelled. The "poor, poor Shelley" period has set in in earnest.

The critics seem to have just discovered, probably at the suggestion of Poe's article,[4] that Tennyson was influenced by Shelley. In the *American Whig Review*[5] for August, 1850, is found an article, "A Few Words about Tennyson," in which the writer states that while Tennyson does not imitate either Shelley or

Keats, he seems to posses a certain combination of the qualities of both. Tennyson, he states, does not reveal the intense idealism of Shelley, and does not, like Shelley, "soar on too high a pinion." He praises Wordsworth, Coleridge, Shelley, and Keats as poets who originated a new school of poetry, who despised conventionalities of expression, the formal monotony of rhyme and measure, the tiresome inversions and ridiculous figures of speech, and who introduced into verse the true melody in place of the monotonous jingle which had usurped its name. In January, 1851, the *Democratic Review* [6] published an article on "Shelley and Tennyson." The writer believes that Shelley and Tennyson are alike in many respects. Neither poet, he says, was skilled in the feelings of the herd, but Tennyson, who had more of earthiness and humor, overcame this deficiency. He studied to accommodate himself to a nation of listeners. Tennyson, he contends, was influenced by Shelley in poetical melody and rhythm. Vivid imagination, delicate and ethereal fancy, graceful personification, reach of thought, purity and nicety of diction, harmony of allusion are all Tennysonian qualities which this writer attributes to Shelleyan influence. This was a generous number, one must agree, even in 1851. Both poets, he avers, loved harmony; but Shelley had the greater melody, the music of his abstract thoughts being impossible as Mozart to translate into prose. The article "Death Verses, or a stroll through the shadow of death with Tennyson, in company with Shelley, Milton, Blair, Swift, Coleridge, and others," [7] as its title indicates, is a comparison of the poems written on the subject of death by these poets. Shelley's *Adonais* the writer characterizes as "the grandest, the most imaginative, and most beautiful production of the kind in the language. . . . Its brilliancy of illustration, depth of thought, height of imagination, harrowing strength, and Grecian completeness, are unparalleled." This is rather overpowering praise, even for the *Adonais*, but it is better than the sentimentalism that follows. In the latter part of the article, however, is a comparison of the Shelley and Tennyson elegies. *In Memoriam* is described as less imaginative and less grand but as having a calmer dignity than *Adonais:*

Shelley, from being so grandly and wildly imaginative, often found language to convey but an obscure translation of his thoughts. . . . Tennyson, from not being so great a poet, is a greater economist of his powers, and preserves the dignity of a certain position.

Tennyson's Pegasus is characterized as a sure-footed steed, speeding at a pleasant and steady pace; Shelley's, a war-steed, breathing inspiration for a fight.

The *Democratic Review* [8] for December, 1850, in a review of

Hunt's *Autiobiography,* gives expression to some of the over-praise of the period regarding Shelley. In referring to Hunt's friendship with Shelley, the reviewer exclaims, "And well may he pride in it, and glory in it, for that alone was worth a lifetime to accomplish. The friendship of Shelley!—in itself sounds like footsteps on the ladder of immortality."

Harper's New Monthly Magazine [9] noticed Shelley only once and that in its third year. In September, 1851, in an article entitled "Wordsworth, Byron, Scott and Shelley," a great deal of attention is given to Shelley as reformer and as poet. The writer, evidently a person with socialistic tendencies, states that Shelley "united in himself many of the mightiest tendencies of our times—its democratic, its skeptical, its pantheistic, its scholastic spirit." He believes that Shelley was fitted by nature and circumstances for the task of social reformer: "Gentle, sensitive, and fervid, he shrank from the least touch of wrong, and hated injustice with the zeal and passion of a martyr." Among English poets, Shelley is ranked by this writer as second only to Shakespeare. Of Shelley's future as a poet he writes in glowing terms:

> After the passions and the theories which supplied Shelley with the subject-matter of his poems have passed away and become mere matters of history, there will still remain a song, such as mortal man never sung before, of inarticulate rapture and of freezing pain—of a blinding light of truth and a dazzling weight of glory, translated into English speech, as colored as a painted window, as suggestive, as penetrating, as intense as music.

Such was the effusiveness to which Shelley was subjected by his would-be admirers of the sentimental fifties.

The *American Whig Review,* a magazine which, as has been seen, seems to have contained a high type of criticism, noticed Shelley several times during the year 1851. In a July article entitled "Wordsworth," [10] the writer, discussing the spiritual element in Wordsworth's poetry, calls attention to this German influence on the English romantic poets:

> This spiritualism, modified in various ways, has deeply tinged all the literature of Germany. . . . It colors the best poetry of England and America to-day. The leaders in this direction were Coleridge, Wordsworth, and Shelley; Tennyson, Keats, and others followed.

In a review of Mulchinock's poems,[11] August, 1851, the reviewer, rather discriminatingly discusses the Shelleyan influence:

> Shelley, with infinitely more genius, but it must be owned, with less common sense . . . talked like this when he boasted of his acquaintance with the Alps and the glaciers and his unsuitableness for the companionship of his fellow Englishmen. And consequently, Shelley is read by nobody but poets. He loved the people well enough, but he never learned

how to write for them. He let his great soul go out over mountains and midnights, and his poems are one prolonged rhapsody. He is a good study, but a bad model. But Mr. Mulchinock has copied his error.

A writer in the November, 1851, issue of the same magazine [12] voices the opinion that James Thomson's poetry is received more favorably than is Shelley's because Shelley's is too imaginative, too far removed from human associations.

The *Southern Literary Messenger* did not give Shelley or any poet much attention in the fifties. The magazine was becoming too much absorbed in the political situation to have much space for letters. Nevertheless, a reviewer of Poe's works in 1850 [13] holds Shelley responsible for Poe's peculiarities in writing: "All his peculiar compositions were marked with that galvanic and unnatural characteristic which marks the movements of Shelley's mind." And in "A Pair of Poets," [14] a review of volumes of poetry by Taylor and by Stoddard, the reviewer in discussing what he terms "the poetic status" of a poet, gives Shelley credit for possessing a transcendent imagination and mastery of the art of verse, but add that because he had a false philosophy, he is read only by scholars and infidels.

Russell's Magazine,[15] of which Paul Hamilton Hayne was editor, published in its "Editor's Table" an article entitled "Kingsley and Shelley," preceded by an explanatory note: "The following article was received too late to be inserted into the body of the work; and in giving it a place in our 'Table,' it is proper to state, that we dissent from some of its views." The writer, whose name is not given, objects to Kingsley's comments on Shelley as given in his "Thoughts on Shelley and Byron." He says that Kingsley could not appreciate Shelley because he could not understand modern English poetry. He then examines charges brought against Shelley by Kingsley and refutes them. Mr. Kingsley, he states, revives the exploded notion of the Satanic poetry in order to lay the responsibility at Shelley's door. He resents Kingsley's accusing Shelley of immorality and declares that the unanimous testimony of all who knew the man gives the lie to such accusations. He states that many divines have written on Shelley and that it is on record that Shelley was one of the purest of beings. He objects to Kingsley's criticism of Shelley for living with Mary as his wife and acknowledging her as such before the world. This writer approves of Shelley's honesty. He does not excuse the poet's laxity regarding marriage, but he accounts for it by stating that the whole scheme of Christian society was hateful to Shelley. He does not condone Shelley's attitude towards Christianity, but excuses it on the grounds that many good and pure men have dreamed dreams and endeavored to reduce similar theories to practice. Shelley's adoption of the new life shows his sincerity. He was not, as Kingsley termed him, a hypocrite.

Shelley received mention during this period in two western periodicals, the *Monthly Literary Miscellany* [16] of Detroit and the *Genius of the West*,[17] a Cincinnati publication. In the latter magazine, P. Fishe Reed, in "Principles of Poetry—No. III," September, 1855, says of Shelley as a poet:

> But our language is not destitute of this passion poetry. Shelley, who is preëminently at the head of Britannia's bards, in delicacy and imagery, has written some excellent lines. The "Sensitive Plant" is not to be excelled.

He extols the first few stanzas of *Queen Mab* for their beauty, and analyzes at some length the following quotation from this poem as an example of lines which carry the reader to the climax of ethereal ecstasy:

> Hark! whence that rushing sound?
> 'Tis the wondrous strain
> That round a lonely ruin swells
>
> .   .   .   .
>
> 'Tis softer than the west wind's sigh,
> 'Tis wilder than the unmeasured notes
> Of that strange lyre, whose springs
> The Genii of the breezes sweep!

He also quotes again from Shelley lines, including "a delicate metaphor" which he says is pure poetry:

> Tresses *shade*
> Her bosom's *stainless* pride;
> Curling the tendrils of the *parasites*
> *Around* a marble column.

These quotations, he says, show "that impulse of excitment, which expresses the *hight* of feeling." He believes that the "Sensitive Plant" is a good example of pathos. He devotes about one-fifth of this article to Shelley.

Graham's Magazine for this decade contains several notices of Shelley.[18] In an article "Tom Moore,—the Poet of Erin," [19] by Bon Gaultier, June, 1852, the writer calls attention to Moore's fears that Byron would adopt the atheistical ideas of Shelley. The article, "The Graves of Shelley and Keats," [20] by William Porter Day, contains information that is interesting in view of the time in which it was written:

> The part of the cemetery in which Shelley is buried, lies at considerable distance from that which contains the dust of Keats, and is both naturally and artificially of exceeding beauty. It rises gradually from the entrance up to the ancient wall of Rome, and is filled with lofty musical cypresses. . . .

Around the grave is a rim of box-plants, and within this stands a row of rose-bushes, which have suffered to a considerable degree from the numberless "souvenirs" they have been forced to furnish. It is cared for with the greatest attention and seems to be very much visited.

The writer then tells of the neglected condition of the grave of Keats, where there were no flowers, but "tall, lank grass and ugly weeds." Keats was not so well known as was Shelley at this time.

In the *Cosmopolitan Art Journal*,[21] 1858, was published an article, "Percy Bysshe Shelley," occasioned by the reading of Trelawny's *Recollections of Byron and Shelley*. This writer assigns to Shelley the position of "one of the greatest spirits whose divine illumination would have contributed most gloriously to the flood of light poured upon the nineteenth century." He continues, however, with the idea that Shelley's early death prevented his retracting many things that he had said. He believes that had Shelley lived to temper his genius with more discretion, his influence would have been for good. He states that Shelley had an almost Christ-like love for humanity, but that he "fell into the mistake of accusing the inaccusable Majesty for the perversions which man alone was guilty of." He says that Shelley was a Christian, unkown to himself, but he forgot the doctrines preached and looked at the results. He believes that in a few more years Shelley would have become a Christian.

After a long period of silence regarding Shelley, the *Knickerbocker* [22] for March, 1857, publishes an article "Shelley," by E. N. V. Easton. This article is tinged with sentimentalism and, on the whole, is weak but contains some fair criticism. Mr. Easton characterizes Shelley as the "perfection of that rare analogy between the author and the man," and gives a brief sketch of the chief events of his life, particularly those influencing his religious views and his development. Shelley's genius, he says, was abstract and logical, his reasoning coherent, his diction searching and vigorous, yet musical. He was susceptible to music in nature and art, declares Easton; no poet has left a greater wealth of imagery. He believes that it is erroneous to associate Shelley with Keats: Beauty was the essence of Keat's poetry; it was but the adornment of Shelley's. Their individuality, he believes, is complete, but they belonged to the same school.

The 1860's brought a few more articles on Shelley, one in the *Universalist Quarterly* and two in the early numbers of the *Atlantic Monthly*. In the first article in the *Atlantic Monthly*, "More Words about Shelley," [23] the writer, W. Dowe, criticizes Shelley's biographers, Middleton, Hogg, and Trelawny, as not pretending to explain his eccentric nature or harmonize in any way his thoughts and feelings. He likewise criticizes these biographers for their attitude towards Harriet. Dowe contends that Shelley was betrayed through enthusiasm and through credulity, and allowed himself to be imposed upon by a designing boarding school girl and her relatives. He believes that Trelawny may have been overlooked, slighted by Shelley, and that Hogg may have been puzzled by some of his acts, the result being their biographies ridiculing him. Mary Shelley, he says, did not attempt a complete biography, but left it for later writers. "Some marked Shelley with charcoal, others with chalk,"—a reprobate or a high-souled lover of human happiness or human liberty, according to Dowe, who believes that he was something of both together. This article is of interest as the first of the series of articles on Shelley's biographers that still appear occasionally in the pages of the magazines.

An article, "Atheism and Its Exponents," by Rev. Sumner Ellis, published in the *Universalist Quarterly*,[24] Boston, January, 1864, contains some interesting comments on Shelley's religious views. This writer begins:

> Shelley was the atheistic poet. His abberation from his true line of development is easy to trace. Nature had formed him for a religious character of a peculiar stamp; not a common, but an uncommon Churchman, a priest of the abstract and subtle ethereal in Christianity. He was by nature sincere and virtuous; sensitive, also, to all grossness of doctrine, his own materialism being made attractive by the dress in which his imagination robed it; more sensitive still, to personal abuse and unkind treatment.

He believes that Shelley's atheism is due (1) to unfortunate early religious training when the "current creed was fearful to anyone, odious to him;" (2) to his reading of Hume and the French philosophers, who hated the religion of the day; (3) to his "bitter experience, the reproach, the neglect, the enmity of his fellows." He concludes, "Shelley was an atheist to the end of his days, the 'Spirit of Nature' his only God." This discussion of Shelley's ideas regarding religion reveals not only a more tolerant attitude towards Shelley in the religious periodicals but also a broadening of their views on questions of religion.

The second article in the *Atlantic Monthly,* "Shelley, by One Who Knew Him," [25] written by Thornton Hunt and published in the February, 1863, number of the magazine, is one of the most illuminating and best known articles on Shelley published in the nineteenth century. It was probably written at the suggestion of the Shelley family and friends and for the very purpose it served, to alleviate misconceptions regarding Shelley as a man. Hunt takes the view that Shelley has been misrepresented, that is, regarded either as a victim of persecution or as a rebel against authority. His friends, however, regard him as a philosopher-patriot. The article is filled with personal recollections of Shelley and with explanations of facts that had been misrepresented. Hunt tells of his first meeting with Shelley who, when threatened with the removal of his children, had come to Hunt's home for support and consolation. He relates incidents to show Shelley's sympathy and kindness towards others, tells of his love for making paper boats, and of his own preference for Shelley on walks because he walked faster and talked more than Leigh Hunt did. He gives the enlightening information that the change in Shelley after Harriet's death was greater than anyone knew. Of Shelley's marriage to Harriet, he states that Harriet served "as an object for his disengaged affection and a subject for his liberating theories, and as a substratum for the idealizing process upon which he constructed a fictitious creation of Harriet Westbrook." The heroine of *Epipsychidion* he explains as an imaginary creature, copied from no living model, but from one certain idea, created by Shelley and suggested by the living portrait, Emilia, the bride of a dream.

While these ideas seem very familiar to the twentieth century reader, it must be remembered that they were very new then and must have caused quite a stir in literary circles when the article appeared in 1863, particularly in England. His criticism of those who wrote on Shelley is so discriminating that one feels that he, Thornton Hunt, was the one person qualified to write an authentic biography of Shelley. Hogg's account of Shelley, he says, is like "a figure seen through fantastically distorting panes of glass." Peacock's dry wit, he declares, could not "discern the form of Shelley's mind" or "portray it with accuracy or distinctness." Leigh Hunt's mind, checked by over-refinement, cultivated rather than corrected by the trials of life, was not suited to comprehend "the strong instincts, indomitable will, and complete unity of idea which distinguished Shelley." Byron was likely to have formed a better design. Mary Shelley's writings, he believes, contain the best materials for forming an estimate of his character. He declares that Shelley had undergone a great physical change after going to Italy:

He had an oval face and delicate features, not unlike those given him in the well-known miniature. His forehead was high. His fine, dark brown hair, when not cut close, disposed itself in playful and very beautiful curls over his brows and round the back of his neck. He had brown eyes, with a color in his cheek "like a girl's;" but as he grew older, his complexion bronzed. . . . The outlines of his features and face possessed a firmness and *hardness* entirely inconsistent with a feminine character.

The outline was sharp and firm; the markings distinct, and indicating an energetic *physique*. The outline of the bone was distinctly perceptible at the temples, on the bridge of the nose, at the back portion of the cheeks, and in the jaw, and the artist could trace the principal muscles of the face. The beard also, although the reverse of the strong, was clearly marked, especially about the chin. Thus, although the general aspect was peculiarly slight, youthful, and delicate, yet, when you looked to 'the points' of the animal, you saw well enough the indications of a masculine vigor, in many respects far above average.

This article is one of the last on Shelley in the American periodicals of this period. During the Civil War and the years immediately following, Shelley, as well as other poets, was neglected. While the criticism of Shelley in the periodicals of the fifties and sixties contained a great deal of sentimentalim, there is in it some hint of a new tendency. He is gradually being recognized as the poet of music and melody, a forecast of the recognition later accorded him as a lyrist. Thorton Hunt's article must have helped to make Shelley a less spectacular figure and thus tended to center attention on the poet rather than on the man.

The "Imitators"

The group of American writers who attempted to cultivate art for art's sake is but a weak representative of the English brotherhood that existed at the same time. Like the Pre-Raphaelites, many of the young Americans, notably Read and Taylor, attempted painting as well as poetry. But conditions in America were not conducive to the development of the aesthetic as were conditions in England. The country was too new and raw. Aesthetic culture was adopted and worn as a holiday dress, but not lived. It could not be a part of the daily life of these writers who dwelt in the midst of commercial activity. It was necessary to form a group who could come together in the leisure hours. Even had they been possessed of great native ability, it would not have been possible, therefore, for these devotees of art to have accomplished much. That they were affected by the sentimentalism of the age, there is no better proof than their attitudes towards Shelley and Keats, especially towards Shelley. They formed a veritable Shelley cult. They conversed about him, imitated him, imagined his soul had entered theirs, and wrote about him. Had they been greater poets, all this attention might have increased Shelley's influence, but because they were of lesser caliber, their unbounded admiration and worship was detrimental to his popularity.

H. C. Lea's remark earlier in regard to the English imitators of Shelley might well apply to the American group: "If Shelley fails in attaining th ᵕ high place he deserves, it will be solely on account of the number of his imitators." [26] The extent of the devotion of these young poets who were in the habit of worshipping at the shrine of Shelley and Keats is best exemplified in such instances as that given in a letter from Bayard Taylor to John B. Phillips in which he states that the spirit of Keats is now sitting at the other side of the table,[27] or in his sonnet to Stoddard with whom, according to his wife, Marie Hansen-Taylor, he worshipped at the altar of Divine Poesy: [28]

> When first we twain the pleasant land of Rhyme
> Discovered, choosing side by side our seats
> Below our separate Gods; in midnight streets,
> In haunted attics flattered by the chime
> Of silver words, and, fed by faith sublime,
> I Shelley's mantle wore, you that of Keats.

Taylor's entry in his *Views Afoot; or Europe Seen with Knapsack and Staff*, for January 1, 1846, shows an acquaintance with and an ardent admiration for Shelley's poetry. After describing Shelley's grave, which he had visited, he adds: [29]

Glorious Shelley! He sleeps calmly in that silent nook, and the air around his grave is filled with sighs from those who mourn that so pure a star of poetry should have been blotted out before it reached its meridian.

Whether or not Taylor, in his early poems, was indebted to Shelley is still a question. While he acknowledged his admiration for the English poet, he seems to have denied his influence. In a letter to Phillips in 1849, he writes: [30]

You know Shelley and love him, but scarcely so much as I do. I have read him this summer for the first time, and found many of my best thoughts forestalled by his utterance. His *Alastor* in the commencement is born of every feeling which inspired my "Angel of the Soul," but I had never seen it when that was written.[31]

In this same letter he states that he has written quite a number of poems lately, the last and greatest being his "Ode to Shelley." Marie Hansen-Taylor believed that her husband was influenced by Shelley in the two poems, the "Ode to Shelley" and "Ariel in the Cloven Pine." [32] The former not only shows a feeling of kinship for Shelley, but certain lines bear a close resemblance to lines in Shelley's "Hymn to Intellectual Beauty." [33] The Shelleyan influence in "Ariel" is restricted to a few lines in the second stanza that faintly recall, in a general way, the "Lines Written among the Euganean Hills." Mrs. Taylor also contended that her husband was influenced less by Shelley than by other writers, such as Schiller and Goethe. But Mrs. Taylor was desirous of establishing a relation between her husband and the German poets. The indebtedness of Taylor to Shelley, however, is generally conceded by critics. This indebtedness is, in general, in the style of writing rather than in the subject matter and it is most prominent in a few of the early poems. *Prince Deukalion,* a late poem, is an exception. In the general plan, structure, style, and form of the lyrics, and even in the subject matter, it is an obvious imitation of Shelley's *Prometheus Unbound.*[34]

It is possible, however, that many critics attach too much importance to Taylor's indebtedness to Shelley. Many of the Shelleyan characteristics in Taylor's poetry could have come through imitation of Tennyson, whose poetry Taylor must have found more to his taste than that of Shelley and whose poetic heights he might have aspired to reach. Taylor did not have the poetic abandon to attain the lyrical heights reached by Shelley, and he probably knew it. But he recognized the Shelleyan tendencies in Tennyson's poetry. He believed that the poems of 1830 had echoes of Shelley which were later omitted. Shelley's most conspicuous and most permanent influence on Tennyson, Taylor believes, was on sound and meter: "Examples of poetry written for pure delight in sound and movement are rare before Shelley's day; and his influence on Tennyson was very transient." [35] He believes that it is this element "which marks Tennyson's place in English literature and accounts for his almost phenomenal popularity." He finds "premonitions" of this type of writing in Byron's "Stanzas for Music," in passages of Keats's *Hyperion,* and in Shelley's "Skylark," "Arethusa," and the choruses in *Prometheus Unbound.* But in Tennyson, he declares, this method of writing found its first superb embodiment, for Tennyson learned to use sound and meter as a painter uses form and color. Taylor calls this "decorative poetry," which he believes occupies an intermediate ground between poetry and music. Since this essay was not published until 1877, there is no means of determining when Taylor first became an admirer of Tennyson or when he discovered Tennyson's indebtedness to Shelley. As a poet, Taylor may be classed as a poor imitator of Shelley, Keats, and Tennyson. His best work was probably his translations. At least his translation of *Faust* is conceded to be one of the best. His work as a critic, however, has never been given the recognition it deserves.

Richard Henry Stoddard, a second member of the group who wrote for the sake of art, in later years recalls the youthful worship of the Romantic poets by himself and Taylor: [36]

My favorite poet was Keats and his was Shelley, and we pretended to believe that the souls of these poets had returned to earth in our own bodies. . . . My comrade's worship of his mater took the form of an "Ode to Shelley" which I thought and still think, the noblest poem that his immortal genius had inspired.

In only one of Stoddard's poems does there appear to be any direct influence of Shelley. His "Hymn to the Beautiful," which is an obvious imitation of Wordsworth's "Ode on Intimations of Immortality," contains occasional lines and groups of lines from Keats and Shelley and some lines that are a mixture of borrowings from both.

Although E. C. Stedman's relation to Shelley belongs, for the most part, to the last quarter of the century, particularly to the period of the centennial, because he was a member of the same group as Taylor and Stoddard and was also early influenced by Shelley, he must be mentioned here. Certain early poems by Stedman reveal an acquaintance with Shelley's poetry. In the second stanza of "The Sleigh Ride" there is a slight resemblance to Shelley. The "Elfin Song" from *The Rime of the Elle-King* is filled with reminiscences of the "Lines Written among the Euganean Hills" and other poems by Shelley: [37]

> Far in the western ocean's breast
>   The summer fairies have found a nest;
> The heavens ever unclouded smile
> Over the breadth of their beautiful isle;
> Through it a hundred streamlets flow,
> In spangled paths, to the sea below,
> And woo the vales that beside them lie
> With a low and tremulous minstrelsy
>
> .   .   .   .
>
> And many an Ariel, blithesome, airy,
> And each laughing Fay and blithesome Fairy,
> Know well the mystical way in the West
>   To the sweet isle of Canary.
> Lustrously sailing here and there,
> Afloat in the beatific air,
> Birds of purple and blue and gold,
> Pour out their music manifold;
> Wafted along in a magic boat,
> By fairy wings that fan the sails,
> And eddying through enchanted vales,
> Through walls of amber and crystal gates.

The poem "The Singer" was undoubtedly inspired by Shelley's "Skylark":

> O lark! sweet lark!
> Where learn you all your minstrelsy?
> What realms are those to which you fly?
> While robins feed their young from dawn till dark,
>   You soar on high,—

> Forever in the sky.
> O child! dear child!
> Above the clouds I lift my wing,
> To hear the bells of Heaven ring;
> Some of their music, though my flight be wild,
> To earth I bring;
> Then let me soar and sing.

Although Thomas Bailey Aldrich is not generally considered to have given Shelley much attention, there are indications that he knew Shelley's poetry and that some of his own early poems were likewise influenced by the English lyrist. His slight comments on Shelley show a high regard for the poet's work. In a discussion on Leigh Hunt, he remarks: "Hunt was not a Keats nor a Shelley nor a Coleridge, but he was a most excellent Hunt." [38] And, in an essay "Leigh Hunt and Barry Cornwall," he says: "Imagine Byron or Shelley, who knew the ocean in all its Protean moods, piping such thin feebleness as 'The blue, the fresh, the ever free.' " [39] Several of the early poems by Aldrich are sufficiently Shelley-like that imitation may be suspected. His "Palabras Carinasas" was undoubtedly inspired by Shelley's "Good-night": [40]

> Good-night! I have to say good-night
> To such a host of peerless things!
> Good-night unto the slender hand
> All queenly with its weight of rings;
>
> .   .   .   .
>
> The snowy hand detains me, then
> I'll have to say good-night again!

The first stanza of "An Old Castle" in form bears a slight resemblance to the first stanza of "Arethusa": [41]

> The gray arch crumbles,
> And totters and tumbles;
> The bat has built in the banquet hall;
> In the donjan-keep
> Sly mosses creep;
> The ivy has scaled the southern wall.
> No man- at -arms
> Sounds quick alarms
> A-top of the cracked martello tower . . .

The first stanza of "Pompina" in movement and in content likewise recalls "Lines Written among the Euganean Hills": [42]

> Lying by the summer sea
> I had a dream of Italy.
> Chalky cliffs and miles of sand.
> Dripping reefs and salty caves,
> Then the sparkling emerald waves,

> Faded; and I seemed to stand
> Myself an old-time Florentine,
> In the heart of that fair land.
> And in a garden cool and green,
> Boccaccio's own enchanted place,
> I met Pompina face to face—
>
> .   .   .   .
>
> Where one gem glistened sunnily
> Like Venice, when first seen at sea . . .

George Henry Boker's interest in Shelley was made known through his friend, Charles Godfrey Leland, who stated that while at Princeton College he passed a great deal of his time in Boker's room reading Wordsworth, Shelley, and Byron. Although Byron was Boker's favorite, Leland says that they both loved Shelley passionately. Boker, however, could not share Leland's love for Southey whose poem "On Gooseberry Pie" caused the practical Boker to declare that "the poor old man was in his dotage," [43] an opinion with which Shelley would have acquiesced many years earlier. As a man of letters, Boker is probably best known for his dramas. Boker's "The Song of the Wind" and "A Snow Storm in April" were possibly inspired by Shelley's "Ode to the West Wind." Thomas Buchanan Read's "Drifting" likewise shows a distinct Shelley influence. The indebtedness is in the verse form, and to some extent in the subject matter. It is obviously an attempt at imitation of the Shelleyan style but lacks the movement and musical quality of Shelley's poetry. Nor does the poet have sufficient command of diction to approach the poet he imitates.

> My soul to-day
> Is far away,
> Sailing the Vesuvian Bay;
> My winged boat,
> A bird afloat,
> Swings round the purple peaks remote: —   (St. I)
> Round purple peaks
> It sails and seeks
> Blue inlets and their crystal creeks,
> Where high rocks throw,
> Through deeps below,
> A duplicated golden glow.   (St. II)

One of the very interesting imitators of Shelley was a New York poet who was not a member of any group, Forceythe Willson. Willson not only attempted to write poems in the Shelleyan manner but occasionally inserted phrases from Shelley's poems. In a "Sphere Song," the lines,

> Once upon a time,
> Through the crevice of mine ear,

> The Music of the Sphere
> Ran into rhyme . . . ,

are distinctly Shelleyan in atsmosphere and in the phrasing of the third line.[44] Another poem in the same group, "A Valedictory," reveals an attempt to use the Shelley stanza and verse:

> The Infinite fills one and all:
> The little animated mote,
> That on a rose's breath might float,
> Or on a sunbeam rise and doat,
> God lived in him still and small, . . .

These poems, however, become religious in character. It is possible that the author was attempting to reconcile Shelley's half-pantheistic ideas with his own orthodox beliefs. It is in a group of poems entitled "The Poet's Epilogue," however, that the Shelleyan characteristics are most apparent. All these poems are Shelleyan in stanza form, in diction, in borrowed phrasing, in movement, or in subject matter. Many of these little poems contain lines and stanzas of a lyrical quality that reveals promise of better poetry to come. One poem, "No More," is an imitation of Shelley in the subject matter and of Poe in the manner or repetition:

> There is a time for tears to start,—
> For dews to fall and larks to soar:
> The Time for Tears is when we part
> To meet upon the earth no more:
> The Time for Tears is when we part
> To meet on this wide earth no more.   (St. 2)

Other poems in this group that reflect Shelleyan characteristics are "La Scintilla," "Autumn Song," "The Enemy," "L'Incoronato," and the beautiful lyric "I Said to the Rose."

> I said to the Rose
> "Thy Palace close,
> For the Summer is gone before!"
> I said to the Lark
> "The night is dark,
> And the morning will come no more!"

It is apparent from these quotations that Forceythe Willson was studying Shelley's poems with a view to improving his own style. These poems and others not in the Shelleyan manner contain enough original lines to lead one to believe that had his life been prolonged beyond his thirty years he might have become a poet of note.

CHAPTER VIII

THE REACTION

Walt Whitman

The period of reaction against sentimentalism really belongs to the last third of the century, the period beginning after the close of the Civil War. F. L. Pattee, who places the division at 1890, summarizes the reactionary movement in literature as follows:[1]

> The new era of vulgarity in literature, complained of by Stedman, came as a revolt against mid-century tendencies. The movement was not confined to America. In the early seventies, as we have seen, Millet and his Wessex natives caught the ear of England; Bjornson made the dis-his Wessex natives caught the ear of England; Bpornson made the discovery that in the Scandinavian peasant lay the only survival of the old Norse spirit; and the Russians Tourgenieff and Tolstoy cast aside the old mythology and told with minuteness the life of the peasant and the serf. Everywhere there was a swing toward the wild and unconventional, even toward the coarse and repulsive. The effeminacy of early Tennysonianism, the cloying sweetness of the mid-century annual, Keatsism, Hyperionism, Heineism, had culminated in reaction.

The best representative in America of this new age of reaction is Walt Whitman. Whitman's long life, with his very productive period of writing, extends from the latter part of the romantic revival through the age of sentimentalism and well into the period of reaction and realism. His poetry gave stimulus to the later free verse and many of the other characteristics of later decades. The lives of other writers, as has been seen,[2] spanned almost the whole nineteenth century as well, but these writers did not represent or introduce any new movement in poetry as did Whitman. Other poets who belong to this period, because their works were published in the latter part of the century, are Sidney Lanier and Henry Timrod. Some attention must also be given to poets whose work extended over into the twentieth century.

Whitman is often associated with Shelley in the minds of those writers who are interested in him as poet, as philosopher, or merely as a man. There is so much in Whitman that is like and yet so much that is unlike Shelley that it seems futile for the most careful investigator to state that he was or was not influenced by Shelley. It is also difficult after the middle of the century, to separate the various influences of the earlier and later English romanticists and to state precisely what may have been derived from each, such as Shelley, Tennyson, or Swinburne. There seems to be a rather wide divergence of opinion among the Whitman biographers and critics as to his acquaintance with Shelley and as to the question of his indebtedness. The similarity of ideas likewise furnishes a subject for some comment.

At least it is of importance to know that Whitman was acquainted with and interested in Shelley at an early date as indicated by a clipping from his scrapbook [3] and an item in his notebook under 'Preparatory Reading and Thought," made before writing *Leaves of Grass,* according to one of his editors, Dr. R. Bucke.[4] The clipping is a copy of Shelley's "Ode to a Skylark," torn from a book and pasted in the scrapbook. The item, entitled "Characteristics of Shelley," is as follows:

Stock—English gentry—must have been quite such another as T. L. Harris . . . screamed loud in talking when enthusiastic . . . fed simply, liked bread and raisins—expelled from college 1811, married same year—separated 1813—wife died—married second 1816. Was not healthy, or rather not rudely so.

Since the notebook includes items regarding all the foremost writers of English literature, this entry is important as indicating the facts of Shelley's life in which Whitman was interested. His generosity, benevolence, and love of man must have appealed to Whitman. His early rising and simple diet would likewise meet with approval. His rebellion at college and his marital relations probably evoked Whitman's sympathy. The last comment, regarding his health, may have been made ironically in view of the writer's own robust health. The item as a whole would argue that it was Shelley the man rather than Shelley the poet in whom Whitman was interested. This fact is further borne out in the report of a conversation between Traubel and Whitman in 1888,[5] in which the latter is recorded as saying:

Shelley is interesting to me as Burns is, chiefly as a person: I read with most avidity, not their poems, but their lives: the Burns letters, for instance.

As to whether Whitman approved of Shelley in general, there seems to be no direct evidence forthcoming. H. B. Binns, who finds parallels in the works of the two poets, states that Whitman's preference was for ballads rather than for lyrics: [6]

Ballads he loved when they came from the folk; but Blake and Shelley, the purely lyrical writers of the new era, do not seem to have touched him; perhaps they were hardly virile enough, for when he came to know and appreciate Burns, it was as a lyrist who was at once the poet of the people and a full-blooded man.

Binns believes that Whitman and Shelley received inspiration from similar sources. He says:[7]

> There is much which Whitman obviously shares with Shelley. Their kinship of inspiration is too significant for a passing note, and might well be followed over many pages. The writer of *Leaves of Grass* and the youthful author of *Queen Mab* had drunk at the same fountain of love and wonder.

Two of Whitman's early poems, "Ambition" and "Resurgemus," reflect the influence of Shelley. The first of these, written in 1842, faintly recalls *Alastor* in the "obscure youth, a wanderer," who had very high aspirations. The second, written in 1850, recalls the *Revolt of Islam* in many expressions, as in railing at kings, "liars paid to defile the people," in "bullets of tyrants," and in the reference to corpses lying in new-made graves. Both poems abound in similes of the Shelley type. Edgar Lee Masters is of the opinion that Whitman in his conception of the power of Love was influenced by Shelley. He writes: [8]

> The work of Shelley inevitably comes to mind in connection with words like these. The wonderful choruses of *Prometheus Unbound* with their prophecies of a happier world based on love; a new day of earth happiness created by social love, are things which Shelley looked forward to and sang in many poems and fragments. In his *Epipsychidion* he transmuted into verse the words of Diotima and Agathon. Of himself he spoke as "a love in desolation." In a fragment he wrote,
>
> > But love, though misdirected, is among
> > The things which are immortal, and surpass
> > All that frail stuff which will be—or which was.
>
> In *Marenghi*, he showed how superior is the love of comrades to that supposedly greatest test of virtue to love one's enemies,
>
> > I am a spirit who has dwelt
> > Within the Heart of hearts, and I have felt
> > His feelings, and have thought his thoughts and known
> > The inmost converse of his soul.

Whitman may have derived from Shelley the idea that there should be no distinction between poetry and prose.[9] At least this is the view of Emory Holloway in his discussion of Whitman's prose: [10]

> Since Whitman, following the lead of Shelley and to a certain extent that of Wordsworth, took the position that the conventional distinction between poetry and prose was invalid, a thorough knowledge of his verse presupposes an acquaintance with his prose compositions.

H. B. Binns recommends that Shelley's *Defence of Poetry* be read "alongside of Whitman's *Preface of 1855.*" [11]

Here, as in Whitman's pages, the permanency of poetry is asserted; its significance is not to be exhausted by the generation in which it found expression. Poetry is the motive power of action and creates utilities. It is the root and blossom of science and philosophy. Poetry is the inter-penetration of a diviner nature with our own; it turns all things to love-liness, and strips off the film of use and wont which holds our eyes from the vision of wonder. The great poets are men of supreme virtue and consummate prudence. They are the world law-givers.

John G. Symonds finds the resemblance to be in the philo-sophy of the two poets:[12]

But now appears the fourth conception, which, according to Whitman's feeling of the world, unites and fuses law, love, revolt in a more ethereal essence—what Shelley phrased the "Life of Life"— the true spirituality, the essential vitality of the vast complex.

.   .   .   .   .

The harmony which merges in eternal, concrete, spiritual energy, Whitman calls "Santa Spirita," Shelley, "Life of Life." Under any name it connotes the individual's conviction that he is an inviolable factor of the universal order.

And here, as far as Symonds is concerned, the similarity ends. If, however, we accept Symonds' interpretation of Whitman's "Square Deific,"—that there are four main conceptions which he considers necessary to the Divine Idea: inexorable destiny or implacable fact; consolation, healing, or affection; revolt or Satan; and the "true spirituality, the essential vitality of the vast com-plex," or Shelley's "Life of Life"—it will be possible to draw a comparison between the philosophy of Whitman and that of Shelley regarding the Divine plan. Symonds is mistaken in interpreting Shelley's "Life of Life" and Whitman's "Santa Spirita" as the same. Shelley's "Life of Life" is the element that permeates all; it is felt but not seen. It enkindles and brightens, but it is not inclusive.[13]

> Life of Life, thy lips enkindle
>   With their love the breath between them;
> And thy smiles before they dwindle
>   Make the cold air fire; then screen them . . .
>
> .   .   .   .
>
> Child of Light! thy limbs are burning
>   Through the vest which seems to hide them; . . .
>
> .   .   .   .
>
> Fair are others; none beholds thee,
>   But thy voice sounds low and tender
> Like the fairest, for it folds thee
>   From the sight, that liquid splendor,
> And all feel, yet see thee never,
> As I feel now, lost forever! . . .

Whitman's "Santa Spirita" both pervades and includes:

> Santa Spirita, breather, life,
> Beyond the light, lighter than light
>
> .   .   .   .
>
> Including all life on earth, touching, including
>   God, including Saviour, and Satan,
> Ethereal, pervading all. . . .
>
> .   .   .   .
>
> Life of the great world, the sun and stars, and
>   of man, I, the general soul,
> Here the square finishing, the solid, I the most solid,
> Breathe my breath also through these songs. . . .

Shelley's "Life of Life" is a part of the Divine plan, the guiding force. Whitman's "Santa Spirita" is the whole; it includes all. Shelley is not so certain:

> Lamp of Earth! where'er thou movest
>   Its dim shapes are clad with brightness,
> And the souls of whom thou lovest
>   Walk upon the winds with lightness,
> Till they fail, as I am failing,
>   Dizzy, lost, yet unbewailing!

If, however, we would accept "Santa Spirita," as does Symonds, as uniting and fusing law, love, and revolt in a more ethereal essence, then it would accord with Shelley's idea in his "Life of Life."

If now we consider Symond's interpretation of the four sides of the "Square Deific" as Whitman's philosophy of life, which is probably the interpretation that Whitman had in mind when he wrote the poem, we would have a basis on which to compare his views with those of Shelley. The first of these is "inexorable destiny or implacable fact." Shelley was never ready to accept destiny or fact, as was Whitman, for in Shelley the reform instinct was inborn. Whitman, on the contrary, accepted all facts of life as facts, regardless of how hideous or repulsive they might be. To him what was ugly was so because that was a part of the Divine plan.[14] Shelley would clothe the ugly in beautiful garments or would look beyond the ugly and see the beautiful.[15] The second side of the square, the humanitarian side, would be in full accord with Shelley's views, both in theory and in practice. The third side, the idea of revolt, of Satan, if taken to represent evil in the world, an element that Whitman recognizes as a part of the world and probably as necessary, Shelley, the idealist, hoped to eliminate.[16] Whitman recognized no millennium as did Shelley; he believed that the world should be accepted and enjoyed. In completing the square with man, "the general soul," Whitman comes nearer to Emerson than to Shelley. Shelley was not yet ready to complete the square.

Dr. Richard Maurice Bucke, in his *Cosmic Consciousness*, attributes to Whitman unusual development of the cosmic sense: [17]

Walt Whitman is the best, the most perfect, example the world has so far had of the Cosmic Sense, first because he is the man in whom the new faculty has been, probably most perfectly developed, and especially because he is, par excellence, the man who in modern times has written distinctly and at large from the point of view of Cosmic Consciousness, and who also has referred to its facts and phenomena more plainly than any other writer either ancient or modern.

Shelley possessed the cosmic sense in even greater proportion than did Whitman. Shelley recognized no limits in space or time. The whole universe was his realm; the millennium was the point to which he looked forward. To him the world was one nation, one family; the birds and the beasts, the trees and the flowers were a part of it. Saurat calls this cosmic sense the "gregarious sense," which makes poets "intensely conscious of the group, the nation, and beyond that, the earth itself, and of their kinship with all beings, with nature, with the Cosmos; their indifference to contradictions between different parts of their conceptions; their power of intuition and expression; all qualities which make a primitive of the poet." [18] And it is in this characteristic, "the cosmic sense," that the greatest resemblance between Shelley and Whitman is noticeable.

Whitman's admiration for Robert G. Ingersoll and Ingersoll's admiration for Shelley might be taken as a further link between the two poets.[19] Ingersoll's comments on Shelley, however, are of interest chiefly because of the fact that Shelley was looked upon as an atheist. His assertion that "Shelley, whose soul, like his own 'Skylark,' was a winged joy, has been damned for many years," [20] is but consistent with Ingersoll's line of thought, as is the following criticism: "I read Shelley's *Queen Mab*—a poem filled with beauty, courage, thought, sympathy, tears, and scorn, in which a brave soul tears down the prison walls and floods the cells with light. I read his 'Skylark'—a winged flame—passionate as blood—tender as tears—pure as light." [21] His observation on Shelley, the poet, meets with approval: "There is none with the subtle delicacy, the aerial footstep, the flame-like motion of Shelley." [22] His criticism as a whole,[23] however, belongs to the super-sentimentalism of those would-be followers of Shelley who find in him some one quality with which they agree and consider themselves ever after as Shelley satellites shining in a sort of reflected glory.

Sidney Lanier

Since Sidney Lanier did not publish anything of importance until 1875 and his first volume of poems did not appear until 1877, he may be considered as belonging to the period just following the Civil War. That Lanier was an early admirer of Shelley as well as of Keats is attested to by T. F. Newell, who had been Lanier's classmate at college and who stated that Lanier had introduced him to the poems of Keats and Shelley.[24] S. T. Williams, in commenting on Lanier, remarks that "one day the Yankees captured along with the Confederate camp, his copies of Shelley and Keats."[25] Aubrey Harrison Starke is more specific in his statement that "the enemy had taken their clothes, their books, among them a volume of poems by Coleridge, Shelley, and Keats."[26] The indebtedness of Lanier to Shelley, however, must remain to some extent a question. The statement of his biographer, Edwin Mims, and his own statement would indicate that he was not in accord with many of Shelley's beliefs. Mims, in commenting on Lanier's religious belief, compares him with Shelley: "He maintained throughout his life a reverent faith; he could distinguish, as Browning said Shelley could not, between churchdom and Christianity."[27] Lanier himself was very critical of Shelley's ideas, as will be seen in the following paragraph, and considered them very immature: [28]

> In truth, Shelley appears always to have labored under an essential immaturity: it is very possible that if he had lived a hundred years he would never have become a man; he was penetrated with modern ideas, but penetrated as a boy would be, crudely, overmuch, and with a constant tendency to the extravagant and the illogical; so that I call him the modern boy.

Regardless of Lanier's personal feeling towards Shelley, it is now quite generally conceded that he owed something to the influence of the English poet. Starke, his latest biographer, believes that Lanier was influenced by Shelley: [29]

> Lanier's poetic fires had been stirred, in part, by the reading of Shelley and Carlyle, the former with his high sense of the nobility, even the usefulness of the poet's calling.

Norman Foerster finds in Lanier a romantic tendency like that of Shelley: [30]

> It is only in the unbridled romanticists, such as Rousseau and Shelley and Jefferies, who have given their imagination freely to nympholeptic longing, and in Lanier's lines we have the *reductio ad absurdum* of the tendency.

Pattee is inclined to attribute to Lanier's poetry at least some Shelleyan characteristics. The *Symphony,* he avers, is "a cry against the materialism that Lanier felt was crushing the higher things out of American life. The solution of the problem was the same that Shelley had brought. Love alone could master the evils of the time." And he finds in other poems similarities to Shelley: "His lyrics like 'Evening Song' and 'The Trees and the Master' and 'The Song of the Chattahoochee' have strains in them almost Shelley-like, but there is always the fatal defect somewhere. Nothing is perfect." [31] Morgan Callaway undoubtedly comes nearer to solving the problem when he sees in Lanier's poetry possibly the product of several influences: [32]

> For in technique, he was akin to Tennyson; in the love of beauty and in lyric sweetness, to Keats and Shelley; in the love of nature, to Wordsworth; in spirituality, to Ruskin, the gist of whose training is that we are souls temporarily having bodies; to Milton "God-gifted organ voice of England;" and to Browning "subtlest assertor of the soul in song." To be sure, Lanier's genius is not equal to that of any of the poets mentioned, but I venture to believe it is of the same order, and, therefore deserving of remembrance.

Callaway, however, neglects to mention Shakespeare, whom Starke finds to be a later influence, but mingled with the early influence of the Romantics. In 1877, according to Starke, "the influence of Shelley, Keats, and Wordsworth is less apparent than that of Shakespeare, but it is real, and we know that Lanier was still reading the works of these poets." [33]

Lanier's opinion of Shelley as a poet may be found in the fifth chapter of *The English Novel,* where he discusses *Prometheus Unbound.* Lanier uses as an example of inartistic writing the part containing the replies to the question, "What is that curse?" He believes that had Shelley considered this poem later, he would have drawn his pen through this part. Nor does he approve of the fourth act: "Shelley drags in Act IV . . . in which voices of unseen spirits, the chorus of Hours, Jove, etc., pelt each other with endless sweetish speeches that rain like ineffectual conflicts in a carnival of silliness." And he criticizes this act as a "long lyric outburst, wholly unnecessary to an action which was already complete." He approves, however, of some parts of Shelley's poem and gives three quotations in which Shelley's "modernness of detail and subtlety,—being exercised upon matters capable of such treatment—has made for us some strong and beautiful poetry." The quotations are the opening lines of Act II, Scene ii, the conversation of the two fauns (Act II, Scene ii), and Asia's description of her vision (Act II, Scene i). Regarding the conversation of the fauns, he says: "I scarcely know anything more compact of pellucid beauty; it seems quite worthy of Shakespeare." Asia's description of her vision in which the successive deposits of the earth's crust are revealed to her, he praises highly: "The whole treatment is detailed, modern, vivid, powerful." [34]

Whether or not Lanier approved of Shelley, it is interesting to note that the two poets had much in common. There is something in this resemblance that causes the name of Shelley to recur again and again on the pages of writings on Lanier. Edwin Mims, in his biography, attributes to Lanier certain characteristics that are also found in the life of Shelley. "Sweetness of disposition, and depth of emotion," "a sense of melody that found vent . . . in words that moved with a certain rhythmic cadence," a lack of clearness and interest in science, all are Shelleyan characteristics. And his habit of "coming, of an evening, unannounced, into the room where we then were, rising like a phantom," as told by a lady friend, is strangely reminiscent of the remark made by Jane Williams regarding Shelley: "Oh, he comes and goes like a spirit, no one knows when or where." [35]

Henry Timrod

Although Henry Timrod has been accorded some recognition in recent years, his poetry is not so well known as it should be. Timrod is truly a poet. His poetry shows, to some extent, the influence of the Romantic school, but it likewise reveals some classical tendencies. His longest poem, "A Vision of Poesy," owes something to the poetry of Shelley, particularly to the *Alastor*.[36] A few passages from the poem will show the similarity.[37]

> In a far country and a distant age,
>> Ere sprites and fays had bid farewell to earth,
> A boy was born of humble parentage;
>> The stars that shone upon his lonely birth
> Did seem to promise sovereignty and fame—
> Yet no tradition hath preserved his name.
>
> .   .   .
>
> 'Tis said that on the night when he was born,
>> A beauteous shape swept slowly through the room;
>
> .   .   .
>
> The child was very beautiful in sooth,
>> And as he waxed in years grew lovelier still;
> On his fair brow the aureole of truth
>> Beamed, and the purest maidens, with a thrill,
> Looked in his eyes, and from their heaven of blue
> Saw thoughts like sinless Angels peering through.
>
> .   .   .
>
> A childish dream is now a deathless need
>> Which drives him to far hills and distant wilds.
>
> .   .   .

> The eagle knew him as she knew the blast
> And the deer did not flee him as he passed.
>
> .   .   .   .
>
> Thither one night of mist and moonlight came
> The youth, with nothing deeper in his thoughts
> Than to behold beneath the silver flame
> New aspects of his fair and favorite spot. . . .

The vision comes to him just as that of the maiden came to the youth in *Alastor*. She tells him that she is called "Poesy" in heaven, and she gives him the poet's creed. This concludes the first part. In the second part, which resembles Wordsworth's *Excursion*, there are some Shelleyan lines:

> Thou knowest how I went forth, my youthful breast
> On fire with thee, amid the paths of men;
> Once in my wanderings, my lone footsteps pressed
> A mountain forest; in a mountain glen,
> Down which its thundrous boom a cataract flung,
> A little bird, unheeded, built and sung.
>
> .   .   .   .
>
> . . . if any Poet-heart
> Hath kindled at my songs its light divine
> I know it not; no ray came back to mine. . . .

In the "Cotton Boll," the Shelleyan influence is noticeable in a few lines and passages:

> Yonder bird,
> Which floats, as if at rest,
> In those blue tracts above the thunder, where
> No vapors cloud the stainless air, . . .

recalls Shelley's "Skylark," and

> Through lands which look one sea of billowy gold
> Broad rivers wind their devious ways;
> A hundred isles in their embraces fold
> A hundred luminous bays;
> And through yon purple haze . . .

reminds one of lines from the "Euganean Hills."

Later Shelleyans

Other writers of the latter part of the nineteenth century were admirers of Shelley or were influenced by him. Although Amy Lowell's father would not allow a volume of Shelley in his house because he considered him to be an atheist, Miss Lowell states that she found Moxon's Shelley at the book shops and enjoyed his poetry.[38] John Burroughs refers to Shelley several times in his letters and writes of a poem sent to Whitman by John Addington Symonds: "It is lofty and symphonous, and reminds of

Shelley." [39] Louise Imogen Guiney was a youthful Shelley admirer who became so interested in Claire Claremont when she learned that she was still alive that she "wished tremendously to sit on a fence somewhere and see her pass by." And, in 1894, she wrote to Dr. Richard Garnett: "I must tell you, however, what a joyful shock it gave me to find (though I was dense not to guess at it before) that the four votive lines for Shelley's birth-room were yours. I have them by heart, and with infinite satisfaction, for years and years." [40] Richard Watson Gilder, whose favorite poet was Keats, also placed Shelley in the list of poets who were "most" to him. He believed that Shelley was a greater artist than Poe: "The poet of mood who is also the poet of action seems to me the greater artist: Shelley . . . or Browning . . . greater than Poe." [41] Gilder's "Ode" and his sonnet "The Celestial Passion" are reminiscent of Shelley's "The Cloud."

> I am the spirit of the morning sea;
> I am the awakening and the glad surprise;
> I fill the skies
> With laughter and with light.
>
> . . . . .
>
> I am the wind that shakes the glittering wave,
> Hurries the snowy spume along the shore
> And dies at last in some far-murmuring cave.
>
> . . . . .
>
> I light the sea and wake the sleeping land,
> My footsteps on the hills make music. . . .

There are other lines that indicate the influence of Shelley's "Ode to the West Wind":

> Receive my soul, ye burning, awful deeps;
> Touch and baptize me with the mighty power
> That in ye thrills, while the dark planet sleeps;
> Make me all yours for one blest, secret hour!
>
> . . . . .
>
> Fill me even as an urn with thy white fire
> Till all I am is kindred to the stars!
> Make me thy child, thou infinite, holy night—
> So shall my days be full of heavenly light!

Richard Hovey, associate of Bliss Carman, seems to have been influenced by Shelley in some of his verse. The lyrics show some indebtedness to those of Shelley, and "Seaward," an elegy on the death of Thomas W. Parsons, is modelled on Shelley's *Adonais*.[42] Harriet Monroe was also a youthful admirer of Shelley. Her first published poem, which appeared in the *Century* in the eighties, was a sonnet on Shelley. About the same time she read a paper on Shelley before the Fortnightly Club. A little later, she and

Stedman defended the poet in a discussion at a Sunday night supper at the home of the latter.[43]

James Huneker, artist and poet, was a late nineteenth- and early twentieth-century Shelleyan. He relates an anecdote that shows his early enthusiasm for Shelley: "After reading that Shelley lived on fried bread, I upset our kitchen by frying bread and writing verse under its greasy inspiration." [44] Another demonstration of his devotion to his beloved poets, Keats and Shelley, took a more aesthetic form. He had formed the habit of visiting the cemetery in Rome and there reading poetry on the graves of Shelley and Keats and transposing their poetry to the key of Chopin and Schuman. He believed that Keats and Shelley touched his imagination here as nowhere else, and he had become selfish about the place and resented the intrusion of strangers.[45] Regarding the tendency to criticize Shelley's genius as "abnormal," Huneker declares: [46]

Shelley? Ah! he is a pronounced case for the specialists. Any man who could eat dry bread, drink water, and write such angelic poetry must have been quite mad. Admitted. Would there were more Shelleys.

Father J. B. Tabb, who possessed a lyrical gift, was one of the most ardent of this late nineteenth-century group of Shelley admirers, acording to a student at St. Charles College, where Father Tabb was a teacher. He gives the following incident as an illustration: [47]

Toward the end of one session, the teacher went to one corner of the classroom, crouched, and began to recite "The Skylark." The students were transfixed. When he had finished, he was on tiptoe at the opposite corner of the room, breathless, as if eager to follow the bird in its flight. Instinctively, the class broke into tumultuous applause. He modestly repressed the enthusiasm with the remark: "Gentlemen, did you see that skylark soar? Did you hear him sing? If there is a single boy in this class who did not see that bird and hear him, I forbid him ever again to open a book of poetry, for it would be a sheer waste of time." Need it be said that most of those present saw the bird and heard it sing?

Father Tabb also wrote two poems on Shelley, a sonnet entitled "Shelley" and a short poem of two stanzas, "To Shelley," in the Shelleyan manner.[48] The Shelley centennial called forth a number of poems on Shelley by other admirers, among them poems entitled "Shelley" by Katherine Lee Bates, Bliss Carman, and Kenyon West.[49] E. C. Stedman, who in 1892 was an even greater admirer of the poet than in his early years, wrote a long poem, "Ariel" in honor of the centennial. The following passage is characteristic of the poem as a whole:

The slaves of air and light obeyed afar
    Thy summons, Ariel; their elf-horns wound
Strange notes which all uncapturable are
    Of broken sound.
That music thou alone could rightly hear
    (O rare impressionist!)
And mimic. Therefore still we list
To its ethereal fall in this thy cyclic year.
Be then the poet's poet still! for none
    Of them whose minstresly the stars have blessed
Has from expression's wonderland so won
    The unexpressed,—
So wrought the charm of its elusive note
    On us,who yearn in vain
    To mock the paen and the plain
Of tides that rise and fall with sweet mysterious rote.

But the poets of the late nineteenth and early twentieth centuries are too far removed from Shelley in time to trace indebtedness in their works to any great extent. The Shelleyan influence has passed through the hands of so many poets where it has been subjected to the influence of other movements and modified according to the tastes of each, that by the end of the century a Shelley pattern is not always recognizable because of the varicolored threads interwoven throughout.

THE REALISTIC PERIOD
(1872-1900)

CHAPTER IX

ESTABLISHING SHELLEY'S REPUTATION

Lady Shelley and the Shelley Scholars

IN THE LAST quarter of the century Shelley's acceptance or rejection no longer depends on the various movements in American literature. A number of factors contribute to this change. As nationalism in America develops and the periodicals become more tolerant of the opinions and customs of the people of diverse sections, they likewise assume a more tolerant attitude towards writers from other countries. Shelley, among other authors, receives consideration as a poet regardless of the views expressed in his poetry and exemplified by his life. The Emersonian view that poetry must be ethical gradually gives place to the view that poetry is an art and that freedom must be allowed the individual in the expression of his art. Whitman is hailed in England as the representative of a new American poetry and Shelley and Keats are assuming their places as poets worthy of recognition among the best. The change in viewpoint regarding poetry, together with the constant efforts of many literary critics in both England and America to persuade the reading public to recognize Shelley's poetry, results in a tendency to separate his lyrics from his didactic poetry. Shelley becomes better known as a lyric poet. In the latter part of the century less attention is given to his immature views on politics and reform, his ideas on religion are being seen from a new viewpoint, and attempts are being made to trace his philosophy to its various sources. With these changes Shelley as an individual gains in general appreciation. No longer is he merely the eccentric young student at Oxford, the husband of a deserted wife, or a member of the Godwin circle. But this recognition of Shelley the man was not wholly a matter of natural development. It took time and effort to bring about the change. To the diligence of Lady Shelley and the Shelley circle is due much of the credit for the new attitude towards Shelley the man.

In the third quarter of the nineteenth century in England, the relatives and friends of Shelley felt that the time had now come to establish the reputation of Shelley the man—to remove any stigma that might be attached to his name and to correct misstatements that had been made regarding his life. Medwin's biography of the poet in 1847 had not been a success. It had brought criticism upon the poet as well as upon the biographer.

And it was not an authentic biograghy. This work was followed by Hogg's very unsatisfactory *Life of Percy Bysshe Shelley,* in 1858, which met not only with serious objection in the Shelley family but with general disapproval in the few periodicals of the time in which it was reviewed. The *New Monthly* [1] called it a "provoking work" which gave too much time to the discussions of food, "a subject in which Shelley was not interested." The *Literary Gazette* [2] condemned the work as exaggerating all the small weaknesses common to humanity, and accused Hogg of being guilty of a breach of trust in a misuse of the documents entrusted to his care. The *Quarterly Review* [3] was inclined to agree with the view of the Shelley family that the biography contained too much caricature. "Hogg made poor use of valuable material," asserts the writer in the *Quarterly.* "He speaks of Shelley as a Divine Poet, but represents him as a silly, conceited, half-crazy buffoon." Mary Shelley had passed away in 1851. Sir Percy Shelley, the poet's son, was not aggressive. Leigh Hunt, who was now an ageing man, rallied sufficiently to criticize Hogg's *Life of Shelley* in one of the most scathing letters of all time. [4] In his letter to Sir Percy and Lady Shelley, Hunt gives vent to an outburst of pent-up feeling against Hogg, not only for his attitude towards Shelley, but for that towards Keats as well, and for his assuming to be a critic and a scholar. Trelawny had already published his *Recollections of Shelley, Byron, and the Author,* 1858, in which he shows his appreciation of Shelley. Peacock replied to the biographies of Middleton, Trelawny, and Hogg in an article in *Fraser's Magazine* [5] in June, 1858, and to Lady Shelley's *Memorials* in the same magazine in January, 1860. [6] The first article was a defense of Shelley against his biographers and the second a defense of Harriet against Lady Shelley.

There was, however, but one person who was sufficiently interested and sufficiently aggressive to take charge of the campaign to promote Shelley. That person was Lady Shelley, the wife of Sir Percy and the most persistent and determined supporter that ever poet had. Her purpose was not wholly unselfish, for Lady Shelley was probably thinking more of the Shelley name than she was of the poet Shelley. For Shelley's reputation as a poet she had no fears. That was well established. Her anxiety was for his reputation as a man. Thus began one of the best planned campaigns in all literary history to remove all stigma from the reputation of a man whose personal views and life had met with countless criticisms, some just and some unjust. Shelley, who valued his beliefs and cared very little, if at all, for what the world thought, would not have approved of such a course. He was always willing to accept criticism, and he rarely complained.

An enviable stoicism was one of his redeeming qualities. To further her plan and to gain her desire, Lady Shelley formed a Shelley cult and enlisted as members some of the foremost scholars of England, men who were known to be enthusiastic over Shelley—Richard Garnett, Edward Dowden, and W. M. Rossetti. She probably had profited by the experience of Mary Shelley with the cult formed in the twenties. But these two leaders were women of different types. Mary Shelley was a professional woman who followed the ethics of the professionald world. Lady Shelley was a member of that feminine class who set a goal and combine all their energies in an effort to attain that goal—a more temperate Lady Macbeth. How near, in her overzeal, she approached to destroying what she attempted to build up, only those scholars who worked with her knew. Only the diplomacy of Richard Garnett held the group together. It was his especial duty to keep the irreconcilable Dowden placated and to act as mediator between him and Lady Shelley.[7] The first step taken by Lady Shelley was to edit the Shelley *Memorials*,[8] which consisted of a sketch of Shelley's life, supposedly written by Lady Shelley (but now generally conceded to have been written by Garnett), to which was added Shelley's "An Essay on Christtianty." This book, according to Lady Shelley, was published to refute the "numerous misstatements" of Medwin's *Life of Shelley*, which was published in both French and German, and of the recent volumes by Hogg, who had made of the biography a "caricature."

The work of Lady Shelley was not without its worthwhile results. For her part in perpetuating and honoring the name of Shelley, she deserves great praise. She was untiring in her efforts and unselfish of her time and energy. She was willing to make any sacrifice in order that the name of the poet should live. Her fault lay in her judgment as to what would contribute to and what would detract from the immortal fame of a truly great poet. The two direct results of her work were Edward Dowden's *Life of Shelley* and the organization of the Shelley Society. Although Dowden was limited in the handling of his material by the constant demands of Lady Shelley, his *Life* is the best biography of the poet that has been thus far produced. It is to Dowden's credit as a scholar and as a writer and to Lady Shelley's credit as a persistent worker that we now have this biography.

The Periodicals

The emergence of the United States from the Civil War as one nation politically, economically, and culturally had its effect on the literature of America. Boston still kept its position as a center of important educational and publishing institutions and as the home of much that was cultural. Philadelphia retained some of its old prestige as a literary center, New York was the cosmopolitan center for publishers and magazines, and Chicago was to become a rival of the older cities in the publishing business. The magazines were in the East, but the contributors came from all sections of the country. These magazines, dependent for their upkeep to a great extent on the commercial advertising within their pages, were eager for a large circulation and had a tendency, therefore, to accept what was popular in letters. This tendency applied to literary and scholarly subjects as well as to fiction and the popular article.

The Shelley Society [9] had succeeded in making Shelley a popular subject in both England and America, so that from 1885 onward the industrious editors of the American periodicals were alert for anything that might be written regarding him. The *Literary World,* during the years 1879 to 1899, contained no less than 50 mentions of Shelley. The *Nation,* during the same period, contained 14, and the *Critic,* from 1885 to 1894, had 56. *Poet-Lore,* between 1892 and 1898, published more than 50 mentions in all, many being comments and articles by prominent critics. Other magazines contributed a smaller number of articles, but all manifested an increasing interest in Shelley. The Shelley centennial in 1892 and the work of the Shelley Society furnished the impetus for many articles, but biographies and other works prompted the writing of some excellent reviews. The mentions of Shelley in the magazines offer a variety of material. Included in the 56 mentions in the *Critic* are a few brief reviews, several longer articles, a few reprints from English magazines, a number of items containing interesting information, and four short poems on Shelley by writers of this period. The tendency of the magazine as a whole is to be critical of Shelley as a man. The 50 items in the *Literary World* are for the most part notices and brief comments on works published. The list includes several brief book reviews, one long article of interest, and a few poems, including those by Katharine Lee Bates and Bliss Carman. Like the *Critic,* the *Literary World* takes an unfavorable attitude towards Shelley because of its disapproval of his personal qualities. The material in the *Nation,* though less in quantity, is an improvement over that in the other two magazines mentioned. The reviews are longer and contain better criticism and the shorter items are on subjects of scholarly interest. The *Dial,* like the *Critic,* contains a variety of material and fewer reviews but is more favorable to Shelley. The material in *Poet-Lore* consists of scholarly articles on Shelley, mention in other articles, and items of importance. It contains ten articles, a "Song from *Prometheus*" with music, and numerous notices and comments. The *Atlantic Monthly*, the most scholarly of the general magazines of the period, contains a very discriminating review of Dowden's *Life of Shelley*, Vida D. Scudder's well known criticism of *Prometheus Unbound*, and two shorter articles. Other articles of value were published in various magazines, such as the *New Princeton Review*, the *Western*, the *Lakeside Monthly*, the *New Englander and Yale Review*, the *Sewanee Review*, and the *Journal of Speculative Philosophy*.

The latter part of the century brought forth a number of short articles, comments, and poems in the various magazines. Among the articles are two in the *Critic* by James A. Harrison. The first of these articles, published in 1885, "Two Views of Shelley," [10] is a discussion of the views of Brandes and of M. James Darmesteter. Brandes, Harrison states, discusses Shelley as a poet of Love and Nature—"a Love and Nature glorified, cleaned, and purged—transcendental in their aspects—immaterial." Darmesteter's essay, he believes, shows that Shelley is now recognized in France as superior to either Byron or Wordsworth. He states that Darmesteter "takes as a type of the poet, the *Epipsychidion*, which is the flame of the torment of eternal love ignited by the *veux profonds* of Emilia Viviani, but which passes from her to the ideal, the divine." The second article, "A Few Words about Shelley," [11] is a rather amusing, ultra-modern view, unusual in the nineteenth century. Harrison calls Shelley "the Poetic efflorescence, the brilliant incarnation of the French Revolution." He then proceeds to characterize him as follows:

An organism of exquisite sensibilities, his nature vibrated like a string to every passing phenomenon, whether it were a storm or a butterfly. Brooded upon by the *incubi* of the time, it is no wonder that his genius at first evolved only scarecrows, Hoffmannesque romances, passionate controversial pamphlets" on the necessity of atheism"; or the maundering talk of vegetarianism. It was his period of Leiden, of Wertherism, of intellectual sickness; and that he eventually wrote it off was one of the triumphs of his strong personality and his later genius.

Harrison was undoubtedly the first critic to classify Shelley as an example of "the *homme-femme,* the dual nature powerful in its masculinity and yet delicate with all the delicacy of the most intimately feminine organization." He explains Shelley's acts, including his attitude towards Harriet, as the result of a sort of madness: "Like the great Swedish poet Tegner, whom in so many ways he resembles, Shelley had one of those unevenly poised natures which a trifle could make vibrate and could throw out of equilibrium." He concludes with a comment on Shelley's "hallucinations" a seemingly favorite subject with critics until Margaret L. Croft proved that Shelley's veracity was greater than some who knew him had believed.[12]

The same periodical, the *Critic*, for September 6, 1884,[13] contains an article of four columns on Shelley, an unusually long article for this magazine. This is a very appreciative criticism in which the writer discussed Shelley's unselfishness towards contemporary poets and his friendship for women, which the writer believes was Platonic. The January 4, 1890, issue [14] of the magazine contains an interesting short article on Shelley occasioned by the death of his son, Sir Percy Florence Shelley. In the *Nation* for February 7, 1889, is an article entitled "Shelley with Byron,"[15] containing a letter from Este signed "E. S." In this letter the writer describes the house at Este in which the Shelley's lived for a short time and discusses some incidents concerning the relation between Byron and Shelley in Italy, including Byron's weekly dinners which Shelley attended. E. S. believes that Claire and Hunt were responsible for the dissension between Shelley and Byron.

Dowden's *Life of Shelley*, published in 1886, was reviewed in several American periodicals. A reviewer in the *Critic* [16] for December 18, 1886, comments on the work in a disparaging manner when he sarcastically remarks that it will be read especially by the sect of Shelleyites, whose capacity for making a noise is considerable. The publishing of this new biography, he declares, will be an excellent pretext for reasserting all the old arguments in favor of Shelley's supremacy as a poet and his perfection as a human being. The *Critic*, however, is prejudiced against Shelley, but is not prejudiced against his biographer, as is revealed in a second review of the same work in the following April.[17] In this review, Shelley and his work are subjected to severe criticism, but the reviewer concludes with the comment that this is "one of the most perfect of living biographies, worthy to go on the shelf with Boswell or with Moore's *Byron*," a combination which shows the lack of discrimination of the reviewer. The *Literary World* [18] for January 27, 1887, likewise gives a very favorable criticism of Dowden as a biographer, but closes with a would-be-righteous criticism of Shelley because of his "social theories" and the "cruel selfishness with which he cast off a wife." The reviewer in the *Nation* [19] for February 17, 1887, is inclined to favor Shelley, but spends too much time on the subject of Shelley and Harriet. He objects to the biography because he believes that Dowden is concerned with Shelley the man, not with Shelley the poet.

It was Dowden's *Life of Shelley* that called forth that voluminous and erratic article "In Defense of Harriet Shelley," by

Mark Twain, published in the *North American Review* in three parts.[20] The article is not a criticism of Shelley, as seems to be the general impression, but an attack on Dowden's biography of Shelley. Mark Twain shows an acute understanding of many of Shelley's characteristics and a fine appreciation of his best qualities. He likewise reveals a sympathetic attitude towards the problems encountered by Shelley and Harriet. It is Mary Shelley who receives the onslaught from his vitriolic pen and who is judged wholly by his narrow Puritanical standards. Even the meddlesome and ambitious Eliza Westbrook, Harriet's sister, is called an "estimable woman." Too much importance is attached to Shelley's friendship with Cornelia Turner. While the thesis of Twain's defense of Harriet is commendable, his article, a rather insipid attempt at school-boy humor, reveals a lack of acquaintance with facts and a marked prejudice against Shelley's biographer, Edward Dowden.

It is necessary to turn to the *Atlantic Monthly* [21] for the one worthwhile review of Dowden's *Shelley* in American periodicals. The reviewer proves to be a discriminating critic and one who is acquainted with his subject. He praises Dowden's work for its fresh information, patient investigation, frankness, and scrupulous justice in stating all sides of those delicate and important matters in which there is room for private judgment. He feels, however, after reading the narrative, that he has been in rather disagreeable company, this company being Shelley's friends, whom he believes Shelley knew at their true value. Hogg, he states, deceived Shelley in many ways but did not borrow money from him, as did Godwin, Hunt, and Peacock. For Horace Smith, the reviewer has a feeling of "amazed respect" because of his attitude towards Shelley. He considers Shelley's worst misfortune to have been his marriage to Harriet, for whom he had affection, not love. Miss Clairmont he regards as an annoyance to Shelley. He characterizes Shelley's feeling for Mary as love, with an appreciation of her faults, and that for Jane Williams as the poetic affection of a tired man to whom she represented the spirit of restfulness and peace. The reviewer expresses his own attitude towards Shelley in the following tribute: "There is no thought of eulogizing him in saying that he represents the ideal of personal and social aspiration, of the love of beauty and of virtue equally, and of the hope of eradicating misery from the world." The reviewer justly criticizes Dowden for adopting an apologetic tone towards Shelley and for his patronizing style. Dowden, he states, did not need to pity Shelley because he differed from him in fundamentals of faith and opinion.

The *Literary World* [22] for February 15, 1879, contains a brief review of Symonds' *Shelley.* The biographer is commented on favorably: "To refined tastes and broad scholarship he unites an unbounded admiration for the poet," and "His estimate of Shelley's character and rank as a poet, and the critical passages relating to his various works are just as discriminating." The reviewer, however, cannot withstand the temptation to discuss Shelley's character and morals. In the earlier review of the same work in the *Nation,*[23] the biography is recommended as an excellent, brief compendium of facts, pervaded by sympathetic and rational criticism. The reviewer believes that Symonds expresses one extreme view of Shelley's religion, that as Christianity passes beyond its mediaeval phase, it will conform to Shelley's belief, and that F. W. Robertson expresses the other extreme, that Shelley eventually would have been reconciled to Christianity. The reviewer agrees with Trelawny that Shelley rejected what is properly known as Christianity in his youth violently and with hatred and in later years came to care less about it. The marriage of Shelley to Harriet he considers to be the result of "knight errantry" rather than of affection, and the separation he believes to have been by mutual consent. This view is interesting for the time in that it reveals a better understanding of the problems of Shelley and a more tolerant attitude towards his views than is generally shown. The change in the attitude toward his works is noted in the statement that "of his two most powerful works, one is acknowledged the highest sustained lyrical flight in English song, and the other is widely believed to be the most perfect English drama since Shakespeare."

Reviews of other biographies of less importance are given in the periodicals of the time. The *Critic* [24] quotes from two interesting reviews of C. Jeaffreson's *The Real Shelley,* one from the *Saturday Review* and the other from the *Pall Mall Gazette.* William Sharp's *Life of Percy Bysshe Shelley* receives very favorable criticism at the hands of the reviewer in the *Critic* [25] for March 31, 1888. He calls Sharp "an accomplished Englishman who writes of his author with true love and yet true discernment." He gives Sharp credit for working Dowden's long biography of Shelley down into a choice short biography, "artistic, well-proportioned, refined, and full." The *Literary World* [26] for March 3, 1888, likewise gives a brief but favorable review of the same work. H. S. Salt's *Percy Bysshe Shelley,* 1896, received a notice in the *Critic* [27] for October 10, 1896, with the comment that it is a concise biography and criticism of the poet, the purpose being to interpret Shelley. The *Literary World,*[28] in an article entitled "Shelley—Salted," gives a brief review of the same work and a criticism of Salt's "revolutionary and iconoclastic sentiments."

The reviewer in the *Nation* [29] declares that Mr. Salt should have called his work "The Socialist Shelley" because Salt's interest is in Shelley the revolutionist. He calls Mr. Salt "a particularly full-fledged social democrat, with a taste for rhetoric and a lively aversion to the married state." He approves of Salt's "sledgehammer blow in rhyme of Matthew Arnold" which he says is worth the price of the book.

Other works on Shelley appearing at this time received attention in the magazines. The *Literary World* [30] for September 11, 1880, contains a notice of Foreman's edition of *The Works of Shelley in Verse and Prose* with a comment as to the contents. W. M. Rossetti's edition of *The Complete Poetical Works of Percy Bysshe Shelley* received a notice in the same magazine [31] for February 6, 1886. R. Garnett's edition of *Shelley's Letters* was given an advance notice in the issue for February 10, 1883, and a favorable review on April 7, 1883. [32] This article begins: "A perennial interest attaches to Shelley, and any publication concerning itself with the man or his works will always be welcome." The *Nation* [33] likewise contributes a good review in which the writer reveals that he has read and appreciated the work. He praises the "spontaneous beauty of form" in both Shelley's poetry and his letters. He criticizes Shelley's lack of knowledge of sculpture and paintings as revealed in the letters. He refutes the charge that Shelley plagiarized Lodge's lyrics and remarks that "Shelley often paints the picture over upon the outline of the old canvas." Like Garnett, he considers the letters as a revelation of Shelley's character: "He lived life as he felt it and wrote about it—on a high plane." A S. Cook's edition of Shelley's *The Defence of Poetry*, 1891, prompted a notice in the *Critic*, [34] and also a comment in the *Dial* [35] to the effect that the *Defence* is "one of the best of the many critical essays on the nature and office of poetry since the days of Aristotle."

The *Literary World* [36] and the *Critic*, [37] 1893, comment favorably on Vida Scudder's edition of *Prometheus Unbound,* and the *Dial* [38] gives a short but favorable review of the work. The *Literary World* recommends it for the student of English literature who must work independently. The *Critic* calls it "a model piece of work" and recommends the introduction as "equally creditable to her scholarship and critical acumen." The writer in the *Dial* characterizes it as a class room edition with good critical apparatus in the shape of notes, extracts from criticism on the poem, and an introduction in three parts.

The most complete and most accurate edition of Shelley up to this time and the one that called forth the greatest amount of comment in American was the centennial edition of the *Complete*

Poetical Works of Percy Bysshe Shelley, edited by George E. Woodberry. This work brings a front-page review from the *Critic* [39] for December 24, 1892. "The definitive edition before us is an honor to the scholars and is more complete than any yet undertaken by English editors," declares this writer. "Woodberry," he states, "has had the advantage of having at hand the previous texts of English scholars plus the library of C. W. Frederickson and the Harvard manuscripts, and also the assistance of a member of the Shelley family." Mr. Woodberry's excellent memoir shows us the man just as he was, continues this reviewer, "a natural being, subject to no more of eccentricity or disease than exists within the bounds of an ordinary healthy nature." The *Literary World* [40] also contains an appreciative criticism for March 11, 1893:

> Professor Woodberry has long established his reputation as one of the most capable and reliable editors of Shelley. A Centenary Edition, therefore, of the works of this ethereal poet from his hand was one of the most fit and worthy tributes which last year saw paid to the poet's memory.

The reviewer then praises Woodberry for his sympathetic attitude towards Shelley and quotes from his "Memoir" of the poet. The *Nation* [41] gives a review of the Woodberry edition in two parts, both of which are very favorable. Woodberry is commended for his "painstaking drudgery in details which few can appreciate and which can be lightened and illuminated only by a special loyalty and devotion." He is praised for adding valuable additions from the "Harvard Manuscripts" and the printed books in the collection of C. W. Frederickson. The reviewer believes that the portrait of Shelley as painted by Woodberry is somewhat idealized, but adds that Woodberry "does not forget his good sense as Professor Dowden sometimes does." He believes that Woodberry praised Shelley highly because he really knew him. The second part of the criticism is concerned with the discussion and approval of Woodberry's notes. The review of Woodberry's edition in the *Dial* is by Melville B. Anderson. Mr. Anderson regrets that Lowell was, as he believes, silent about Shelley and Emerson cold towards him. He calls Woodberry a critic of "taste, solidity, and sobriety." He believes that one could hardly ask for a better edition of a poet than this edition of Shelley. He refers to the stupendous amount of work involved, quotes from the preface, praises the memoir for brevity and reserve, and approves of the notes. He makes the observation that "The production of this admirable edition at this time is a most auspicious sign of renewed interest in a poet to whom neither the critics nor the reading public have yet done justice."

The long articles on Shelley in these late nineteenth-century periodicals comprise an illuminating collection on a variety of subjects. Most of these articles are concerned with Shelley's poetry rather than with his life and character. This change in the attitude of the magazine writers is indicative of the change that had gradually taken place in Shelley criticism during the latter half of the century. Shelley was gradually taking his place among the great poets of the world. A few writers still consider him in the light of his religious beliefs, his youthful political theories, his separation from Harriet. But, for the most part, even the writers who discuss his theories on religion try to reconcile his views with those of Christianity. Two such writers, practically unknown, may be taken as representative of the views of many of the ministers of this period. The Reverend Howard Mac-Quearry, author of "Shelley, the Sceptic," in the *Arena*[43] for March, 1891, attempts in a very rational manner to reconcile Shelley's views with the most intellectual and progressive theology of the day. He states that the great law of evolution proves the design in nature that Shelley demanded. He would now find leading theologians agreeing with him that God is the Infinite Spirit pervading all nature and upholding it by the word of His power. He objects, however, to other views of Shelley regarding Christianity, but believes Shelley would have become reconciled had he lived longer. Reverend D. H. Wheeler, in his "Shelley's Place in English Poetry," published in the *Methodist Review*[44] in 1894, accepts Shelley as a poet and a pagan. He says that he does not expect a poet to be an authority on other subjects, although he may be. He believes that Byron, Poe, and Heine, as well as Shelley, were only singers. This minister, who proves to be a fair critic of lyrical poetry, extols the lyrical qualities of Shelley's poems. The one article on Shelley's philosophy, entitled "The Philosophical Element in Shelley," written by George Spencer Bowen and published in the *Journal of Speculative Philosophy*[45] in 1880, contains a complete discussion of Shelley's philosophy from his adoption of French materialism, through Baconian or Spinozistic materialism, to a modified form of Berkeleianism. Charles Dudley Warner, in reviewing the criticism of the early part of the century, in the *New Princeton Review*,[46] expresses the opinion that Shelley would have been accepted at once had it not been for his democratic ideas. He calls Hunt's *Examiner* Shelley's only defender and states that *Blackwood's* is the only one of the great periodicals that wrote of the poet with authority and discrimination. He declares that the interest in Shelley is perennial. Towards the late biographers of Shelley he assumes a satirical tone: Dowden's *Life of Shelley* is "the last word for the Shelley Society," Rossetti's sketch is "admirable though adoring," and Symonds' biography is a "capital résumé."

One of the very best articles of the century is "The Soul of Shelley," by R. A. Holland, March 1876, in the *Western*,[47] a periodical published at St. Louis. Holland divides poets into two classes, the observant and the speculative. He lists Shelley, with Job, Dante, Milton, and Goethe, in the latter class, and Homer and Shakespeare in the former. He places Shelley here because of promise of power unfulfilled as well as for his achievement. He believes that Shelley's place is not fixed in literature because of the characteristics of the era in which he lived. He was at war with the society of his age. And because at that time poetry seemed to consist more in finish of form than in richness of material, Shelley would not submit to the shackles of the criticism of his time. "He set up the standard of revolt, and the revolt has since become a successful revolution. Melody is to be measured by accents and not by thumb rule." Imagination and Fancy, he says, rule over Shelley's poetry. He took his themes from the present and the future. "Shelley's soul was poetry itself and whatever passed through it become a poem. Artist he can scarcely be called." His critical faculty was overborne by the mightier impulse of creation. "But limit, Shelley's imagination scacely ever reached. It could not pause long enough to look calmly back on its course. Its very rests were lyric pantings," Thus, and in very eloquent language, does Holland pay tribute to Shelley.

Hence the rapt bard sang, albeit without hope of audience from his own time—sang because his soul overflowed with music pouring into it through every sense, and from all the air of thought.

He declares that in no other poet has speculation been so ultimately identified with feeling, desire, and being itself: Shelley animated the things of sense with the most delicate traits of thought.

Holland believes that Shelley's philosophy is that of Berkeley and quotes from *Hellas* and other poems in proof. He then discusses Shelley's social ideas, particularly those on reform, and their development in his life from childhood. Shelley's direct contact with and study of nature, Holland states, made him the most musical of poets. He regrets that Swinburne disputed this fact and makes the following comparison between the two poets:

Swinburne is a musician of words, Shelley a born singer. Swinburne's excellence is technical brilliancy of variation, Shelley's is essentially grace of tune. Swinburn'e sonatas are masterly tricks of art, . . . Shelley's profuse strains are but the audible pulses of his thought, spontaneous, easy and versatile in modulation, . . .

Shelley's love of nature, says Holland, was not only a passion and an inspiration, but sometimes a worship, when nature became an apparition of God. He declares that Shelley never was an atheist, for in his creed, mind alone existed, and that mind was eternal. He did not believe the universal mind to be similar to the individual; the latter was marked by limitations which could not bound the former. "Nature communicated to his life the spirit of her own—the spirit of an all-pervading Beauty that does not differ from Truth and Goodness, but is one with them and the same." Beauty, he avers, swayed every impulse of the poet's being. He is concerned with Shelley's attitude towards marriage rather than with his marital relations. He states that although Shelley's views of marriage were immoral in their tendencies, they were not a sign of immorality in his character. "Shelley's mistake," he declares, "consisted in transferring the ideal life of a perfect society to the conditions of one malformed and mischievous."

Holland recognizes *Prometheus Unbound* as the greatest of Shelley's poems and discusses it at some length:

> To be duly esteemed *Prometheus Unbound* must not only be read but studied— . . . Thus studied in addition to the music and painting and colossal sculpture of impersonation which the most careless reading acknowledges to be wonderful—it will disclose a breadth and depth and height of philosophy that make it the Epic of Modern Thought.

The articles on Shelley's poetry, except for those in *Poet-Lore,* which will be discussed separately, include four of interest. The first of these is an interesting article in the *Lakeside Monthly,* a Chicago publication, for November 1876.[48] This writer states that the dialect school of poetry is a reaction against the school of poetry that has prevailed for the last fifty years, commencing with Shelley and culminating in Whitman. Shelley, he terms the prince of all poets of the imagination, and adds that no poet is so little known and so little appreciated. This lack he attributes to the poet's seeming obscurity of expression.

> With a mind turned in upon itself in rapt contemplation of its own operations and laws, his habits of thought were shaped from the very depths, and took their complexion from that world of metaphysical research into which he was plunged from boyhood. With him the ordinary methods of thought were reversed. To him the material world was but an assemblage of types of the intellectual. . . . Thus he became pantheistic in the loftiest sense of the word, endowing every subject of nature with a living, breathing spirit. . . .

Shelley's writings, this critic believes, are misty and vague to the majority of readers, but not to the student and man of deep thought. "To him who places himself upon the poet's own standpoint, and, like him, looks rather inward upon the spirit and its workings than outward upon the material objects of sense, his works are as a child's primer for simplicity." The works of Shelley, he insists, are the foundation of two schools, the one a legitimate and the other an illegitimate. Members of the first school were not servile imitators, but seers. Among these, he names Ruskin, Carlyle, and Mrs. Browning. In the second, which he characterizes as a part of the Della Cruscan school, he places Tupper, Swinburne, and Walt Whitman, each of whom represents a different type. He states that Tennyson has at last fallen in with the current and babbles of "Loves of the Wrens." He criticizes Whitman and Swinburne, and some of the poetry of Tennyson severely. He says that the poetry published in the magazines during the last ten years is the very antipodes of the verse of Shelley, its professed prototype.

"Shelley—the Poet," by Julia H. Gulliver, appeared in the *New England and Yale Review* [49] for February, 1890. Miss Gulliver, who discusses Shelley as a lyric poet, states that his poetry is music, and his feeling has the immediacy of a wood-thrush's song. He has been able, she adds, as has no other poet, to imprison in the mesh of language some of the evanescent potencies of music. She compares Shelley with Tennyson, Wordsworth, and Keats, and quotes from the "Skylark," which she declares has an effect similar to that produced by the music of Schubert and Chopin, "an entrancing sense of overflowing, all-embracing melody." Miss Gulliver also gives lyrical sections from the other poems, such as the "Chorus of Spirits" from *Prometheus Unbound*. She quotes Jenny Lind as saying that Shelley's lyrics could not be sung because the verbal melody seemed to be self-sufficing. She gives lines from "To the Night" in proof of Miss Lind's assertion, and adds that the emotional intensity of the language of tones is more powerful than words.

Miss Vida D. Scudder's articles on *Prometheus Unbound,* published in the *Atlantic Monthly,* [50] and later as an introduction to her edition of the same poem, are well known. Miss Scudder divides her discussion into three parts: I, The Drama and the Time; II, The Myth of the Drama; III, The Drama as a Work of Art. In the first part, she discusses *Prometheus Unbound* as a myth born originally of the early childhood of the race, but for Shelley of the world born anew, of the dawn of a new cosmic day, at the begining of the nineteenth century. It is a poem of youth, of the eager thought, the ardent faith of adolescence. The tone is of youth, freshness, exuberance of life. It has a deeper note than the wistful dream of the child; in the eyes of Prometheus and Asia is seen the shadow of a suffering world. A hatred of oppression, a yearning for freedom, a belief in the possibility of universal love pervade the poem. Shelley is representative of his time, of the French Revolution; Prometheus of the culmination of the democratic idea. *Prometheus Unbound* is crude where the Revolution was crude, weak where it was weak, strong where it was strong—spiritually. The second part of the article contains an analysis of the myth of the drama: Prometheus is the Mind of Man; Asia, the Spirit of Divine Love; Ione, Hope; Panthea, Faith; Mercury, Spirit of Compromise; Demogorgon, Fate. Miss Scudder assigns to the four acts of the poem the following titles: I, Torture of Prometheus; II, Journey of Asia; III, Fall of Jupiter and Liberation of Asia; IV. (an afterthought). In the third part, she outlines the acts as follows: I. The calm of proud endurance; II. Hope and promise; III. Calm of fulfillment; IV. A full paean of triumph sweeping us along with tumultuous and unequalled harmony. The drama, she says, is shaped to an organic whole by the use of light and color.

A fourth article of poetic interest is "Shelley's *The Triumph of Life*," by Stockton Axson, published in the *Citizen* [51] for November, 1895. Mr. Axson calls the *The Triumph of Life* one of the "sublimest poems of the century, an absolute creation, a revelation, like an apocalypse; a revelation, in that it portrays no mechanism, no insight into the manner of its conception and growth." He explains that the cosmic character of the theme gives it universal interest and makes of the work an epic. He interprets the poem allegorically. The shape within is Life and the driver is Time or perhaps Destiny; the chariot is drawn by captive slaves, the men and women of all ages; two only are absent, Socrates and Christ. "Triumph," he believes, is used in the sense of "pageant" rather than of "victory." Axson finds a certain monotony that gives the sense of inevitability in the Dantesque rhyme scheme. He interprets the Platonic "Idea" as "pure reason" which dwells in self-sufficiency behind the perishable world. In this aloofness from all interest is the soul's freedom. The moment the soul yields to any desire, however pure, it loses its sight of Pure Reason and becomes a bondman to Life.

The articles in *Poet-Lore* represent a fair cross section of Shelley criticism in the last ten years of the century. The more than fifty mentions in this magazine between 1890 and 1899 include articles by prominent literary critics and lovers of literature and numerous items of interest regarding Shelley. Since the chief interest of the magazine was Browning, many of the mentions are concerning Shelley and Browning. The first volume [52] contains a note on Browning's "Introduction to Shelley's Letters," 1852, and an account of the discovery of the "forged letters of Shelley" as taken from an article in the *Book-lover*. The second volume contains an article entitled "Personal Recollections of Browning" [53] in which Browning relates the incident that led to his writing "Memorabilia." In the third volume William G. Kingsland,[54] the London correspondent for the magazine, tells of Browning's refusal to become president of the Shelley Society because he did not appreciate Shelley's treatment of Harriet. Kingsland, who also does not approve of Shelley's treatment of Harriet, hopes that Dowden has closed this topic forever. The next mention of Shelley and Browning is in the seventh volume.[55] Florence Convers traces Shelley's influence on Browning's *Paracelsus* through parallel passages. She reviews the story of Browning's strong interest in Shelley and of his early worship of the poet. She believes that Shelley might have influenced Browning to attempt to include nature description in his poetry but states that there is seemingly no direct influence and no parallel passages. In an article on "Robert Browning as a Letter Writer," [56] extracts are given from two letters from Browning regarding Shelley, one to Hunt and the other to Forman. In both letters Browning reveals himself as the Shelley scholar.

An article of interest is Jane H. Simpson's "Shelley at Essex Hall" [57] which is, in reality, a report of a lecture on "The Lyrical Poetry of Shelley," by Stopford A. Brooke. Miss Simpson states that Brooke's lecture was attended by a large number of working men, the result of the efforts of the Shelley Society to arouse interest in Shelley. Miss Simpson seems to be interested in Shelley as a social reformer rather than as a poet. For his reform work, she believes that all, particularly women, owe him a debt of gratitude. In the same volume, F. G. Fleay discusses "The Story of Shelley's Life in his *Epipsychidion*." [58] The first part of the article is given to identifying the women mentioned in the *Epipsychidion*. Then follows a discussion of Claire's relation to Shelley and Mary in which Fleay mentions a number of poems which he believes were written to Claire and states that Mary was jealous of Claire. He gives the information that Shelley in 1817 had projected a long autobiographic poem, *Pandemos and Urania*, but had not fulfilled his design because of the suicide of Harriet. Fleay regards the ethical and political teachings in Shelley's poems as dangerous, but admires the poet as an artist. He expresses surprise and disgust that the biographers attempted to whitewash all except Harriet and Claire.

The 1892 volume of *Poet-Lore* is filled with items of interest regarding Shelley. Among these are the comment made by William G. Kingsland that until a fitting monument is placed in Westminster Abbey, due recognition will not have been accorded the memory of Percy Bysshe Shelley,[59] and a comment to the effect that T. J. Wise has published a facsimile of the first edition of *Adonais*, the original of which cost him no less than forty-five pounds.[60] Most important, however, are the three articles by G. W. Alger, Helen A. Clarke, and Kineton Parkes.

G. W. Alger's article, "In Memoriam, Shelley," [61] is a brief but excellent review of the attitude towards Shelley criticism since 1824. Alger begins by stating that the comment of the *Quarterly* in 1824 on Shelley's translation of Euripides and Goethe was the "entering wedge for appreciation of Shelley's work by the critics." This "semi-contemptuous remark" of the *Quarterly* that "one department of our literature has without doubt sustained a heavy loss in the early death of this unfortunate and misguided gentleman," Alger believes, was the beginning of a better understanding of Shelley's genius. The centenaries of Byron, Wordsworth, and Shelley show that the fame of the first two has faded while that of Shelley has increased. He adds that respect for Shelley the man is increasing, and attributes this change to the influence of Dowden's "great biography." He states that Shelley, until quite recently, has been unfortunate in his critics. Ruskin treated him with contempt as shallow and verbose; the learned and usually sympathetic H. B. Reed calls him thin; Professor Shairp, a more recent critic, even goes so far as to deny him a conscience. But Dowden and Hutton and Bagehot have done much to overthrow the older impressions. His popularity has increased because of the cheap editions, the efforts of Todhunter, and the tracts of the Shelley Society. He then refers to Shelley's increasing popularity in France where in the 1890-1891 course in *Le Livret de l'Etudiant de Paris*, under the English literature heading, only Shakespeare and Shelley are considered and are given equal amounts of space. He expresses satisfaction with the new tendency to disregard all the old arguments that Shelley is weak and senescent, lacks quotable passages, and is vague. His belief is that Shelley's position is secure.

Helen A. Clarke, in "A Sketch of the Prometheus Myth in Poetry," [62] compares the Prometheus of Shelley with that of Goethe. She states that the Prometheus of Shelley, modelled much more closely on the Prometheus of Aeschylus, embodies the democratic idea in a far more widely-embracing form than does the Prometheus of Goethe. Goethe's drama seems to typify the progressive spirit of art; Shelley's the progressive mind of the human race struggling to combat error with truth. In comparing Shelley's treatment of the myth with that of Browning, she states that to Shelley must be accorded the honor of dethroning Jupiter; to Robert Browning, of recognizing the philosophic truth that evil is not an accident, but one of the means through which higher good is evolved. Browning, Miss Clarke believes, treats Prometheus as a link between the infinite and the finite; the Prometheus of Browning [63] is a type of evolution rather than of revolution. She then gives an illuminating discussion of the first connected account of Prometheus as found in Hesiod.

The discussion entitled "Shelley's Faith: I. Its Development and Relativity; II. Its Prophecy," in *Poet-Lore*,[64] constitutes one of the interesting additions to Shelley criticism for the year 1892. In the first part of the discussion Mr. Parkes divides Shelley's writing into three periods: the negative period, in which there is a constant denial and all-pervading feeling of destruction, the intermediate period, in which denial gives place to investigation and seeking, and the positive period, in which the work is of a constructive character with definite statements and bold propositions regarding the poet's faith. The first period shows Shelley's desire for knowledge on the subject of religion, the second that his pantheism did not satisfy him, and the third that his religious belief developed into a lofty and noble Deism. If Christianity consists of the moral teachings of Christ, says Parkes, then Shelley might eventually have ranged himself with the Christians, as Browning believed. Shelley's aim, he insists, was to establish a system of philosophy that should cooperate with Christ's teachings as it did with the teachings of all the world's great prophets— Jesus, Buddha, Mohammed. In the second section of the article, Parkes attempts to establish a relation between the ideas of Shelley and those of Herbert Spencer. He states that Shelley would destroy superstition, would have man stand forth in intellectual superiority boldly to claim liberty to think and to seek for himself the truth, and would remove the ideas men have of God and substitute his own high conceptions of the Infinite Power. Spencer, he states, believed that all religions had the same origin, as revealed in the first chapter of his *Ecclesiastical Institutions*.

Other comments and articles appear later in the nineties. In 1893, Helen A. Clarke, in her article "How to Study Tennyson's *In Memoriam*," [65] expresses appreciation of Shelley's *Adonais:* "But while Shelley illuminates the theme with the glorious light of his own wonderfully imaginative faculty, he has not quite escaped Greek poems," particularly those of Moschus. In 1895, in "The Critical Work of Margaret Fuller," [66] Carolyn B. La Monte praises Miss Fuller for not failing to appreciate the beauty and power of Shelley's verse although she fully realized its shortcomings, and quotes in proof from Miss Fuller's criticism of Shelley. The 1897 volume of *Poet-Lore* contains "The School of Literature," [67] by "The Editors," in which Shelley's poetry is discussed, and suggestions are made for the study of the poet. Longer articles of interest are the comparisons of Shelley with Browning and Verlaine. In fact, during the late nineties, enthusiasm for Shelley seems to have taken the form of comparison with other poets. Alice Wilson, a regular contributor to *Poet-Lore,* makes a very interesting and complete comparison of Shelley and Verlaine.[68] Miss Wilson succeeds in finding similarity in the lives as well as in the works of the two poets. She says: "Shelley reaches out to Verlaine from the Romantic epoch; Verlaine reaches back to Shelley from his analytic Today." Some of the similarities in the poetry are: absence of delineation of human character; intensity, the overflow of the lyric quality; music, in which is a touching brokenness, a lifting motion, with a quick flight which seems their own; fondness for the long rolling effect of the alexandrine and for certain expressive words as "winged," "weave," "sinuous," "panting," "expire." While alike in creation of nature imagery, the two poets, believing that nature has a life of its own similar to human life, differ in their description of nature. Verlaine holds that landscape is almost a reproduction of man's brain. He is a mysic. Shelley believes the intellect could pierce through the mystery of existence. Isaac Hull Platt discusses "Shelley and Whitman: a Comparison and a Contrast." [69] The comparison is in similarity of ideas, while the contrast is in difference in attitudes, in means of approach. Thus while both were religious and there was undoubtedly spiritual affinity, Shelley "walked upon the winds of lightness," and Whitman kept his feet firmly planted upon the ground, but "his head sometimes turned to the ethereal regions where Shelley moved." To Shelley, the triumph of Democracy meant the overthrow of all tyrants; to Whitman, it meant their more peaceful subjugation and assimilation.

In 1899, Edwin W. Bowen attempts to establish a likeness between Catullus and Shelley.[70] The resemblance is so general that it might be applied to many lyric poets. Some of the points of resemblance are as follows: Both poets sing out their own feelings; the lyrics of both have a vein of sadness; the poetry of both terminates with the present world; their poetry appeals directly and chiefly to the young.

The last comparison in this group, paradoxical as it may seem, is between Carlyle and Shelley.[71] It is entitled "Carlyle and Shelley: a Parallel and a Contrast." The writer succeeds in finding several likenesses between these men. Both were imaginative and not logical; both wrote, not for artistic, but for missionary ends; both drew their subjects from the politico-social class; both belong to the French eighteenth-century type of writers who invent or take up general ideas, abstractions of the widest order, preach them with all the fervor of religious enthusiasm, and render them attractive by aid of resources of eloquence and literary art. But it is in their attitudes towards Christianity that the writer finds the strongest resemblance. Both rejected the dogmatic claims of Christianity and had a natural religion of a pantheistic cast. Carlyle felt the awe of the life in the universe, but Shelley the love; Carlyle's religion lacked the human element, while Shelley's was a religion of love; to Carlyle, man was a vision, a revealing force, but to Shelley, man was an ally of God. Richard Garnett finds a resemblance between the personalities of Shelley and Novalis [72] in that both are independently compared to ideal representations of Saint John. This likeness is true, believes Garnett, as regards facial contour, and more as regards facial expression: "The rapt gaze of the German poet and mystic is precisely that attributed to Shelley by the person who described him as 'looking as if he were beholding some beautiful sight.' "

The periodical criticism in America at the close of the century was, on the whole, very favorable to Shelley. The unfavorable criticism was most conspicuous in the eighties, at the time of the publication of Dowden's biography of the poet. This criticism likewise came only from the smaller and less important magazines, such as the *Critic* and the *Literary World,* and these periodicals soon gave up their prejudices and joined the Shelley supporters. The *Nation* was almost wholly favorable. In only a few instances was reference made in this magazine to Shelley's morals. Attention was centered on Shelley's ideas and on the merits of his poetry in a general way. His religion, his philosophy, his ideas on reform, his progress, and even the influences on his writings were receiving attention, but only a few articles were devoted wholly to a consideration of his poetry as poetry. Among these were the article by Julia Gulliver on Shelley as a lyric poet and some of the comparisons with other poets, such as Alice Wilson's article on Shelley and Verlaine. That Shelley had at last gained recognition was evidenced by his almost complete adoption by *Poet-Lore,* a magazine established to further the interests of Browning as a poet. A number of factors contributed to the favorable reception of Shelley by the American periodicals at this time. Among these were the numerous favorable articles in the British magazines, the many biographies, the American edition of his poems by George E. Woodberry, and the general popularity of Shelley as a subject owing to the efforts of the Shelley Society and the fact that the Shelley centennial came in 1892. By the close of the century Shelley was so well established that he would never again be a stranger to the American public.

CHAPTER X

THE CLOSE OF THE CENTURY

The Essayists

During the latter part of the century a number of well-known critics published essays on Shelley. Foremost among these writers was George H. Calvert, whose *Coleridge, Shelley, and Goethe*,[1] an essay in seven parts, is worthy to take its place with the best critical work of the century. The author reveals an understanding and appreciation of the problems of Shelley's life not often shown by his biographers and critics and remarkable for the time in which the essay was written. Calvert, owing to his temperament and his appreciation of literature, was an ideal biographer for Shelley. He had appreciation for beauty, for poetic ability, and for human nature, without the sentimentality that is so detrimental to much of the Shelley criticism not only of this period but of later times as well. And he had the judgment and taste to stress the important points and to pass over lightly or omit the minor details.

The first part of the essay, "Up to the Time of Entering Oxford," is an interesting biographical sketch. Calvert uses facts as given by other biographers but brightens them with comments that reveal a knowledge and understanding gained from a study of the poet and his work. For Shelley's life at Oxford he wisely uses Hogg's *Life of Shelley*, but his own comments add much. He refers to the marriage of Shelley and Harriet which he considers to have been a misfortune to both. He holds Eliza responsible to a great extent for both the marriage and the separation. He states that Shelley had a pure love and a high respect for women, but from the purity of his feelings and the impetuosity of his nature, he was prone to act out hastily his desires and conceptions.

In the fourth section, Calvert begins his criticism of Shelley's poetry. Of *Queen Mab* he says: "This promising, but juvenile and crude, performance was probably a bravado thrown by a defiant athlete into the teeth of hoary Oxford—a bravado tempered by rhythmic verse, but flanked by very outspoken prose in the shape of long, elaborate, heterodox notes." He believes that Shelley's youth should excuse him. *Alastor*, he states, is purely subjective. In it Shelley does not attempt to solve problems. As a lover of beauty, he was ever pouring forth admiration. "Any event or person or object could become the vent for drawing from his deep, general spring and individual stream of felicitous verse."

He makes the acute observation that Shelley delighted in Byron's company at Geneva because he craved sympathy and congenial companionship which he seldom got. He calls *Prometheus Unbound* "the grandest of lyrics in dramatic form." He says that Prometheus is the resplendent embodiment of a prolific idea, that man as a soul is not indestructible, but, through high will, inspired by love, is creative. Love is the redeemer of mankind. He refers enthusiastically to the music of the poem. On the *Cenci* he has less comment. He believes that Cenci is a prosperous Caliban: "Cenci is a fiend, a demon, a blazé demon, not a man."

Calvert says of Shelley's poetic development in Italy that his outward senses were daily cultivated by the beauty of the country, while his inward, luxuriating at the feast of memories, were fed by the records of the words and deeds of the lofty men who, from generation to generation, drew to Italy. He declares that no matter how high Shelley soared, the cord that bound his heart to humanity was never broken. "The closer he comes to his fellows, the more musical is the ring of his verse, the more poetical its tissue." And he quotes from the "Witch of Atlas" in proof. Shelley, he believes, is an unsurpassed master of artistic presentation. He knew the futility of making poetry the direct teacher of anything. In his discussion of Shelley's later poetry, he says of *Epipsychidion:* "In his imaginative ecstasy Emilia became to Shelley the embodiment of that heavenly dream in *Alastor*, . . . *Epipsychidion* is the subtlest picture of ideal, uncarnal love." The subject of *Adonais*, he believes, is far higher and richer than is that of *Lycidas:*

> The sustained splendor of *Adonais* is astonishing. Fifty-five Spenserian stanzas, each a new bar of musical thought, each resting to the eye on, and to the ear supported by, the rhythmic strength of the final alexandrine; each as fresh and original as a succession of May mornings, every one of which seems to surpass the preceding in the glittering beauty of its auroral dewiness; all glorified by the mysterious, creative life out of which spring the earth and stars.

> . . . . .

> The fineness and freshness of Shelley's poetic invention is nowhere more effectively exhibited than where he represents the "quick Dreams" mourning round the body of Keats. No one knew better than Shelley what a gift to the poet—it might be called his capital outfit—is the power of day-dreaming.

He believes that stanzas IX and X are the most typical of Shelley of all the stanzas in the poem; they are "so new, so springy, so laden with musical mind, so inwardly lucent."

Calvert's first essay on Shelley,[2] published in 1874, but probably written much earlier, is concerned chiefly with the minor poems. This essay is one of those rare gems of poetic criticism that are found occasionally among the contributions of the writers of the nineteenth century. It contains beautiful sentiment without sentimentality, and appreciation without exaggeration. It is the work of a competent and sympathetic critic whose original powers of appreciation have been enhanced by study. Calvert believes that Shelley takes rank with the foremost of those poets "whose function it is to enkindle and refine, elevate and liberate, their fellowmen." The "Ode to the West Wind," he observes, "is especially characteristic of Shelley because it is so purely poetical; for when Shelley is most himself, his mind is most creative, being essentially, predominately, a poet." The "rapid procreative energy" of the "West Wind," he says, "is a mark of the highest mental resources, involving mental originality with swift and wide imaginative swing." He quotes a passage to show that image shoots out of image with cumulative effect. "Each of the five stanzas," he continues, "furnishes similar poetically cumulative passages, passages piled up by an insatiate mental liveliness, ever feeding itself on fresh beauties of its own begetting." He adds that the fineness of the mental fibre transparent in the "West Wind" was visible in all that Shelley wrote:

One of the most richly endowed of men, Shelley was at the same time one of the most exquisitely organized. His sensibilities kept his life in a frequent tremor, and at times, when his imagination fastened upon images of terror . . . his agony almost convulsed him. . . . This suseptibility made him recoil from the gross and robust and even from the palpable, while his intellectual subtlety, and his keen sense of the beautiful, ever tempted him into visionary fields, where he fashioned creatures who were largely absolved from the cumbersome conditions of earthly being.

Referring to Mary Shelley's complaint that "The Witch of Atlas" contained no human interest, Calvert states that this objection cannot be made to *Prometheus Unbound*, which he characterizes as "grandly, intensely human." He explains that "Shelley's incarnations lack the earthly element; he had too much nerve and not enough muscle. Hence in his *Prometheus Unbound* . . . the conception is not vividly accomplished. "The *Cenci*, he declares, is not a poetic reality. Shelley, he believes, was drawn to this subject by his imaginative delight in excess. "The Witch of Atlas" he calls "the most exquisitely ideal and ethereal of all poems." But *Adonais*, he believes, is the masterpiece of Shelley. "In it there is more of the poet Shelley and more of the man Shelley, than in any other of his works."

William P. Trent, a leading literary critic of the late nineteenth and early twentieth centuries, in his essay "Apropos of Shelley," [3] finds the poet "an entrancing, perplexing, irritating subject for

study" because of the wide variety of opinions regarding the
man and his poetry. He cites opinions of Carlyle, Browning,
Rossetti, Swinburne, and Kingsley among the critics and of
Dowden and Sharp among the biographers. In the second part
of the essay he discusses Shelley's life and character. He attributes Shelley's difficulties to his early environment in which he
believes there was an "utter absence of all that is spiritual,
elevated, and refined." Dr. Lind he calls an "unwholesome" and
Godwin a "bad" influence. Shelley's lack of wisdom, because of
this unpropitious environment, he contends, caused his expulsion
from Oxford and his marriage with and separation from Harriet.
But he approves of "one gain" that Shelley made by his contact
with Godwin—"a noble and sympathetic woman for his wife."
He recognizes Shelley's devotion to beauty when he says that he
"loved beauty whether in woman or flower, or wave, or sky, or
in the creation of art, or in the abstractions of the human mind."
He criticizes Shelley for not seeing that theories which for the
time were true for him were not good for others, as for Harriet
and Emilia Viviani. In the third part of the essay, in which he
discusses Shelley's poetry, Trent is less valid. He depends too
much on the opinions of Matthew Arnold, although he does not
agree with Arnold that Shelley is to be remembered as a translator and prose writer. "Shelley's star has been steadily rising
since his death," says Trent in defense of the poet. But his criticisms of the poems all suffer from the Arnold-complex.

Trent's attitude towards Shelley, however, is best exemplified
in his essay "The Byron Revival," [4] in which he is rather severe
with the critics who favor Shelley rather than Byron. Of Swinburne and Saintsbury, he sardonically remarks, "As might have
been expected, Mr. Swinburne, too, had a pair of chief poets to
set up—to wit, Shelley and Coleridge," and Professor George
Saintsbury could maintain, without serious loss to his reputation
as a critic, that ". . . Byron . . . could not be read in close juxta-
position with a real poet like Shelley without disastrous results
to his fame." He blames Carlyle for the reaction against Byron,
and adds that Wordsworth, Shelley, Keats, Tennyson, and Browning can count their partisans by the score. But he asks, "What
has Shelley whose *Prometheus Unbound* and the *Cenci,* though
in some respects wonderful, are neither fully unique nor representative?" Of the genius of Shelley and Tennyson, he remarks:
"The abberations of men of genius, even of almost consummate
artists, are not to be accounted for; and there are things perilously
near doggerel in the mature work of poets like Shelley and
Tennyson." Byron's dramatic productions he praises, three of

which he says are not to be matched in the works of any of Byron's modern rivals, save Shelley. In comparing Byron and Shelley as poets, he states: "The British critics have almost unanimously rendered their verdict in favor of Shelley; and from the point of view of technical art, they are doubtless in the right. Yet I question whether the sheer vigor of Byron does not balance the art of Shelley in a class of compositions in which neither could attain perfection."

One of the most enlightening of the late nineteenth century discussions of Shelley's ideas is the essay "Shelley",[5] by Alfred Elmer Hancock. Mr. Hancock's essay contains so many views not generally held at this time that it is surprising that it has not been quoted or referred to more often by twentieth-century writers on Shelley. Hancock discusses Shelley's ideas in relation to the French Revolution. He begins his essay: "Shelley was a true child of the Revolution; he inherited its vehement temper, he shared its impossible illusions, he was the apt pupil of its doctrines; among his brother poets he must therefore take precedence." He believes that Godwin's influence on Shelley during the formative period has been overestimated. This view of Hancock's was unusual in the nineteenth century. Godwin, he contends, was a minor influence in the composition of *Queen Mab*, as Shelley was a born freethinker. A first principle of truth to him was, "Whatever is, is not right." He suggests that Godwin probably phrased for Shelley in mature language his own ill-defined and germinating ideas. He then proceeds to discuss at some length the sources for *Queen Mab*, for which he divides the poem into three parts. For Cantos I and II, Volney's *Les Ruines* was used; for the second part, Cantos III–VI, Holbach was referred to; and for the third part, the picture of the Golden Age, Godwin's theories were kept in mind. All these sources, however, were not used at one writing of the poem, according to Hancock. There was an earlier draft of *Queen Mab*, probably the *Poetical Essay* which had Volney's *Les Ruines* for its source, and the last draft was written under the inspiration of Holbach's *System de la Nature*, which Shelley translated in 1812. From Volney, Hancock asserts, Shelley drew his inspiration for invective against kings, from Holbach the militant faith for the profession of atheism and also the philosophical doctrine of necessity, but in the fundamental principles of government, he followed Godwin, not the French writers. Hancock proves his assertions by quoting parallel passages. This essay is important in that it looks forward to the work of the Shelley scholars of the twentieth century.

Thomas Wentworth Higginson seems to have been well acquainted with the work of Shelley, but his chief interest in him and in other poets evidently was in their personalities and in incidents of their lives, which he used as a source of material for his essays. As an essayist and critic of human relations, Higginson was discerning, humorous, and sympathetic. His observations on Shelley, to whom he has a habit of referring in his essays, are both illuminating and entertaining. In *Literature as an Art*,[6] he quotes Shelley, who, he says, described Southey "as a talking album, filled with long extracts from forgotten books on unimportant subjects." In his biography of Longfellow,[7] he remarks that "Byron and Shelley gained in fame by the supposition that the domestic and law-abiding gifts were far from them." He makes a similar observation in his essay "Concerning Giants":[8]

Had Shelley been the contented husband of one wife, or had Poe selected any one city to dwell in, it is certain that the Shelley literature and the Poe literature would have been far slenderer in dimensions though the genius of the poets might have remained the same. It is the personal qualities in such cases that multiply the publications, though it is quite true, on the other side, that Poe might have lived unnoticed in more cities than claimed Homer had it not been for *The Raven* and that Shelley might have had as many wives as a Mormon but for *The Skylark*.

Higginson adds, however, that "As time goes on, it is the thought of the poet more than the gossip about his life which holds and creates literature." His descriptions of Shelley's cottage at Keswick,[9] which Higginson had visited, furnishes a further example of the essayist's enthusiasm for Shelley and adds to the store of knowledge concerning him:

You go from Keswick up over Windy Brow to Chestnut Hill, and still find in its garden and among its rhododendrons the pretty cottage whither Shelley. . . . The visitor finds himself in the very room where the young poet wrote his address to the Irish people and many poems; where he tried chemical experiments after dark, and his landloard, Gideon Dare, drove him out of the house next day as being concerned in what he called "black art."

George E. Woodberry

The century comes to a close with the work of the distinguished Shelley scholar, George E. Woodberry. Professor Woodberry's contribution to Shelley criticism far exceeds both in quality and quantity that of any other American of the century and is the equal of that of the English scholars. It is doubtful if any other person who wrote about Shelley was so well qualified by temperament, by general scholarship, and by appreciation and knowledge of Shelley to edit a text of his poems or to pass judgment on the poet and his works. Had he made no other contribution than to edit the Shelley text, he would be deserving of a high place among the Shelley scholars. He edited the Harvard *Shelley Notebook*, and his essays on Shelley would make a small volume of valuable critical material. Charles Franklin Thwing, who knew Woodberry personally, gives his impressions of this critic's feeling for Shelley.[10] He says that Woodberry's deepest devotion was not to his teachers but to Shelley: "For at times he seemed to be almost 'Shelley-mad.' " Thwing finds a similarity in the poetic feeling of the two men: "The flights of Shelley and of Woodberry seem to be in the same atmosphere, a highly rarefied atmosphere indeed." As to a singular likeness in temperament, he writes of Woodberry, "One would say, as he says of Shelley, 'He would stand preëminent and almost solitary for his services to the struggling world, for what he did as a quickener of men's hearts by his passion for supreme and simple truths.' " And he continues, "Likewise, it may be said of Woodberry as he again says of Shelley:

> . . . he put persuasion in the place of force, and love in the place of hate, and the genius of victory which he invoked was the conversion of society by the stricken cheek and the lost cloak.
> This partial service moreover takes on the form and force of the imagination. In *Prometheus Unbound* it becomes the millennium of mankind. Other poems, like the *Adonais*, are filled with these and other like emotions: "personal pathos, of meditation on life, of divine philosophy . . . under the spontaneous and unreflecting impulse of poetic passion." But all are held in both the older and the younger poet within the bounds of beauty.

Woodberry himself expressed his great love for Shelley when he said:[11]

> People in general know me little for my Shelley. Yet Shelley, from back in my college days, has always been one of my enthusiasms. This is the Centenary Edition of his poems, which I edited in 1892, giving, as you will notice, all the variations, line for line, with complete notes. Much of my examination studies for this I did in the private library (since dispersed) of Mr. Frederickson, then a famous collector living in Brooklyn. This old gentleman had the finest Shelley library to be found anywhere. . . . He had collected in Shelleyana over two thousand volumes, including the very earliest and rarest editions.

In addition to editing Shelley's poems and the Harvard *Shelley Notebook*, Woodberry wrote six essays on Shelley and devoted the greater part of a seventh, "The Titan Myth," to the same poet. He likewise gives Shelley considerable mention in at least eight other essays. These lectures and essays extend over a period of years and into the twentieth century.[12] The first of the essays, "Remarks on Shelley," published as early as 1890,[13] is divided into three parts: "His Career," "His Acquaintance," and "His Italian Letters." In the first part, Woodberry in a sympathetic manner criticizes Shelley's poor judgment in attempting to reform the world, discusses his religious belief and concludes that his atheism could not be denied, and finally refutes the charge that Shelley was selfish. In the second part, he discusses Shelley's acquaintances, whom he does not consider friends, and dwells on his disillusionment and loneliness in the last two years of his life when "his ideals removed into the eternal world." It is possible that Woodberry, in his love for Shelley, attaches too much importance to this disillusionment.[14] That Shelley did not lower his ideals is but an indication of the true nobility in him, a characteristic conferred on an occasional soul at birth. The third part of the essay is a fitting tribute to Shelley's prose work, as exemplified in his letters, and was a valuable contribution at the time it was written.

The second essay, "Shelley's Work," [15] was published in 1892 to commemorate the centenary of his birth. Shelley's difficulty, as seen by Woodberry, was "that the artistic and the practical instincts in him worked together imperfectly," but to this quality, Woodberry likewise believes that we owe some of his lyrical effusions. Shelley, to Woodberry, as to so many other critics, was a child of the Revolution: "So far as the Revolution was specu-lative or moral, he reflected it completely." Even his crudities were not merely those of immature and boyish development; they belonged quite as much to the youth of the cause. His political, social, and intellectual beliefs were not superficial, argues Woodberry, any more than are principles of democracy, philanthropy, and intellectual liberty. Woodberry explains the "tenets" that caused Shelley's voluntary exile, that is, his atheism and his belief that legal marriage was not a proper social institu-tion, and discusses his idea of the perfectibility of man. He describes Shelley's atheism as his difficulty in reconciling "an anthropomorphic conception of deity with a philosophical de-finition" and in "the humanizing of a pre-Christian and medieval idea of God in accordance with that moral enlightenment which Christianity itself has spread throughout the world." Of Shelley's view regarding marriage, he says: "The belief of Shelley in love without marriage was an extreme way of stating his disbelief in marriage without love, as the law of England then was." Shelley's genius, Woodberry believes, was prophetic in that it "seized the elements of the future yet inchoate, and glorified them, and won the hearts of men to worship them as in imagined hope, and fervently to desire their coming."

The third essay, published in 1900, but probably written earlier, "Shelley's Poetry: a Sketch," [16] may be summed up as follows: Shelley's earliest poems on the regeneration of society differ widely as to poetic method. *Queen Mab*, "the precipitate from the fermant of his boyish years," is a "crude poem after the style of Southey;" the *Revolt of Islam* shows an increase of his poetic faculty "by his denial of a didactic aim and by the series of scenes from nature and human life which is the web of verse;" *Prometheus Unbound,* the third and greatest of his works of this kind, reveals the Greek influence in "a new type in English— the lyrical drama." Shelley's extraordinary myth-making faculty, as revealed in nearly all his poetry, gives the impression that he dwelt in an imaginary and unsubstantial world. His love of a romantic tale is best exemplified in his *Rosalind and Helen,* his *Witch of Atlas,* and his drama *The Cenci* and the fragment *Charles I.* The poems that deal primarily with individual nobility and happiness apart from society show "the recoil of Shelley's mind from the task of reform he had undertaken." This group of poems includes *Alastor, Prince Athanese,* and *Epipsychidion.* His popular fame, however, rests on the lyrics, "impulsive, overflowing, irresistible in their spontaneity," which express "his world-weary yet still aspiring soul." Of these, the most perfect is the "Ode to the West Wind," to which only the *Adonais* can compare for personal power.

The remaining essays by Woodberry belong to the twentieth century. In "The Titan Myth",[17] a lecture published in 1905, Woodberry interprets *Prometheus Unbound* wholly in relation to the French Revolution: "In this poem the Revolution as a moral idea reached its height; that is what makes it, from the social point of view, the race-point of view, the greatest work of the last century in creative imagination." He explains the myth and then concludes: "Thus Shelley, as is the universal way of genius, had created a great work by fusing in it two divergent products of the human spirit—the Hellenic idea of a higher power superseding the lower, and the Christian idea that this power was one of non-resistance, of forgiveness, of love. In his lecture entitled "Shelley",[18] after explaining the process of attaining the spiritual life, he adds: "It sometimes happens that a man who goes through the process of this high spiritual life, becoming more and more deeply, variously, and potently human, developing this power of man in him, has also passion for accomplishment—and that is one of the marks of a man of genius. Shelley was such a man, and I desire to present him, as a man with a passion for accomplishment but also as an extraordinarily good illustration of the mode in which a man, through literature, evolves the highest self of which mankind is capable." Of Shelley's *Cenci,*[19] published in 1820, Woodberry states that the theme is displayed through the two leading characters, and that this is not a playwright's, but a poet's play. Although he agrees that the drama shows the influence of Shakespeare, Woodberry believes that the personality of Shelley pervades the whole play.

Numerous references to Shelley and his works are found in other essays and lectures of Woodberry. In "A New Defense of Poetry,"[20] he recognizes Shelley and Sidney as his masters: "And thou, O Youth, . . . idealize your masters and take Shelley and Sidney to your bosom, so shall they serve you more nobly and more sweetly than if the touch and sight of their mortality had been yours indeed." In "Man and the Race," [21] he states that the "immanence of the divine" is an "immanence of sublime power" in Shelley, "an immanence of transcendent love." In his essay entitled "Lyrical Poetry," [22] he discusses the necessity of repose as the end of all art and gives Shelley's *Adonais* and "Stanzas Written in Dejection near Naples" as examples. He states that he does not include "The Indian Serenade" because it ends in a note of climbing passion.

The criticism of Shelley by Woodberry testifies to the place held by Shelley in the world of American letters at the close of the nineteenth century and the dawn of the twentieth. Woodberry's place in America was like that of the distinguished Shelley scholars in England—Dowden, Garnett, Forman, W. M. Rossetti. He not only contributed to knowledge regarding Shelley, but he helped to make Shelley's position in America secure.

CONCLUSION

Shelley criticism in America may be considered as representative of American literary criticism of the nineteenth century. As in England, criticism in America in the early part of the century was largely a matter of personal prejudice. Thus Shelley was lauded or maligned to the extent that the writer agreed or disagreed with the acts of his life or the opinions expressed in his poems. A few independent critics, such as E. P. Whipple and the anonymous writers in the *New York Literary Gazette*, the *American Quarterly Review,* and the *Yale Literary Magazine,* were interested in Shelley as a poet and expressed their approval of his poetry in some discriminating criticism. They appreciated poetry as an art and had the foresight to know that it was the poetic qualities in Shelley's works that would stand the test of time. Orestes W. Brownson and Parke Godwin were likewise interested in Shelley as a poet, but the former came to his defense through sympathy for the persecuted and to oppose his detractors, while the latter probably was first attracted to the poetry because of the ideas of social reform contained therein. Both were critics of judgment and were able to appraise Shelley's poetry at its true value. Otway Curry, of the *Hesperian,* and H. C. Lea and Henry T. Tuckerman, who wrote for the *Southern Literary Messenger,* were critics of importance who were able to appreciate Shelley and to make some valuable contributions to the criticism of the period. Margaret Fuller's enthusiasm for Shelley's poetry was constant, but her feeling for the poet was inclined to vacillate according to the influences of the period. George W. Curtis, the most ardent of the youthful admirers of Shelley, has left a few appreciative criticisms, beautiful tributes to the poet, characteristic of Curtis's youthful ardor. The few comments made by Edgar Allan Poe were favorable, but his silent approval cannot be weighed. His constant study of Shelley and his imitation of his style are ample proof of the esteem in which he held the English poet. The reaction of the leading critics and the literary periodicals for the first half of the century was, on the whole, very favorable to Shelley.

Shelley's most severe critics were those who were opposed to him on religious and moral grounds. It was to be expected that such conservatives as Andrews Norton and W. B. O. Peabody would object to his views on religion and to his reputed morals as well. But to these men, as to other leaders among the conservatives, Shelley was not sufficiently important to deserve a great deal of attention. Any consideration given to him was as

183

a member of a group. To Norton he was one of the representatives of the evil thinking in religion and morals that was creeping in from the continent directly and through England. To Peabody he was one of the Byronic group who represented a sort of Satanic evil in the form of Pegasus that would instantly corrupt all readers of his works. To Mrs. Seba Smith and several anonymous writers the spirit of Shelley assumed a diabolical form with the purpose of wrecking the morals of the young. But Mrs. Smith was confident that the power of a comforting hand extended would change this satanic form to one more angelic. Even the great William Ellery Channing, accepting too readily the opinion of Southey, considered Shelley a seraph gone astray. Whittier's youthful effusion may be considered merely as an outburst of outraged Puritanical feelings.

Among the more liberal minded of the religious group as a whole, however, Shelley always received his share of sympathy. As early as 1834 he was defended by the anonymous writer in the *Literary Journal and Weekly Register of Providence,* and later by James Freeman Clarke in the *Western Messenger* and Amory D. Mayo in the *Massachusetts Quarterly Review.* And in the middle of the century he is accorded understanding sympathy and recognition by Phillips Brooks. The Shelley admirers likewise numbered in their ranks such men as Nathaniel Hawthorne and John Lothrop Motley, who were able to estimate Shelley at his true worth.

The many socialists in America who adopted Shelley because of his ideas are not to be overlooked. Most enthusiastic of these was G. G. Foster, who was the editor of the first American edition of Shelley's complete poems. Foster's preface to the first edition shows him to belong to the early sentimental admirers of the poet, but the prefaces in the later editions show improvement, probably owing to the severe criticism of the first and to the kindly advice of friends. Other socialists were "D. L.," who contributed to the *Western Messenger,* and several anonymous writers. There is also a tinge of socialism in some other articles, including Parke Godwin's excellent criticism in the *Democratic Review.* In America, as in England, however, Shelley's greatest admirers and most ardent supporters during the first half of the century came from the literary class.

The poetry of Shelley met with the approval of almost all the major poets in America. Even Whittier was willing to admit that Shelley was a lyrical poet of ability, even a genius. Emerson probably formed his opinion of the poet's ability too quickly, and being a very determined Emerson, could not change his mind. Lowell early became a follower of Shelley, but under the influence

of Maria White and "the gang" relinquished Shelley in favor of
Keats. Holmes assumed that benevolent attitude towards him
which was so characteristic of the good Doctor. Longfellow, who
seems not to have been especially interested in the English
Romantic poets as a class, found Shelley to be a poet very much
to his liking and enjoyed his lyrics. The long list of minor poets
who attempted during the thirties and forties to write in the style
of Shelley is indicative of the esteem in which he was held by
these admiring poets. Proper guidance, more of Poe and less of
Emerson, might have developed some of these poets into lyrists of
note. Less attention to reform measures, including the abolition
of slavery, and more attention to literature and art would have
afforded the opportunities necessary for the making of poets.
But the age of sentimentalism which set in during the late
forties engulfed Shelley, so that he almost became lost in the
maelstrom of gushing sentimentalists and would-be-followers.
The period of Romantic poetry in America virtually came to a
close with the death of its greatest singer, Edgar Allan Poe, the
only person who could have combatted the forces working for
its ruin. Poe, however, had already completed for Shelley what
Tennyson had begun in England, the popularization of onomato-
poetic poetry. He might have advanced Shelley's cause directly
had he acknowledged the influence of the English poet on his
own poetry.

Periodical criticism during the first half of the century fluctuated somewhat in accordance with the character and interests
of the magazines as well as with the changes in editors. Of the
approximately seventy-five mentions of Shelley two-thirds were
favorable. The periodicals of a literary character, as has been
noted, were favorable because they considered Shelley as a poet
and were willing to ignore or pass over lightly or even to sympa-
thize with his faults. The magazines of a socialistic turn, such as
the *Harbinger,* were interested in him because of his advanced
ideas on social reform. Wholehearted and sympathetic editors of
the James Freeman Clarke and Orestes Brownson type found in
Shelley not only a poet to their taste but also an object for their
kindly and philanthropic sympathies. That they were sincere in
their defense of the poet there can be no doubt. The interest of
Godey's Lady's Book lay wholly in the fact that Shelley was the
husband of Mary Wollstonecraft Shelley, the daughter of the
defender of the rights of women. Of the twenty mentions in the
Southern Literary Messenger seventeen were favorable, two of
the unfavorable being in reply to Tuckerman's articles. The other
unfavorable articles, except those by Andrews Norton in the
Boston Daily Advertiser, were either mentions in longer articles

or brief articles in ephemeral magazines, such as the *North American Magazine,* the *Philadelphia Monthly,* and the *American Monthly.* Of the two unfavorable articles in the *Whig Review,* one was occasioned by disgust with Foster's unlimited praise of Shelley and the other prompted by Gilfillan's attitude towards Shelley and Keats. It may be concluded, therefore, that periodical criticism in America during the first half of the century was not only favorable but partial to Shelley.

Of the poets who belong to the latter half of the century, but few show any direct indebtedness to Shelley. About the middle of the century, when Romanticism in America was on the decline, Shelley, together with Keats, was adopted by a group of writers from New York and Philadelphia who were supposedly interested in art for art's sake and who seem to have made of these poets a "cult" and to have tried to imitate them. This imitation, coming at the same time as the "poor, poor Shelley" reaction, created a wrong impression of Shelley's status in America. It led to the erroneous idea that his influence on American literature had been detrimental and that the only writers who gave any heed to his work were these imitators, a belief which has been carried over into the twentieth century. Of the poets of the Transition Period, Whitman, in his early work of the forties, came under the influence of Shelley. Any indication of indebtedness in Whitman's later work lies in the similarity of ideas. The poetry of Henry Timrod likewise shows some indebtedness, and it is possible that Sidney Lanier also owed something to the early inspiration of Shelley. A group of poets in the latter part of the century, including Moody, Lodge, and Stickney, seem to have attempted to write in the style of Shelley, but poetry as a whole had felt the effects of too many movements, including the free verse, to make it possible to resuscitate the style of any one poet.

The periodical criticism in the latter half of the century reveals the extent to which Shelley was recognized as a poet. Even in the fifties and sixties, when literary criticism was at a low ebb, Shelley receives a fair amount of recognition in the periodicals. Mentions in the seventies were few, the two most important articles being in the more literary magazines, the *Lakeside Monthly* and the *Western.* After the publication of Symonds' biographical sketch of Shelley in 1878, the notices in American magazines become more numerous. With the publication of succeeding works on Shelley, including Dowden's *Life of Shelley,* in two volumes, in 1886, the number of notices increase, reaching their climax in 1892, the year of the centenary of Shelley's birth.

A number of essays appear independently and in volumes in the latter part of the century. Such able writers and critics as

George H. Calvert, Alfred Hancock, and William P. Trent found him to be an inspiring subject for lengthy essays. Thomas Wentworth Higginson and James Gibbons Huneker related numerous incidents about him. And George Edward Woodberry wrote lectures, essays, and magazine articles about him and edited the *Harvard Manuscripts.* Woodberry's greatest contribution, however, was his centenary edition of Shelley's complete poetical works, a work which was compiled and edited with the meticulous care that only a lover of his work can give. To Woodberry must be accorded recognition as the greatest American scholar of Shelley of the nineteenth century.

The century closes with Shelley in the foreground as one of the major English poets. With his general recognition in American periodicals and his adoption by *Poet Lore,* the most literary of the magazines, he needed no further introduction to the American public and no further recommendation to the literati. And his many biographies made him a subject of curiosity to the multitude.

As the twentieth century dawns, Shelley is gradually being recognized as one of England's foremost poets. The road to success was not an easy one. It was crooked and rough. The efforts of the Shelley family and friends straightened it and made it smooth. Certain factors make for security in the work of a poet. That the poetry of Shelley had these qualities of timeliness his relatives and friends knew. Thus they were willing to strive to keep his work in the foreground and to remove all obstacles to progress, especially those prejudices against the character of Shelley. The quality in Shelley's poetry that made it live in the nineteenth century, as has been seen, is the poetical quality. Shelley's poetry as poetry has been appreciated by the poets and even by the critics of every period. His ideas will never cease to arouse interest among the thoughtful, and his life will always be a source of curiosity to the many. Just as the nineteenth century was interested in his views on social problems and his ideas on religion, so the twentieth century continues to be interested in these and other problems. His ideas on religion and on science are found to be absorbing topics. His place as a lyrist has been established.

American interest in Shelley seems to hav no limits. Bennett Weaver has investigated his study of the Bible, Ellsworth Barnard, his views on religion, Carl Grabo, his knowledge of science and philosophy, and Benjamin Kurtz, his ideas on death. W. E. Peck has engaged in research concerning various Shelleyan problems and has brought to light knowledge hitherto little known. N. I.

White has made available information on various matters touching the poet and has given us a complete study of the periodical criticism of Shelley during the poet's life. Other works are probably in progress. Perhaps America will yet supply the desired Shelley biography.

APPENDICES, NOTES
AND
BIBLIOGRAPHY

Shelley in the Central West

Shelley seems to have been fairly well known in the section known as the Central West during the fourth and fifth decades, although he was hardly known earlier. R. L. Rusk states that the earliest sign of Shelley he has found is a copy of the posthumous "Song" beginning "Rarely, rarely comest thou," in *The New Harmony Gazette,* May 14, 1928.[*] He gives the interesting information that in a forty-page list of books advertised by one of the chief Ohio booksellers in 1831, none of the four authors, Wordsworth, Coleridge, Shelley, or Keats, was included, but that in a catalogue of the same firm in 1833, all were included but Wordsworth. In 1835, a minor list of a Detroit bookseller included a volume of Coleridge, Shelley, and Keats. He adds, "It was this one-volume edition that was usually contained in the lists mentioned."[†] This was undoubtedly the American reprint of the Galignani edition of Coleridge, Shelley, and Keats, which seems to have had a wide circulation in America at this time.

An occasional article on Shelley appeared in the western periodicals during this early period. Those in the *Western Messenger* have been discussed in the text, as were those in later periodicals. An interesting article that was not discussed, was one by Otway Curry, published in the *Hesperian,* at Columbus, Ohio, April, 1839.[‡] Curry was not only assistant editor of the magazine but a poet and critic of considerable reputation. His discussion is that of a superior critic. He discusses Shelley as man, thinker, and poet. He characterizes him as gentle, loving, and unoffending towards individuals. He believed that Shelley suffered because the practices of his life were opposed to many of the great conservative principles, usages, and beliefs of necessity to society in its civilized mode, a very practical and common sense view that was not expressed by the critics of the time. Curry declares that Shelley was not a logical thinker and cites as proof his beliefs concerning religion and marriage. He declares that Shelley practiced and preached Christianity but rejected it as a religion. He regards Shelley as a superior poet whose work shows "eloquence in thought, sublimity and beauty in imagery, power of imagination, and mastery of machinery of versification." He offers the unusual but reasonable explanation for Shelley's seemingly vague diction that because his images are new, he is compelled to make use of words which are the representatives of familiar things. Thus their meanings, especially to the superficial reader, are rendered almost impalpable.

---

[*] *The Literature of the Middle Western Frontier,* II, 23–25, 1925.
[†] *Ibid.,* II, 28, footnote.
[‡] II, 440–447.

The Authorship of the "Memoir" in the Little, Brown, and Company edition of Shelley's Poetry.

The question as to whether James Russell Lowell or Charles E. Norton wrote the "Memoir" for the Little, Brown, and Company edition of *The Poetical Works of Percy Bysshe Shelley* seems never to have been settled. This "Memoir" was long attributed to Lowell, but in the 1866 edition Norton is given as the writer.[§] It is not the object of this discussion to decide the question but rather to give the content of the essay.

The "Memoir" is an interesting essay. The writer seems to take pride in Shelley's American ancestry. He refers to Sir Bysshe Shelley's American "fine manners," a retort to Medwin's criticism regarding his drinking with low people. His style is rather light and jocular when he refers to the ancestry of Timothy Shelley. There are some slight errors as to fact. The only reference used seems to be the comments of Leigh Hunt whom the writer evidently regards as an authority on the subject of Shelley. Interest in Shelley's early education is revealed by the following comment: "At Eton he became a good Latin scholar and a tolerable Greek one. Here began his love of Plato and of boating, the one destined to influence his whole life as an author and a man, and the other to cause his untimely death." As proof of Shelley's sincerity and disinterestedness, he quotes Hunt. On the expulsion from Oxford he takes a definite stand. He does not excuse Shelley. He believes that a milder mode of treatment and a less heroic remedy than expulsion might have been more efficacious. He states that Shelley gave up his seat in Parliament on conviction, whereas Byron gave up his as a whim. Regarding Shelley's separation from Harriett, he says that the circumstances of the disagreement have not been cleared up. His viewpoint is interesting for the time. He does not condone Shelley's act, nor is he too severe. "But now was to come the terrible recoil which almost inevitably results from an attempt to bend an entire social system out of the way of the passions of a single man." He continues: "The greater Shelley's genius, the nobler his character and impulses, so much more startling is the warning. If we make our own inclinations the measure of what is right, we must be the

sterner in curbing them. A woman's heart is too delicate a thing
to serve as a fulcrum for a lever with which a man would over-
turn any system, however conventional." He then quotes at
length from Hunt as to Shelley's habits and his character. He
states that the best narrative of Shelley's death is by Hunt and
quotes it in full. He makes no comment on Shelley's poetry.¶

§ The "Memoir" is not signed, but in the table of contents Norton is given as the
writer. In the 1857 edition Lowell is given as the author (cf. Congressional Library,
or catalogue).

¶ This fact and other internal evidence would lead one to believe that Norton
rather than Lowell was the author of the "Memoir."

Replies to Whittier's Attack on Shelley*

The criticism of Shelley by Whittier in his article "Infidelity" brought an indignant reply in the form of a letter contributed to *Poulson's American Daily Advertiser* by one who signed himself "Justitia" and dated February 10, 1830.* A copy of Whittier's article was published in the *Advertiser* in the morning issue of the same date. The writer refers to this article as "a violent and unwarrantable attack" upon the memory of his deceased friend, Mr. Percy B. Shelley. He defends Shelley against Whittier's accusation of dissipation, and says that "there never existed a man whose life was passed in more total seclusion from all the haunts of the dissipated." He commends Shelley for his interest in the "higher branches of literature" and for his "retiring sensibility. He approves of his early marriage to a "virtuous wife" and his "enjoyment of a very limited circle of friends, to whom his truly amiable deportment, his high attainments, and the universal charity of his heart, especially endeared him." In reply to Whittier's criticism of Shelley's metaphysical opinions, the writer asserts that Shelley had "as good right as any other man to the enjoyment of his speculations, whether on philosophical or religious subjects." He declares that Shelley went to Italy because he sought the shelter of a foreign land and a more congenial climate, and not "to find oblivion from the memory of his guilt," as Whittier stated he had done. The letter concludes with a retort to Whittier's charge that Shelley died with a cloud upon his brow and the seal of infamy upon his memory:

What presumption! what gross and insulting mockery! *who* is there that shall say how *he* died, who perished in the solitude of the whirlwind? Who is there that can declare with what fear, or with what fortitude, he encountered the dark horror of the destroying tempest?

None survived to give a true account. But enough! It was from the bosom of a secluded villa on one of the smiling bays of Italy, that the subject of this letter, accompanied solely by the friend of his heart, departed on his last voyage. Nothing more has ever been known of him than his earthly remains.

That his life was strictly moral, passed in the refined seclusion of literary retirement, giving no food for the tongue of common invective, and even his death unseen by mortal eye,—only aggravates with the enemies of truth the crime of the persecuted.

Whittier answered this letter in his article "Shelley," published in the *Essex Gazette* for February 30, 1830.† To this second attack

---

★ These articles were received too late to be included in the discussion on Whittier.
* February 12, 1830, page 3, column 2.
† Cf. page 31.

by Whittier, a reply, probably written by Robert Morris, was published in the *Philadelphia Album*.‡ The writer defends Mary Shelley against Whittier's criticism with the argument that the child is not to blame "because her mother was profligate." He confuses Mary and Harriet, and refers to Mary as the one who "perished by drowning." § He rebukes Whittier for interpreting Shelley's life through his poetry:

> Must a man's poetry be the index of his life? Have not the most moral poets that ever lived generally been the most intemperate and profligate of men? Truly we should soon win for ourselves a niche in the temple of good works, if a poetical flight were sufficient to give tone to character and history.

He then concludes with a reply to Whittier's remark that genius should never take the precedence of virtue.

> We echo the sentiment in its fullest sense, "that genius should never take the precedence of virtue," but whilst we deprecate the doctrine and practice of infidelity, let us not lose all christian charity[sic], and tinge our reprimands, rather with the bitterness of a fiend, than with the mild benignity of the disciples of a pure and elevated religion.

---

‡ March 13, 1830, pp. 86–87.
§ There seems to be some confusion in the minds of these writers regarding to whom the term "virtuous wife" refers.

NOTES

Introduction

1. "Shelley," *The French Revolution and the English Poets*, 50–57, 1899.
2. "Shelley's Work," *Literary Essays*, 107, 1892.
3. "Shelley in 1892," *Questions at Issue*, 209, 1893.
4. John Malone, "A Search for Shelley's American Ancestor," *Century Magazine*, XXII n.s., 634–636, May, 1892.
5. It would not be difficult to ascribe many of Shelley's characteristics to his American ancestry. Henry James readily makes him an American in "The Aspern Papers," and refers to his muse as American.
6. Canto XI, stanzas XXII-XXIV.
7. Rolleston edition, 6.
8. Thomas Love Peacock, *Memoirs of Shelley* (Brett-Smith edition), 35–37, 1909.
9. *Life of Shelley*, I, 472–473, 1886.
10. *Fred Newton Scott Anniversary Papers*, 1929.
11. "Shelley and Charles Brockden Brown," *Publications of the Modern Language Association*, XLV, 1116–1128, September, 1930.
12. Cf. N. I. White, *The Unextinguished Hearth*, 363.
13. II, 392. Goodrich and Company, New York, Publishers. An advance notice, probably by Ollier, London.
14. 270. Evidently an advance notice.
15. July, 1820, 223–243; January, 1821, 168.
16. 477.
17. XVII, 285.
18. *Ibid.*, 490.
19. I, 372. A Philadelphia magazine published by E. Littell and R. Norris Henry, New York.
20. II, 321.
21. II, 330–331.
22. In addition to the *Posthumous Poems*, 1824, and the number of reprints of individual works by Ollier, there was the Baudry edition of *The Living Poets of England*, which contained poems by Shelley, II, 366–371, and "A Literary Memoir," signed "A. P." (Printed for L. Baudry, evidently by A. and W. Galignani, 1827), and the Galignani edition of Coleridge, Shelley, and Keats, 1829, for which Mary Shelley wrote a preface in 1824.
23. This article and others, 1822–1830, are discussed with the periodical criticism of the Romantic Period. The articles were so few and the limits of the Romantic Period so indefinite that it seemed best to include them with those of the later group.
24. The number of pirated editions of Shelley's work in England during the twenties is still uncertain. The first in America seems to have been an 1821 edition in New York, by William Baldwin and Company.

The next American reprint, probably pirated, of which we have any record is that of the Galignani edition, Philadelphia, 1831. I believe, however, that there are others.

NEW ENGLAND

CHAPTER I

Shelley and the New England Transcendentalists

1. M. A. DeWolfe Howe, *The Life and Letters of George Bancroft,* I, 150, 1903.
2. O. B. Frothingham, *Theodore Parker: a Biography,* 108.
3. 414–428.
4. C. L. F. Goddard, *The Periodicals of American Transcendentalism,* 165, 1931.
5. Hogg's story of Shelley, when a student at Oxford, stopping a woman on Magdalen Bridge and inquiring if her baby could tell them anything about preëxistence is well known. T. J. Hogg, *Life of Percy Bysshe Shelley,* I, 239–241.
6. While he was still a young man, Shelley spoke of desiring to adopt a child and educate it according to his own standards. All through his life he had a penchant for teaching others.
7. F. B. Sanborn and T. W. Harris, *A. Bronson Alcott: His Life and Philosophy,* I, 165, 1893.
8. Elizabeth Palmer Peabody and her father established a circulating library in their home in Boston.
9. Elizabeth Palmer Peabody ,*Reminiscences of William Ellery Channing,* 435–440, Boston, 1880.
10. *Ibid.,* 321–322.
11. W. B. Greene, *A Priori Autobiography,* 41–42, Boston, 1849.
12. W. B. Greene, *Transcendentalism,* 8, Boston, 1871.
13. James Freeman Clarke, *Autobiography, Diary, and Correspondence,* edited by Edward Everett Hale, 329–330, Boston, 1891.
14. T. W. Higginson, *Margaret Fuller Ossoli,* 307, Boston, 1884.
15. *The Poetical Works of Percy Bysshe Shelley,* edited by G. G. Foster, Philadelphia, 1845.
16. Margaret Fuller, *Life Without and Life Within,* 149–152.
17. T. W. Higginson, *Margaret Fuller Ossoli,* 42.
18. *Memoirs of Margaret Fuller Ossoli,* 59, Boston, 1852.
19. *Ibid.,* I, 165–166.
20. *Love-Letters of Margaret Fuller Ossoli,* I, 97, 1845–1846, edited by Julia Ward Howe, New York, 1903.
21. *Love-Letters of Margaret Fuller Ossoli,* 178.
22. *Papers on Literature and Art,* 68–73.
23. M. Fuller Ossoli, *At Home and Abroad,* 119–140, edited by Arthur B. Fuller, 1856.
24. *My Literary Acquaintance,* 61.
25. *Contemporaries,* 21.
26. *Journals,* IV, 198.
27. *Ibid.,* V, 344.
28. October, 1840, 149–150.
29. *Works,* VIII, 25.
30. *Journals,* VI, 114–115.
31. *Ibid.,* 213, June 16, 1842.
32. *Ralph Waldo Emerson,* 233, Boston, 1915.
33. *Literary Anecdotes of the Nineteenth Century,* edited by Nicoll and Wise, 207.
34. Pages 36 and 46.
35. *Complete Works,* VIII, 315–326, Centenary edition.

36. *Journals,* VII, 284–285.
37. Cf. *Prometheus Unbound,* IV.
38. The resemblance is to the "Ode to the West Wind."
39. The use of the elements in poetry is quite general among poets, but the lines,

By one music enchanted,
One deity stirred,—

express a Shelleyan view. Cf. *Prometheus Unbound.*
40. *Adonais,* XLII.
41. *Ibid.,* XLIII, 1–5.
42. According to Arthur Christy (*The Orient in American Transcendentalism,* 68–69), Emerson read Jones before he was nineteen. Shelley likewise read Jones before he had reached that age, or before June 11, 1811. (Peck, *Life of Shelley,* I, 76, ftn., 40.)
43. *The Orient in American Transcendentalism,* 182, 1936.
44. Denis Saurat, *Literature and the Occult Tradition,* 6, 1930.
45. *Ibid.,* 43–44.
46. 470–493.
47. I, 217–218, October, 1840.
48. The first three lines recall "To Jane: the Keen Stars Are Twinkling," and the first line of the last stanza, "The Indian Serenade." The remaining lines are similar to the songs of the Spirits in *Prometheus Unbound.*
49. I, 291, January, 1841.
50. III, 505, April, 1843.
51. *Ibid.,* 505–506.
52. II, 52–53, July, 1841.
53. III, 99–100, July, 1842.
54. In the years between 1830 and 1845, Goethe leads in the number of mentions of German writers in American periodicals, Schiller is a close second, Richter comes next with about one-third as many notices, Körner is fourth, and Fouque, fifth. (Approximated from the bibliography of "German Literature in American Magazines," by Scott H. Goodnight, *Philology and Literature Series,* IV, University of Wisconsin, 1907.)
55. Henry Steele Commager, *Theodore Parker,* 58–59, Boston, 1936.

CHAPTER II

The New England Poets and Shelley

1. *Essex Gazette,* February 6, 1830, Haverhill, Massachusetts.
2. *Ibid.,* February 27, 1830. Cf. Appendix C.
3. 239–240, Riverside edition, 11.
4. *Complete Poems,* 92–93, Cambridge edition.
5. *One Hundred Days in Europe,* X, 18, Riverside edition.
6. *Ralph Waldo Emerson,* 316–317. Boston, 1884.
7. *Ibid.,* 328.
8. *Ibid.,* 33.
9. *Ibid.,* 399.
10. This transfer of identity belongs to the school of the young German Romanticists whose philosophy of love involved the transfer of identity.
11. O. W. Long, *Literary Pioneers,* 188–189, Cambridge, 1935.
12. *Ibid.,* 193, 256.

13. S. Longfellow, *Life of Henry Wadsworth Longfellow*, II, 58, Boston, 1886.
14. *Ibid.*, III, 401–302.
15. *The Waif*, 30–31, "Song." The first stanza is omitted. 1846, Boston.
16. "Coleridge," *Essays*, VI, 68–77, Riverside edition, 1887–1914.
17. J. A. Harrison, *Life and Letters of Edgar Allan Poe*, II, 144, New York, 1903.
18. James R. Lowell, *The Function of the Poet and Other Essays*, 157, edited by Albert Mordell, 1920.
19. This article "Poe" was written at Poe's request and published in *Graham's Magazine*, February, 1845. (Cf. Lowell, *Function of the Poet*, 153, footnote.) According to Harrison, Lowell at this time viewed Poe, his elder by ten years, with reverence and awe. (*Life and Letters of Edgar Allan Poe*, I, 202.)
20. R. H. Stoddard, *Recollections*, 95–96, New York, 1903.
21. *The Function of the Poet*, 70–72.
22. *Literary Essays*, II, 229.
23. *Ibid.*, 143–145.
24. *New Letters of James Russell Lowell*, 206–207, edited by M. A. De-Wolfe Howe, 1932.
25. *Literary Essays*, IV, 369–370; 413.
26. *Letters of James Russell Lowell*, edited by C. E. Norton, 191, 1894.
27. John M. Robertson gives Lowell's criticism of Shelley as an illustration of his contradictory judgment. "Lowell as a Critic," *North American Review*, 246–262, February, 1919.
28. *The Function of the Poet*, 1920.
29. *A Defence of Poetry*, par. 13.
30. Compare the following quotation from the *Defence of Poetry:* ". . . Like the alternations of an ever-changing wind over an Æolian lyre, which move it by their motion to ever-changing melody."
31. Stanzas 1–8.
32. Stanzas I, II, VIII.
33. "A Poet's Hope." Last line.
34. The fifth line resembles Shelley's "The Indian Serenade," 16–19, and the other lines are similar to lines 9–12 and 13–16 of "The Cloud."
35. "Conversations in Rome: between an artist, a Catholic, and a Critic," 56–57. Boston, 1847.
36. *Poems by W. W. Story*. Volume II, *Monologues and Lyrics*, Boston and New York, 1891.
37. V. Knox, 1842, 211–212, 373–375.
38. *Literary Essays*, II, 144–146.
39. Percival could hardly have seen Shelley's *Prometheus Unbound* when he wrote his own *Prometheus*. The subject of the Promethean myth was a favorite one at this time, 1821, when Percival wrote his poem.
40. Richard Hovey called this poem one of the few faultless lyrics in the language.

Some New England Shelleyans

41. Cf. Peacock's *Nightmare Abbey* in which the character Scythrop is supposed to represent a kind but satirical study of Shelley in his desire to reform the world.
42. January 1 to December 1, 1832.
43. "P's Correspondence," *Mosses from an Old Manse*, II, 181–184.

44. *Essays*, 447–448, II.
45. *John Lothrop Motley*, 379. 1879.
46. O. W. Long, *Literary Pioneers*, 200.
47. G. W. Curtis, *Correspondence of John Lothrop Motley*, II, 359–360.
48. "An Autobiographical Sketch," 703–705, *Cosmopolitan, October*, 1894.
49. *Early Letters of George W. Curtis to John S. Dwight*, edited by George W. Cooke, 190, 1898.
50. *Ibid.*, 258–265, (Noverber 22, 1846).
51. *Sartain's Union Magazine of Literature and Art*, edited by Mrs. Kirkland, III–IV, 22–26, July, 1848.
52. W. D. Howell's, *My Literary Acquaintances*, 110.
53. *The Life and Letters of Christopher Pearse Cranch*, 128, by Leonora Cranch Scott, New York, 1917.
54. *Ibid.*, 343.
55. *Orations and Addresses*, II, 354.
56. *Literary and Social Essays*, 197.
57. Alexander V. G. Allen, *Life and Letters of Phillips Brooks*, I, 136–138.
58. *Reminiscences of Reverend William Ellery Channing*, 339.
59. W. H. Channing, *The Life of William Ellery Channing*, 414.
60. Peabody, *Channing*, op. cit., 339.
61. *Ibid.*, 375.
62. The name of J. Lewis Diman, Professor at Brown University, might be added to the list of Shelley admirers. His biographer, Caroline Hazard, says: "For Shelley he always retained his early fondness and admiration." *Memoirs of the Reverend Lewis Diman*, 23, 1887.
63. *A Month in England*, 141–159, New York, 1845.
64. 56–58.
65. Cf. page 94–5.
66. F. B. Sanborn, *Recollections of Seventy Years*, II, 543–545.
67. I, 231–236. 1890.

CHAPTER III

Shelley and the New England Periodicals

1. F. L. Mott, *A History of American Magazines*, 1740–1850, 40, New York, 1930.
2. Volume XXI, 353, October, 1825.
3. Volume XXVIII, 17, January, 1829.
4. Volume XXXVI, 176, January, 1833.
5. Volume XL, 433, April, 1835.
6. Volume I, 1833–1834, edited by Albert G. Grenne.
7. The number for Saturday, May 31, 1834, 409–410 contains a sketch of "Shelley" with those of Byron, Lamb, Keats, and others.
8. Pages 252–253.
9. Page 275. In the July, 1838, number is a poem, "Lines," written in the Shelleyan manner and preceded by a quotation from Shelley.
10. Volume V, 183–189.
11. Volume LVII, 342–343, October, 1843.
12. Volume LVIII, 27, January, 1844.
13. *North American Review*, LXI, 352, 356, 360, 364, for Shelley.
14. *Ibid.*, LX, 67, January, 1845.
15. *Ibid.*, LXI, 468–497, October, 1845.
16. *Ibid.*, LXI, 216–217, July, 1845, a review of Longfellow's *Poets and Poetry of Europe*.
17. Volume LXVI, 458–459, April, 1848.

18. Volume IV, 393–436, October, 1841.
19. Two other periodicals that contained notices of Shelley were the *Biblical Repository and Classical Review*, which published a brief review of G. G. Foster's edition of Shelley's poem, January, 1846, and the *Pictorial National Library*, which contained a brief article on "The Grave of Shelley," October, 1848, 179–180.

The Emerson-Andrews Norton Controversy

20. This group includes the more orthodox Unitarians as well as the Calvinists and others.
21. II and III, 1836–1837, 474–478, February, 1837.
22. *Boston Daily Advertiser*, XLIII, Monday, August 27, 1838, page 2.
23. *Boston Daily Advertiser*, XLIII, 2, Friday, September 28, 1838.
24. *Ibid.*, 2, Friday, October 5, 1838.
25. VI and VII, 42–47, November, 1838.
26. See note 21.
27. *The Biblical Repertory and Princeton Review*, XI, 37–101, January, 1839.
28. II, 87–113, January, 1839.
29. IIII, 323–331.

THE MIDDLE ATLANTIC SECTION

CHAPTER IV

Shelley in Philadelphia

1. 245–247, July 15, 1828.
2. II, 278.
3. VIII, 160–161.
4. XII, 84.
5. II, 312–314.
6. XVIII, 1–19, September, 1835.
7. XIX, 257–287.
8. XXI, 187–213, March, 1837.
9. An edition of Shelley's prose works was published by Lea & Blanchard, Philadelphia, 1840, *Shelley, Letters from Abroad, Translations and Fragments*, edited by Mrs. Shelley.
10. Preface to the *Poetical Works of Percy Bysshe Shelley*, edited by G. G. Foster, Philadelphia, 1845.
11. *Passages from the Correspondence and Other Works of Rufus W. Griswold*, by W. M. Griswold, Cambridge, 1898.
12. Advertisement to the 1857 edition of the *Poetical Works of Percy Bysshe Shelley*, edited by G. G. Foster, Boston, 1857.
13. Some of these were: the third edition, published by J. S. Redfield, New York, 1850; one published in 1852 and one in 1857 by Phillips, Sampson, & Company, Boston.
14. XXVIII, 96.

Shelley in New York

15. 271–272.
16. Cf. II, 7, July, 1833; V, 478, June, 1835.
17. *A Literary History of America*, 229.
18. 84–88, Letter XVI, April, 1833.
19. I, 53–54, September, 1825–March, 1826. James G. Brooks, editor.
20. I–IV, 326, 1828–1832.
21. I, 84.

22. I, 179–184, March, 1833.
23. XI, 346, May, 3, 1834.
24. XVII, 75.
25. The issue for March 30, 1839, contains an article, "Lord Byron of Pisa," in which Shelley is mentioned, and on April 6, 1839, he is again noticed in "Hazlitt in Switzerland."
26. 759–760.
27. 783–784.
28. II, 251–254, September, 1841, Editors, Cornelius Mathews and Evert A. Duychinck.
29. 114.
30. 84.
31. II, 1846.
32. II, 75–76, January 10, 1846.
33. IV, December 12, 1846; II, 251, September 26, 1846, excerpt from Margaret Fuller's "Papers on Literature and Art;" V, 49, April 17, 1846, "Letter from Italy.
34. II, 33–37, July, 1845.
35. III, 673, June, 1846.
36. V, 386–396, April, 1847.
37. *Ibid.*, 534–537, May, 1847.
38. IX, 530–532, May, 1849.
39. *A History of American Magazines*, 677–679.
40. III, 603–623, December, 1843.
41. No biography of Shelley had been written at this time.
42. XIX, 316–320, October, 1846.

THE SOUTH

CHAPTER V

Southern Shelleyans

1. T. S. Perry, *Life and Letters of Francis Lieber*, 151. (See also pages 109, 117, and 141.) 1882.
2. T. O. Mabbott and F. L. Pleadwell, *Edward Coote Pinkney*, 60, 88.
3. It is possible that Simms had Shelley in mind when, in his *Guy Rivers*, he has Colleton, the hero, insist that Lucy Munroe come to live with him and her successful rival.
4. Cf. *Poems by General Albert Pike* with introductory biographical sketch by Mrs. Lilian Pike Roome, daughter of the author. Little Rock, Arkansas, 1900.
5. William Pitt Palmer expresses regret that he was unable to continue with the poetical work of his youth. Cf. *Echoes of Half a Century*, with introduction, by William Pitt Palmer, 1880.
6. Cf. page 58.
7. *Broadway Journal*, August 2, 1845.
8. G. E. Woodberry, "The Poe-Chivers Papers," *The Century*, LXV, 435–447, 545–558, January, February, 1903.
9. Cf. page 97.

The Southern Literary Messenger

10. II, 326–336, April, 1836.
11. VI, 393–396, June, 1840.
12. VI, 717–720.

13. VI, 826–828, December, 1840.
14. VII, 28–29.
15. VI, 470–471, June, 1841.
16. VII, 32, January, 1841.
17. VII, 312, April, 1841.
18. VIII, 194–196.
19. X. 619–629.
20. XI, 238–242, April, 1845.
21. XI, 468.
22. XII, 158, March, 1846.
23. X, 104–106.
24. XII, 737–742.
25. The reference is to Poe's praise of Shelley in his review of Elizabeth Barrett's *Drama of Exile and Other Poems* in the *Broadway Journal,* I, 1–2.
26. XV, 292–293.
NOTE: At least one other periodical of this period contained a mention of Shelley. In the *Southern Quarterly Review,* Charleston, October, 1842, (11, 314), in a review of "Ahasuerus, a Poem. By a Virginian," mention is made of Shelley: "Shelley, sacrificed as his genius was on the altar of England's intellectual tyranny,—though doomed, awhile, to obscurity,— now finds admirers in a distant land, and the mutterings of the *Cenci* will yet be rewarded with a resting-place in the sea-girt isle."

CHAPTER VI

The Influence of Shelley on Poe

1. In Neal's review of Poe's 1829 volume of poetry, *The Yankee and Boston Literary Gazette,* December, 1829; E. C. Stedman's *Poets of America,* 239–240, 245; *Southern Literary Messenger,* XVI, 185, March, 1850, a review of Poe's works.
2. *A History of American Literature,* 420–422; also "Some Notes on 'Al Aaraaf'," *Modern Philology,* XIII, 35–44.
3. The Galignani edition, published in Paris, 1829, had a wide circulation in America in the fourth and fifth decades of the nineteenth century. Cf. R. L. Rusk, *The Literature of the Middle Western Frontier,* II, 23–25; George E. Woodberry, "The Poe-Chivers Papers," *Century Magazine,* XLIII, 438, January, 1903; and Lowell's Essay on Coleridge.
4. This criticism will be discussed later in this chapter.
5. There are, however, indications that Poe might have been acquainted with Shelley's poems as early as 1827. The 1845 text of the "Evening Star," a poem whose composition is assigned to 1827, contains a few lines that are very Shelleyan, so much so that I am inclined to wonder if they were not inserted later than 1827. The lines are, 9–14,

> I gazed a while
> On her cold smile;
> Too cold—too cold for me.
> There passed as a shroud
> A fleecy cloud, . . .

The early text of "Tamerlane" also shows that Poe even at this date experimented with Shelleyan rhyme schemes (Cf. Stanzas III–VII).
6. "Al Aaraaf" likewise reveals acquaintance of the author with *Queen Mab* (Cf. note 11). Both Killis Campbell and W. B. Cairns believe

that "Al Aaraaf" was influenced by Shelley, but the former refers to only one phrase in the 1829 edition that may show indebtedness (*Poems of Edgar Allan Poe*, 181, Notes), while the latter states that the definite Shelley qualities cannot be detected (*Modern Philology*, XIII, 35–49, May, 1915).

7. The following brief outline will reveal the use probably made by Poe of his earlier poems: Part I, 1–121, comprises the early poem on earthly beauty, written under the influence of Milton, Moore, and Byron, with the exception of 94–101, lines probably added later under the influence of Shelley. The stanza, 133–150, may have been added in 1827. Part II, 1–39, was probably a poem written under the influence of Milton, with 40–60 added later or changed to suit the poem as a whole. Lines 60–67 are reminiscent of *Paradise Lost*, (Cf. Campbell, 185, Notes). The poem, 68–99, is Byronic. The lyric, 100–155, is probably an earlier lyric rewritten. The next stanza, 156–173, is Miltonic. The passage, 174–213, belongs to the early poem and follows the first lyric in Part I, 82–117, which is the "hymn" referred to. The original poem, which later was expanded into "Al Aaraaf," probably concluded with 213. The stanza, 214–244, is in imitation of both Milton and Shelley; the next, 245–260, probably belongs to the original poem; and the last four lines could have been written either for the original poem or for "Al Aaraaf."

8. "Lalla Rookh" and "Loves of the Angels," by Moore, are undoubtedly two chief sources for Poe's early poems.

9. *Prometheus Unbound*, I, 25, 30, 635.

10. See also I, 669; II, i, 26; II, v, 86; II, i, 33; III, iii, 81; IV, 51, 366.

11. Ianthe is the name of the heroine in *Queen Mab* and also the name given to Shelley's daughter.

12. See "Letter to B—."

13. Poe could not have recognized the references to science that Grabo calls attention to in that he did not have the modern knowledge of science on which to base his assumptions or the information regarding Shelley's reading.

14. Killis Campbell also calls attention to this resemblance, (*Poems of Poe*, 197–198).

15. Cf. Killis Campbell, 63–69, footnotes, for the 1831 text of "The Sleeper," entitled "Irene."

16. See note 3, on Galignani edition.

17. Cf. Keat's "Isabella: or the Pot of Basil;" Coleridge's "Christabel" and "The Ancient Mariner."

18. Killis Campbell believes that the resemblance is in the general idea of the destruction of a gloriously beautiful city in a sea, and between lines 12-29 of "The City in the Sea" and the third and fourth sections of the "Euganean Hills." (*Poems of Poe*, 208). This is the first of a series of poems by Poe which are influenced by "Lines Written among the Euganean Hills."

19.   To the deep, to the deep,
                    Down, down!
                .   .   .
        Even to the steps of the remotest throne,
                    Down, down!
              (*Prometheus Unbound*, II, iv, 54–98)

20. Campbell believes that the third line is similar to the opening line of "Lines Written among the Euganean Hills." (*Poems of Poe*, 222).

21. Prometheus Unbound, II, v, 48–71.
22. Poe may have felt that the poem was not good enough to be published, or he may have feared that the indebtedness to Shelley would be recognized. It is possible, however, that he published "Israfel" because it was the more nearly perfect of the two poems.
23. This poem was written for "The Fall of the House of Usher," and it does not seem accidental that the discussion of Roderick Usher's belief in "the sentience of all vegetable things" and the reference to his "abandon" immediately follow the introduction of the ballad. Poe must have had Shelley in mind at this point in the story.
24. See *Alastor*, 621–622; *Prometheus Unbound*, II, i, 16; IV, 313; *Julian and Maddalo*, 506–507; "Lines Written among the Euganean Hills," 147–148; "A Summer Evening Churchyard," 22.
25. Cf. discussion of "Al Aaraaf" in this chapter.
26. Lines 100–114.
27. Killis Campbell states that the next stanza bears the closest parallel to Shelley of any he has found, the resemblance being to *Prometheus Unbound*. (*Poems of Poe*, Intro., xlvii–xlix.)
28. Campbell likewise suggests Shelley's poem as a possible source. (*Poems of Poe*, 257).
29. His discussion of pleasure as the aim of poetry was brobably derived from Coleridge's *Biographia Litteraria*.
30. II, 326–336.
31. III, 41–49.
32. Poe mentions the names of Lamartine, Herder, Körner, Tegner, Keats, Shelley, Coleridge, Tennyson, Lowell, Longfellow, and others.
33. This article was never written. Perhaps Shelley's *Defence of Poetry* supplied the need.
34. *A Defence of Poetry*, paragraph 3. (Italics supplied).
35. In the Preface Shelley declares, "Didactic poetry is my abhorrance, etc."
36. Par. 13.
37. Paragraphs 3 and 6 respectively.
38. Par. 12.
39. "To——," 'One word is too often profaned.'
40. Par. 12.
41. Par. 8.
42. Par. 14.
43. Paragraphs 13, 20, 26, 40–43.
44. *Godey's Lady's Book*, January, 1834, 40–43.
45. *Broadway Journal*, I, 1–2.
46. XV, 292–293, May, 1849.

THE PERIOD OF SENTIMENTALISM

CHAPTER VII

1. It is just possible that Hayne's "A Dream of the South Wind" was suggested by Shelley's "Ode to the West Wind," and that his "Midsummer in the South" was influenced by the "Euganean Hills."
2. *Southern Literary Messenger*, XX, 32, January, 1854.
3. The New York members of the group were R. H. Stoddard, E. C. Stedman, T. B. Aldrich, and Bayard Taylor; the Philadelphia members were G. H. Boker, G. Leland, R. M. Bird, and T. B. Read. All except Bird (1803) were born between 1822 and 1836.

The Periodicals

4. *Southern Literary Messenger,* XV, 292–293, May, 1849.
5. XII, 176–181.
6. XXVIII n.s., 49–54.
7. *American Whig Review,* XIII, 534–544, June, 1851.
8. XXVII, 432.
9. III, 502–505.
10. XIV, 73.
11. XIV, 103.
12. XIV, 392–399.
13. XVI, 185.
14. XVIII, 16–17, May, 1852.
15. *Russell's Magazine,* VI, 469–472, February, 1860.
16. VI–VII, 508–509.
17. IV, 268–270.
18. *The International Monthly Magazine* (III, 16–18) contains a memoir of "Mary Wollstonecraft Shelley," including a sketch of Mary and Shelley. New York, 1851.
19. XLVII, 598, *Graham's,* also contains mentions of Shelley for May, 1856, XLVIII, 432, and for May, 1857.
20. XLII, 542–543.
21. II, 84–86, 1857.
22. XLIX, 219–224.
32. III, 59–66, July, 1860.
24. I, 80–93, January, 1864.
25. XI, 184–204, February, 1863.

The "Imitators"

26. *Southern Literary Messenger,* XI, 31–37, January, 1845.
27. *Life and Letters of Bayard Taylor,* edited by Marie Hansen-Taylor and Horace E. Scudder, I, 129–131.
28. *Poetical Works of Bayard Taylor,* with Preface by Marie Hansen-Taylor, iv.
29. 417–418, 1859.
30. *Life and Letters of Bayard Taylor,* I, 131, op. cit.
31. It seems inconsistent that Taylor should deny acquaintance with the poetry of Shelley after the entry in *Views Afoot,* 1846.
32. *Poetical Works,* Preface, iv, op. cit.
33. Taylor, II, 3–4; III, 2–9; Shelley, II, V, VI.
34. It is divided into four acts in blank verse, interspersed with lyrics. There are Spirits of the Wind, Snow, and Streams, and of Dawn. And there are Echoes. Prometheus is likewise the chief character.
35. "Tennyson," *Critical Essays and Literary Notes,* 1–36.
36. *Recollections, Personal and Literary,* 56, 1903.
37. "Heliotrope" may have been influenced by Shelley's "Sensitive Plant." "The Voice of the Western Wind" was probably inspired by the "Ode to the West Wind." "Summer Wind" and "Amavi" are also somewhat Shelleyan.
38. *Ponkapog Papers,* 88, 1903.
39. *Ibid.,* 91.
40.   Good-night? ah! no; the hour is ill
    Which severs those it should unite;
    Let us remain together still,
    Then it will be *good* night.

41.   Arethusa arose
              From her couch of snows
          In the Acroceraunian mountains,—
            From cloud and from crag,
              With many a jag,
      Shepherding her bright fountains, . . .

42. Sections one and four.
43. Edward Sculley Bradley, *George Henry Boker, Poet and Patriot,* 18, 1927.
44. Cf. *The Sergeant and Other Poems,* by Forceythe Willson, 1867.

THE REACTION

CHAPTER VIII

Walt Whitman

1. F. L. Pattee, *A History of American Literature since 1870,* 83.
2. Bryant and the New England Poets.
3. *The Complete Writings of Walt Whitman,* VII, 82. Knickerbocker Press, 1902.
4. *Ibid.,* IX, 84.
5. *Whitman,* 254–255, 1937.
6. *A Life of Walt Whitman,* 59, 1905.
7. *A Life of Whitman,* 107, 1905.
8. *Whitman,* 144–145, 1937.
9. Shelley, in his *Defence of Poetry,* states: "The distinction between poetry and prose is a vulgar error." (Par. 8).
10. E. Holloway, Introduction to *I Sit and Look Out.*
11. *A Life of Walt Whitman,* 107–108, 1905.
12. *Walt Whitman, a Study,* 25–27, 1895.
13. *Prometheus Unbound,* II, v, 48–71.
14. Cf. "The Wound Dresser," *Leaves of Grass.*
15. Cf. Shelley's "The Sensitive Plant" and *Prometheus Unbound.*
16. For Shelley's belief in the millennium, see *Prometheus Unbound.*
17. Cf. Edgar Lee Masters, *Whitman,* 219, 1937.
18. Denis Saurat, *Literature and the Occult Tradition,* 49, 1930.
19. In October, 1890, Ingersoll delivered a benefit lecture for Whitman. He also delivered the "oration" at Whitman's funeral. Masters, *Whitman,* 212, 295, 1937.
20. R. G. Ingersoll, "Orthodoxy," *Works,* II, 416.
21. "Why I Am an Agnistic," *Works,* IV, 39.
22. "Interviews," *Works,* VIII, 609.
23. Cf. "Miscellaney;" "Fragments," XII, 354.

Sidney Lanier

24. Edwin Mims, *Sidney Lanier,* 34, 1905.
25. *American Writers on American Literature,* 328, 1934.
26. *Sidney Lanier, a Biographical and Critical Study,* 57, 1933.
27. *Sidney Lanier,* 318, 1905.
28. *The English Novel,* 99.
29. *Sidney Lanier,* 58, 1933.
30. *Nature in American Literature,* 232, 1923.
31. *American Literature since 1870,* 285, 288.
32. *Select Poems of Sidney Lanier,* Introduction, lv, 1906.

33. *Sidney Lanier,* 120, 1933.
34. Sidney Lanier, *The English Novel,* 102–106.
35. E. J. Trelawny, *Recollections of the Last Days of Shelley and Byron,* 14, London, 1906.

Henry Timrod

36. George Armstrong Wauchope, in his *Henry Timrod: Man and Poet,* states that "A Vision of Poesy" has a theme similar to that of Shelley's *Alastor.* Cf. 22.
37. Cf. *Poems of Henry Timrod,* memorial edition, 74–100, 1901.

Some Later Shelleyans

38. S. Foster Damon, *Amy Lowell: a Chronicle,* 113.
39. Clara Barrus, *Life and Letters of John Burroughs,* I, 157–158.
40. *Louise Imogen Guiney,* edited by Grace Guiney, 54.
41. *Letters of Richard Watson Gilder,* edited by Rosamond Gilder, 434; 430–431.
42. Richard Hovey, *Seaward: an Elegy,* Boston, 1893.
43. Harriet Monroe, *A Poet's Life: Seventy Years in a Changing World.* Pages 82, 78, and 85, respectively.
44. *Steeplejack,* 196.
45. *Ibid.,* 277–280.
46. *Promenades of an Impressionist,* 261–262.
47. Jennie Masters Tabb, *Father Tabb: His Life and Work,* 36–37, 1921.
48. *Ibid.*
49. XVIII, 72–73, August 6, 1892; 82–83, August 13, 1892; XIX, 93–94, February 18, 1893.

ESTABLISHING SHELLEY'S REPUTATION

CHAPTER IX

Lady Shelley and the Shelley Scholars

1. CXIII, 337–343, 1858.
2. Cf. *Living Age,* LXIII, 43–47, 1859.
3. CX, 289–328, October, 1861.
4. *Leigh Hunt's Letter on Hogg's Life of Shelley,* privately printed by L. A. Brewer, Cedar Rapids, Iowa, 1927.
5. LVII, 643–659.
6. LXI, 92–109.
7. E. Dowden, R. Garnett, and W. M. Rossetti, *Letters about Shelley,* 77–80; 113–114; 117; 119; 146–147.
8. *Shelley Memorials: From Authentic Sources,* edited by Lady Shelley.

The Periodicals

9. The Shelley Society was organized in England, December 7, 1885, but it soon had members in America as well. It had for its object, according to the Rules, "the study, discussion, and illustration of the Works and Personality of Shelley, the publication of papers on them, and of Shelleyana, of facsimiles of his first editions and his MSS., and of a concordance-lexicon of his Poetical Works, the performance of his plays, and generally the extension of the study of the Poet."

10. *The Critic*, IV n.s., 97–98, August 29, 1885.
11. *Ibid.*, VII n.s., February 12, 1887.
12. *The Century Magazine*, XLVIII, 905–909, September, 1905.
13. XV, 292–293.
14. XXI, 15.
15. XLVIII, 113–116.
16. VI, 309.
17. VII, 214, April 30, 1887.
18. XVIII, 19–20.
19. XLIV, 146–147.
20. CLIX, 108, 240. 353, July, August, September, respectively, 1894.
21. LIX, 559–567, April, 1887.
22. X, 52.
23. XXVII, 401–412, December 26, 1878.
24. IV,22–23, July 18, 1885, and III, 310–311, June 27, 1885.
25. IX n.s., 151.
26. XIX, 70.
27. XXVI, n.s., 212.
28. XXVII, 244, August 8, 1896.
29. LXIII, 36, July 9, 1896.
30. XI, 314.
31. XVII, 49.
32. XIV, 47, 103–104.
33. XXVII, 100–101, August 2, 1883.
34. XVI, 349, December 19, 1891.
35. XII, 364, February, 1892.
36. XXIV, 75–76, March 11, 1893.
37. XIX, 197, April 1, 1893.
38. XIV, 150–151, March 1, 1893.
39. XVII, 353.
40. XXIV, 69–70.
41. LVI, 68–70, January 26, 1893; 87–88, February 2, 1893.
42. XIV, 244–246, April 16, 1893.
43. III, 221–237.
44. LIX, 574–583, July–August, 1894.
45. XIV, 421–454, October, 1880.
46. IV, 289–305, November, 1887.
47. R. A. Holland, "The Soul of Shelley," *The Western,* 129–161, March, 1876.
48. VIII, 331–339, November, 1872.
49. XVI n.s., 138–146, February, 1891.
50. LXX, 106, 261, 391, July, August, September, 1892.
51. I, 209–212.
52. I, 592, 1889.
53. II, 131, 1890.
54. III, 155, 1891.
55. VII, 18–28, 1895.
56. VIII, 226–227, 1896.
57. II, 78–81, 1890.
58. II, 222–235, 1890.
59. IV, 527.
60. IV, 285.
61. *Poet-Lore*, IV, 315–318, 1892.
62. *Ibid.*, IV, 135–144, 1892.

63. Browning's "Parleying with Bernard de Mandeville" closes with the Promethean myth.
64. IV, 289–304, 397–408, 1892, by Kineton Parkes.
65. V, 578.
66. VII, 483.
67. IX, 585–606.
68. *Poet-Lore*, VIII, 405–420, 1896.
69. *Ibid.*, VIII, 332–342, 1896.
70. *The Sewanee Review*, VII, 335–341, July, 1899.
71. *Contemporary Review*, 728–741, May, 1900.
72. *The Magazine of Art*, XXV, 492–495.

THE CLOSE OF THE CENTURY

CHAPTER X

The Essayists

1. George H. Calvert, *Coleridge, Shelley, and Goethe*, 129–258, 1880.
2. George H. Calvert, *Brief Essays and Brevities*, 129–139, 1874.
3. *The Authority of Criticism*, 137–196.
4. *Ibid.*, 205–232.
5. *The French Revolution and the English Poets*, 50–77, 1899.
6. *Atlantic Essays*, 37, 1881.
7. *Henry Wadsworth Longfellow*, 9, 1902.
8. *The New World and the New Book*, 190–191, 1892.
9. *Part of a Man's Life*, 220–221, 1906.

George Edward Woodberry

10. "Woodberry," *Friends of Man*, 43–52, 1933.
11. Francis W. Halsey, "George E. Woodberry in East Seventeenth Street, New York." In *American Authors and Their Homes*, 223–234.
12. It is impossible to determine from the publication of these essays just when they were written.
13. *Studies in Letters and Life*, 124–166.
14. Disillusionment is a part of life, particularly for idealists.
15. *Literary Essays*, 107–127.
16. *Makers of Literature*, 51–62.
17. *The Torch*, 57–109.
18. *Ibid.*, 201.
19. *Studies of a Litterateur*, 281–296.
20. *Heart of Man*, 51–139.
21. *The Torch*, 3–24.
22. *Appreciation of Literature*, 21–38.

BIBLIOGRAPHY
BOOKS
I. Shelley
A. EDITIONS OF WORKS

FOSTER, G. G., *The Poetical Works of Percy Bysshe Shelley*, with Preface. First American edition. Philadelphia, 1845; New York, 1850; Boston, 1852, 1857.

GALIGNANI, A. AND W., Publishers, *The Poetical Works of Coleridge, Shelley, and Keats*, complete in one volume, with "Memoir of Percy Bysshe Shelley," by Mary W. Shelley, v–xi, London, June 1st, 1824, No. 18 Rue Vivienne, Paris, 1829.

GARNETT, RICHARD, *Relics of Shelley*, London, 1862.

HUTCHINSON, THOMAS, *The Complete Poetical Works of Percy Bysshe Shelley*, with Introduction and Notes by Benjamin Kurtz, New York, 1933.

INGPEN, ROGER, *The Letters of Percy Bysshe Shelley*, London, 1914, 2 vols.

INGPEN, ROGER, AND PECK, WALTER E., *The Complete Works of Percy Bysshe Shelley*. Julian Edition, London, 1926–1930, 10 vols.

KOSZUL, ANDRÉ M., *Shelley's Prose in the Bodleian Manuscript*, London, 1910.

ROLLESTON, THOMAS W., *A Philosophical View of Reform*, Oxford University Press, 1920.

SHELLEY, JANE (LADY), *Shelley Memorials: From Authentic Sources*. (Third edition), London, 1875.

SHELLEY, MARY W., *Essays, Letters from Abroad, Translations and Fragments*, by Percy Bysshe Shelley, Lea & Blanchard, Philadelphia, 1840.

WOODBERRY, GEORGE E., *The Complete Poetical Works of Percy Bysshe Shelley*, Cambridge Edition, New York, 1901.

B. REFERENCES ON SHELLEY
2. BIOGRAPHIES

DOWDEN, EDWARD, *The Life of Percy Bysshe Shelley*, London, 1886, 2 vols.

HOGG, THOMAS JEFFERSON, *The Life of Percy Bysshe Shelley*, edited by Edward Dowden, Lindon and New York, 1906.

INGPEN, ROGER, *Shelley in England*, London, 1917.

MEDWIN, THOMAS, *The Life of Percy Bysshe Shelley*, edited by H. Buxton Forman, Oxford University Press, 1914.

PECK, WALTER E., *Shelley:His Life and Work,* New York, 1927, 2 vols.

TRELAWNY, EDWARD JOHN, *Records of Shelley, Byron, and the Author,* London, 1878.

B. CRITICAL WORKS

BARNARD, ELLSWORTH, *Shelley's Religion*, University of Minnesota Press, 1937.

BUCK, PHILO M., JR., *Goethe and Shelley,* University of Wisconsin Studies in Language and Literature, No. 34, 1932.

CALVERT, GEORGE, "Shelley." In *Brief Essays and Brevities*, Boston, 1874.

CALVERT, GEORGE, "Shelley." In *Coleridge, Shelley, and Goethe*, 129–255, Biographic and Aesthetic Studies, Boston, 1888.

DOWDEN, E., GARNETT, R., AND ROSSETTI, W. M., *Letters about Shelley*, edited with an introduction by R. S. Garnett, London and New York, 1917.

FAIRCHILD, HOXIE NEALE, "Shelley and Transcendentalism." In *The Romantic Quest*, 373–401, Columbia University Press, 1931.

211

FULLER, MARGARET (OSSOLI), Shelley's Poems." In *Life Without and Life Within*, 149–152, edited by Arthur B. Fuller, Boston, 1859.

FULLER, MARGARET (OSSOLI), "Modern British Poets." In *Papers on Literature and Art*, 58–99, London, 1846.

GODWIN, PARKE, "Shelley." In *Out of the Past*, 111–145, New York, 1870.

GOSSE, EDMUND, "Shelley in 1892." In *Questions at Issue*, 201–215, New York, 1893.

GRABO, CARL, *A Newton among Poets: Shelley's Use of Science in "Prometheus Unbound,"* Chapel Hill, 1930.

GRABO, CARL, *Prometheus Unbound: An Interpretation*, Chapel Hill, 1935.

GRABO, CARL, *The Magic Plant: The Growth of Shelley's Thought*, Chapel Hill, 1936.

GRANNISS, RUTH, *A Descriptive Catalogue of the First Editions in Book Form of the Writings of Percy Bysshe Shelley*, The Grolier Club, New York, 1923.

HANCOCK, ALBERT E., "Shelley." In *The French Revolution and the English Poets: A Study in Historical Criticism*, 50–57, New York, 1899.

HUNT, LEIGH, "Mr. Shelley, with a Criticism on His Genius." In *Lord Byron and Some of His Contemporaries*, Philadelphia, 1828.

HUNT, LEIGH, *Letter on Hogg's Life of Shelley with Other Papers*, Preface by Walter E. Peck. Privately printed, Cedar Rapids, Iowa, August, 1927, by Luther A. Brewer (100 copies).

KURTZ, BENJAMIN, *The Pursuit of Death; a Study of Shelley's Poetry*, Oxford University Press, 1933.

LIPTZIN, SOLOMON, *Shelley in Germany*, Columbia University Press, 1924.

PEACOCK, THOMAS LOVE, *Memoirs of Percy Bysshe Shelley*, edited by F. B. Brett-Smith, London, 1909.

PEYRE, HENRI, *Shelley et la France; lyrisme anglais et lyrisme français au XIX siècle*, Paris, 1935.

SALT, HENRY S., *Percy Bysshe Shelley: Poet and Pioneer*, New York and London, 1896.

Shelley Society Papers, Part I, First series, no. 1, London, 1888–1891.

SOLVE, M. T., "Shelley and the Novels of Charles Brockden Brown." In *The Fred Newton Scott Anniversay Papers*, 141–156, Chicago, 1929.

TRENT, WILLIAM P., "Apropos of Shelley." In *The Authority of Criticism and Other Essays*, 37–96, New York, 1899.

WEAVER, BENNETT, *Toward the Understanding of Shelley*, University of Michigan Publications, IX, Ann Arbor, 1932.

WHITE, N. I., *The Unextinguished Hearth: Shelley and His Contemporary Critics*, Duke University Press, 1938.

WOODBERRY, GEORGE E., "Remarks on Shelley." In *Studies in Letters and Life*, 124–166, New York, 1890.

WOODBERRY, GEORGE E., "Shelley's Work." In *Literary Essays*, 107–129, New York, 1892.

WOODBERRY, GEORGE E. "Shelley." In *The Torch*, 193–217, New York, 1905.

WOODBERRY, GEORGE E., "Shelley's Poetry." In *Makers of Literature*, 51–62, New York, 1900.

WOODBERRY, GEORGE E., "Shelley's Poetry;" "Shelley's *Cenci*." In *Studies of a Litterateur*, 261–280; 281–296, New York, 1921.

II. *GENERAL REFERENCES*

(American)

A. LITERATURE, LIFE, ETC.

BLANKENSHIP, RUSSELL, *American Literature as an Expression of the National Mind*, New York, 1931.

BOYNTON, PERCY H., *Literature and American Life*, New York, 1936.

CAIRNS, WILLIAM B., *A History of American Literature*, New York, 1912..

Cambridge History of American Literature, edited by W. P. Trent, John Erskine, Stuart P. Sherman, and Carl van Doren, New York, 1817–1921, 4 vols.

FOERSTER, NORMAN, *Nature in American Literature*, New York, 1923.

FROTHINGHAM, OCTAVIUS BROOKS, *Transcendentalism in New England*, New York, 1886.

FULTON, MAURICE GARLAND, *Southern Life in Southern Literature*, New York, 1917.

GODDARD, HAROLD C., *Studies in New England Transcendentalism*, New York, 1908.

GOHDES, C. L. F., *The Periodicals of American Transcendentalism*, Duke Uni. Press, 1931.

GREENE, W. B., *Transcendentalism*. Dedicated to R. W. Emerson, 4th edition, 1871.

HOWELLS, WILLIAM DEAN, *Literary Friends and Acquaintances*, New York, 1901.

KREYMBORG, ALFRED, *Our Singing Strength: an Outline of American Poetry*, New York, 1929.

LEISY, E. E., *American Literature; an Interpretative Survey*, New York, 1929.

LONG, O. W., *Literary Pioneers*, Harvard University Press, 1935.

MACY, JOHN, editor, *American Writers on American Literature. Thirty-seven Contemporary Writers*, New York, 1934.

MOTT, FRANK LUTHER, *A History of American Magazines*, 1741–1850, New York 1927.

PARRINGTON, VERNON LOUIS, *The Romantic Revolution in America*, 1800–1860, New York, 1927.

PATTEE, FRED LEWIS, *The First Century of American Literature*, 1770–1870, New York, London, 1935.

PATTEE, FRED LEWIS, *A History of American Literature since 1870*, New York, 1915.

PATTEE, FRED LEWIS, *The New American Literature*, 1890–1930, New York, 1930.

PERRY, BLISS, *The American Mind*, Boston, 1912.

RICHARDSON, CHARLES F., *American Literature. I. The Development of American Thought. II. American Poetry and Fiction.* New York, 1899, 2 vols.

Reinterpretation of American Literature, edited by Norman Foerster, New York, 1928.

RUSK, RALPH LESLIE, *The Literature of the Middle Western Frontier*, Columbia University Press, 1925. 2 vols.

Southern Literature. Library of, edited by E. A. Alderman, Joel Chandler Harris. and Charles W. Kent, Atlanta, 1907.

VAN WYCK BROOKS, *The Flowering of New England*, 1815–1865, New York, 1937.

WENDELL, BARRETT. *A Literary History of America*, New York, 1901.

WHIPPLE, THOMAS KING, *Spokesman. Modern Writers and American Life*, New York. 1928.

B. BIOGRAPHY AND LETTERS

ADAMS, CHARLES FRANCIS, *Richard Henry Dana, a Biography*, New York, 1891.

ALLEN. ALEXANDER VIETS GRISWOLD, *Life and Letters of Phillips Brooks*, New York, 1904. 2 vols.

BAILEY, JOHN CANN, *Walt Whitman*, New York. 1926.

BEATTY. R. C., *Bayard Taylor, Laureate of the Gilded Age*, University of Oklahoma Press, 1936.

BEERS, HENRY A., *Nathaniel Parker Willis*. New York, 1885.

BINNS. HENRY BRYAN, *A Life of Walt Whitman*, London, 1905.

BRADLEY, EDWARD SCULLEY, *George Henry Boker, Poet and Patriot*, University of Pennsylvania Press, 1927.

BROOKS, CHARLES T., *William Ellery Channing, A Centennial Memory,* Boston, 1880.

CAPPON, JAMES, *Bliss Carman and the Literary Currents and Influences of His Time,* New York and Montreal, 1939.

Channing, William Ellery, with Extracts from His Correspondence and Manuscripts, London, 1850, 2 vols.

CHANNING, WILLIAM HENRY, *The Life of William Ellery Channing,* Boston, 1890.

CLARKE, JAMES FREEMAN, *Autobiography, Diary, and Correspondence,* edited by Edward Everett Hale, Boston and New York, 1891.

COMMAGER, HENRY STEELE, *Theodore Parker,* Boston, 1936.

CURTIS, GEORGE WILLIAM, *Early Letters to John S. Dwight,* edited by George Willis Cooke, New York, 1898.

DAMON, S. FOSTER, *Thomas Holly Chivers,* Friend of Poe, New York, 1930.

DAMON, S. FOSTER, *Amy Lowell: A Chronicle,* New York, 1935.

FIRKINS, OSCAR W., *Ralph Waldo Emerson,* Boston, 1915.

FROTHINGHAM, OCTAVIUS BROOKS, *Theodore Parker: A Biography,* New York, 1886.

FULLER, MARGARET, (OSSOLI), *Memoirs* edited by R. W. Emerson, W. H. Channing, and J. F. Clarke, Boston, 1857, 2 vols.

FULLER, MARGARET, (OSSOLI), *Love-Letters,* Introduction by Julia Ward Howe, New York, 1903.

FULLER, MARGARET, (OSSOLI), *At Home and Abroad,* edited by Arthur B. Fuller, Boston, 1856.

FURNESS, HORACE HOWARD, *Letters* edited by H. H. Furness Jayne, New York, 1922.

GILDER, RICHARD WATSON, *Letters* edited by Rosamond Gilder, Boston and New York, 1916.

GOODRICH, SAMUEL G., *Recollections of a Lifetime,* New York, 1856, 2 vols.

GREENE, WM. B., *Remarks on the Science of History; followed by an a Priori Autobiography,* Boston, 1849.

GREENSLET, FERRIS, *James Russell Lowell, His Life and Work,* Boston and New York, 1905.

GRISWOLD, RUFUS W., *Passages from the Correspondence and Other Papers* edited by W. M. Griswold, Cambridge, 1898.

Guiney, Louise Imogen, edited by Grace Guiney, with a Preface by Agnes Repplier, New York, 1926, 2 vols.

HALSEY, F. W., "G. E. Woodberry." In *American Authors and Their Homes,* New York, 1901.

HARRISON, JAMES A., *Life and Letters of Edgar Allan Poe,* New York, 2 vols.

HAWTHORNE, JULIAN, *Nathaniel Hawthorne and His Wife,* Boston, 1884, 2 vols.

HAZARD, CAROLINE, *Memoirs of the Reverend Lewis Diman,* New York, 1887.

HIGGINSON, THOMAS WENTWORTH, "Ralph Waldo Emerson;" "Lanier." In *Contemporaries,* Boston, 1899.

HIGGINSON, THOMAS WENTWORTH, *Henry Wadsworth Longfellow,* Boston, 1902.

HIGGINSON, THOMAS WENTWORTH, *Margaret Fuller Ossoli,* Boston, 1886.

HOLMES, OLIVER WENDELL, *Ralph Waldo Emerson,* Boston, 1885.

HOWE, M. A. DEWOLFE, *The Life and Letters of George Bancroft,* New York, 1903, 2 vols.

JAMES, HENRY, *William Wetmore Story and His Friends,* from Letters, Diaries, and Recollections, Boston, 1903, 2 vols.

KENNEDY, WILLIAM SLOANE, *Reminiscences of Walt Whitman,* London, 1896.

LATHROP, ROSE HAWTHORNE, *Memories of Hawthorne,* Boston, 1897.

LELAND, CHARLES GODFREY, *Memoirs,* New York, 1893.

Lieber, Francis, The Life and Letters of, edited by Thomas Sergeant Perry, Boston, 1882.

LONGFELLOW, SAMUEL, *Life of Henry Wadsworth Longfellow*, Boston, 1886 and 1887, 3 vols.
LOWELL, JAMES RUSSELL, *New Letters* edited by M. A. DeWolfe Howe, New York, 1932.
LOWELL, JAMES RUSSELL, *Letters* edited by Charles Eliot Norton, New York, 1894, 2 vols.
MABBOTT, THOMAS C., AND PLEADWELL, F. L., *Edward Coote Pinkney*, New York, 1926.
MASTERS, EDGAR LEE, *Whitman*, New York, 1937.
MIMS, EDWIN, *Sidney Lanier*, Boston, 1905.
MONROE, HARRIETT, *A Poet's Life: Seventy Years in a Changing World*, New York, 1938.
MORDELL, ALBERT, *John Greenleaf Whittier, Quaker Militant*, Boston, 1933.
MOTLEY, JOHN LOTHROP, *Correspondence* edited by George William Curtis, New York, 1902, 2 vols.
NORTON, CHARLES ELIOT, *Letters* with a comment by his daughter, Sara Norton, and M. A. DeWolfe Howe, Boston, 1913, 2 vols.
PEABODY, ELIZABETH PALMER, *Reminiscences of Reverend William Ellery Channing*, Boston, 1880.
PERRY, BLISS, *Walt Whitman: His Life and Work*, Boston, 1906.
PERRY, CHARLES M., *Henry Philip Tappan, Philosopher and University President*, Ann Arbor, 1933.
SANBORN, FRANK B., *Recollections of Seventy Years*, Boston, 1909, 2 vols.
SCOTT, LEONORA CRANCH, *The Life and Letters of Christopher Cranch*, Boston and New York, 1917.
SCUDDER, HORACE E., *James Russell Lowell, a Biography*, Boston, 1901, 2 vols.
SHEPARD, ODELL, *Bliss Carman*, Toronto, 1923.
SHEPARD, ODELL, *Pedlar's Progress: The Life of Bronson Alcott*, Boston, 1937.
SHEPARD, ODELL, editor, *The Journals of Bronson Alcott*, Boston, 1938.
SMYTH, ALBERT, *Bayard Taylor*, Boston and New York, 1896.
STARKE, AUBREY HARRISON, *Sidney Lanier: A Biographical and Critical Study*. Chapel Hill, 1933.
STEARNS, FRANK P., *The Life and Genius of Nathaniel Hawthorne*, Boston, 1906.
STEDMAN, LAURA GOULD AND GEORGE M., M. D., *Life and Letters of Edmund Clarence Stedman*, New York, 1910.
STODDARD, RICHARD HENRY, *Recollections Personal and Literary*, New York, 1903.
STORY, WILLIAM W., *Life of Joseph Story*, Boston, 1851, 2 vols.
TABB, JENNIE MASTERS, *Father Tabb: His Life and Work*. A Memorial by his niece. Introduction by Charles A. Smith, Boston, 1921.
TAYLOR, BAYARD, *Life and Letters* edited by Marie-Hansen Taylor and Horace E. Scudder, Boston, 1850, 2 vols.
THAYER, WILLIAM ROSCOE, *Letters* edited by Charles D. Hazen, New York, 1926.
TIMROD, HENRY, *Poems with Memoir and Portrait*. Memorial Edition, Richmond, 1901.
THWING, CHARLES FRANKLIN, "George E. Woodberry." In *Friends of Men*, New York, 1933.
WAUCHOPE, GEORGE ARMSTRONG, *Henry Timrod: Man and Poet*. A Critical Study, Bulletin of University of South Carolina, no. 41, Part IV, April, 1915.
WOODBERRY, GEORGE E., *Life of Edgar Allan Poe, Personal and Literary*, Boston, 1909, 2 vols.

C. ESSAYS AND CRITICISMS

ALTERTON, MARGARET, *Origins of Poe's Critical Theory*, State University of Iowa Humanistic Studies, II, No. 3, Iowa City, 1925.
BUCK, PHILO M., JR., *The World's Great Age*, New York, 1936.

CALLAWAY, MORGAN, editor, *Select Poems of Sidney Lanier,* with a Preface, New York, 1906.

CAMPBELL, KILLIS, *Poe's Reading.* In University of Texas Studies in English, No. 5, Austin, 1925.

CAMPBELL, KILLIS, editor, *Poetry of Edgar Allan Poe,* Introduction and Notes, New York, 1917.

CHANNING [W.] ELLERY, *Poems of Sixty-five Years,* Selected and edited by Frank B. Sanborn, Philadelphia and Concord, 1902.

CHANNING, W. ELLERY, *Conversations in Rome between an Artist, a Catholic, and a Critic,* Boston, 1847.

CURTIS, GEORGE WILLIAM, *Literary and Social Essays,* New York, 1895.

CURTIS, GEORGE WILLIAM, *Orations and Addresses,* edited by Charles Eliot Norton, New York, 1894, 3 vols.

EMERSON, RALPH WALDO, *Complete Works* edited by Edward Waldo Emerson, Centenary Edition, Boston, 1904, 12 vols.

EMERSON, RALPH WALDO, *Journals,* edited by Edward Waldo Emerson and Waldo Emerson Forbes, Boston, 1909–1914, 10 vols.

FIELDS, MRS. ANNIE ADAMS, *Authors and Friends,* Boston, 1896.

GOODNIGHT, SCOTT H., *German Literature in American Magazines prior to 1846.* Bulletin of the University of Wisconsin, no. 188. Philology and Literature Series, IV, no. 1, Madison, 1907.

GINGERICH, SOLOMON F., *The Conception of Beauty in the Works of Shelley, Keats, and Poe.* Essays and Studies in English and Comparative Literature, University of Michigan, VIII, Ann Arbor, 1932.

GRISWOLD, RUFUS W., *The Poets and Poetry of England in the Nineteenth Century,* 270–272, Carey and Hart, Philadelphia, 1846.

HAWTHORNE, NATHANIEL, "P's Correspondence." In *Mosses from an Old Manse,* II, 181–184, Riverside edition, *Works,* V, Boston, 1903.

HIGGINSON, THOMAS WENTWORTH, *Atlantic Essays,* Boston, 1871.

HIGGINSON, THOMAS WENTWORTH, *Part of a Man's Life,* Boston, 1906.

HIGGINSON, THOMAS WENTWORTH, *The New World and the New Book,* Boston, 1892.

HOLMES, OLIVER WENDELL, *Writings,* Boston, 1858, 14 vols.

HUNEKER, JAMES GIBBONS, *Steeplejack,* New York, 1920.

HUNEKER, JAMES GIBBONS, *Promenades of an Impressionst,* New York, 1920.

HUNEKER, JAMES GIBBONS, *Bedouins,* New York, 1920.

INGERSOLL, ROBERT G., *Works* edited by G. P. Farrell, New York, 1900, 12 vols.

JAMES, HENRY, *The Aspern Papers,* New York, 1928.

JONES, W. ALFRED, *Characters and Criticisms,* New York, 1857, 2 vols.

KINSLEY, WM. W., "Shelley." In *Views on Vexed Questions,* 255–302, Philadelphia, 1881.

LANIER, SIDNEY, *The English Novel, and the Principles of Its Development,* New York, 1883.

LOWELL, JAMES RUSSELL, *Prose Works.* Boston and New York, 1892, 6 vols.

LOWELL, JAMES RUSSELL, *The Function of the Poet and Other Essays,* Collected and edited by Albert Mordell, 1920.

PERCIVAL, JAMES GATES, editor, *Elegant Extracts,* Originally compiled by Vicemus Knox, D.D., Boston, 1842, 6 vols.

PIKE, GENERAL ALBERT, *Poems* with introductory biographical sketch by Mrs. Lilian Pike Roome, daughter, Little Rock, Arkansas, 1900.

POE, EDGAR ALLAN, *The Complete Works* edited by James Harrison, New York, 1902, 17 vols.

SOTHERAN, CHARLES, *Percy Bysshe Shelley as a Philosopher and a Reformer,* New York, 1876.

STEDMAN, EDMUND CLARENCE, *Poets of America,* New York, 1885.

SYMONDS, J. A., *Walt Whitman: A Study,* London, 1893.

TAYLOR, BAYARD, *Views A-foot, or Europe Seen with Knapsack and Staff,* New York, 1859.

TAYLOR, BAYARD, *The Echo Club*, with a Prologue by R. H. Stoddard, 1870.
TAYLOR, BAYARD, "Tennyson." In *Critical Essays and Literary Notes*, 1–36, New York, 1880.
TUCKERMAN, HENRY T., "A Day at Oxford." In *A Month in England*, 141–159, New York, 1854 (Second edition).
TUCKERMAN, HENRY T., *The Italian Sketch Book*, 56–68, 1835.

PERIODICALS

I. General List

(American)

A. BEFORE 1860

Album, 86–87, March 13, 1830.
American Atheneum, IX, 477, September 1, 1821; XII, 480, September 5, 1824.
American Daily Advertiser [Poulson], February 12, 1830, p. 3.
American Literature Magazine, IV, 479–480, February, 1849.
American Monthly Magazine (Boston), I, 646–659, November, 1829; VIII, 275, January, 1835; XII, 63, July, 1838.
American Quarterly Review, XVIII, 1–19, September, 1835; XIX, 257–287, June, 1836; XXI, 187–213, March, 1837.
American Whig Review, II, 33–37, July, 1845; III, 673, June, 1846; V, 534–537, May, 1847; V, 386–396, April, 1847; XII, 176–181, August, 1850; XIII, 534–544, June, 1851; XIV, 392–399, November, 1851.
Arcturus, a Journal of Books and Opinion, II, 251–254, September, 1841.
Atlas, a Select Literary and Historical Journal, I–IV, 376, August 4, 1832.
Belles-Lettres Repository and Monthly Magazine, II, 392, March 1, 1820. (New York, Goodrich & Company).
Biblical Repertory and Princeton Review, XI, 37–101, January, 1839.
Boston Daily Advertiser, XLIII, Monday, August 27, 1838; Friday, September 28, 1838; Friday, October 5, 1838.
Boston Lyceum, I, 179–180, January, 1827.
Boston Quarterly Review, II, 87–113, January, 1839; III, 328–331, July, 1840; IV, 393–436, October, 1841.
Christian Examiner and General Review, XXVII, (3rd series, IX), 146–161, November, 1839.
Corsair, a Gazette of Literature, Art, Dramatic Criticism, Fashion, and Novelty, I, 46–47, March 30, 1839; 72–73, April 6, 1839; 759–760, 783–784, February 8, 1840.
Cosmopolitan Art Journal, a Record of Art, Bigraphy, and General Literature, II, 84–86, March and June, 1858.
Critic: a Weekly Review of Literature, Fine Arts, and the Drama, I, 308, March 14, 1829.
Democratic Review, III, 603–623, December, 1843; XIX, 316–320, October, 1846; XXVII, 432, December, 1850; XXVII n.s., 49–54, January, 1851; XLIX, 219–224, March, 1857.
Dial, The, I, 217–218, October, 1840; I, 291, January, 1841; II, 52–53, July, 1841; III, 99–100, July, 1842.
Genius of the West: a Monthly Magazine of Western Literature, (Cincinnatti), IV, 268–270, September, 1855.
Godey's Lady's Book, II, 278, May, 1831; VIII, 160:161, March, 1834; XII, 84, February, 1836.
Graham's American Monthly Magazine, XXVIII, 96, February, 1846; XXXIV–XXXV, 61, January, 1849; XLII, 542–543, May, 1853; L, 399, May, 1857.
Harbinger, Devoted to Social and Political Progress, II, 75–76, January 10, 1846; III, 249–252, September 26, 1846; IV, 26, December 12, 1846; V, 49–50, July 3, 1847.
Harper's New Monthly Magazine, III, 502–505, September, 1851.

Hesperian, II, 440–447, April, 1839.
International Monthly Magazine of Literature, Science, and Art, III, 16–18, April, 1851.
Ladies' Companion, a Monthly Magazine, Embracing Every Department of Literature, 114, 1841.
Literary Gazette or Journal of Criticism, XVII, 285, 490, May, August, 1821.
Literary Journal and Weekly Register of Science and the Arts, (Providence, Rhode Island), I, 114, 252–253, 409, September 14, 1833, January 11, 1834, May 31, 1834.
Literary and Scientific Repository and Critical Review, (New York), I, 223–243, 270, July, 1820; II, 168, January, 1821.
Massachusetts Quarterly Review, II, 414–428, September, 1849.
Museum, 458–463, December, 1824.
New York Literary Gazette and Phi Beta Kappa Repository, I, 53–54, September, 1825–March, 1826.
New York Mirror, Devoted to Literature and the Fine Arts, XI, 346, May 3, 1834; XVII, 75, August 20, 1839.
New World, a Weekly Journal of Popular Literature, Science, Music, and the Arts, 84, February 5, 1842.
North American Magazine, II, 309–317, May, 1833.
North American Review, VII, 198–211, July, 1818; XXI, 353, October, 1825; XXVIII, 17, January, 1829; XXXVI, 176, January, 1833; XL, 433, April, 1835; LVII, 342–343, October, 1843; LVIII, 27, January, 1844; LIX, 352–383, October, 1844; LX, 67, January, 1845; LXI, 216–217, July, 1845; LXI, 468–497, October, 1845; LXVI, 4581 459, April, 1848.
Philadelphia Monthly Magazine, Devoted to General Literature and the Fine Arts, II, 245–247, July 15, 1828.
Pictorial National Library, a Monthly Miscellaney of Science and Literature, I, 179–180, October, 1848.
Present, The (edited by W. H. Channing), I, 88–93, November 15, 1843.
Russell's Magazine, (edited by Paul H. Hayne), VI, 469–472, February, 1860.
Sartain's Union Magazine, III–IV, 22–25, July, 1848.
Saturday Magazine. Being in Part a Compilation from the British Reviews, Magazines, and Scientific Journals, (Philadelphia), I, 372, August 20, 1821; II, 321, 330–331, April 13, 1822.
Southern Literary Messenger, II 326–336, April, 1836; III, 49, January, 1837; V, 706, October, 1839; VI, 393–396, June, 1840; VI, 470–471, June, 1840; VI, 717–720, November, 1840; VI, 826–828, December, 1840; VII, 28–29, 32, January, 1841; VII, 312, April, 1841; VIII, 194–196, March, 1842; X, 104–106, February, 1844; X, 619–629, October, 1844; XI, 238–242, April, 1845; XI, 468, August, 1845; XII, 737–742, December, 1846; XVI, 185, March, 1850; XVIII, 277–278, May, 1852; XX, 32, January, 1854.
Southern Quarterly Review, (Charleston), II, 814, October, 1842.
Spirit of the Age, II, 15–16, January 5, 1850.
Spirit of the Times, XXVI, 187, May 31, 1856.
Western Messenger, II–III, 474–478, February, 1837; VI–VII, 42–47, November, 1838.
Yale Literary Magazine, V, 183–189, 1839–1840.
Yankee and Boston Literary Gazette. III n.s., 168, December, 1829.
Yankee, The (Portland), May, 1828, 160.

B. 1860–1900

Antiquary, The, III, February, 1881.
Atlantic Monthly, III, 59–66, July, 1860: XI, 184–204, February, 1863; LIX, 559–567, April, 1887; LXX, 106, 261, 321, July, August, September, 1892.
Century Magazine, XVII, 313, December, 1889; XXII n.s., 634–636, August, 1892.

Citizen, The, I, 209–212, November, 1895.
Contemporary Review, LXXVII, 728–741, May, 1900.
Cosmopolitan Magazine, 286–289, October, 1894.
Critic, The, III, 310–311, June, 1885; IV, 22–23, 32–33, July 18, 1885; IV,
   97–98, August 29, 1885; IV, 118, September 5, 1885; V, 104, February
   7, 1886; VI, 292–293, December 11, 1886; VI, 309, December 18, 1886;
   VII, 73, February 12, 1887; IX, 151, March 31, 1888; XII, 306,
   December 21, 1889; XV, 68, February 7, 1891; XVI, 246, April 23,
   1892; XVIII, 72–73, August 6, 1892; XVIII, 82–83, August 13, 1892;
   XX, 29, July 8, 1893; XXII, 249, October 13, 1894; XXVI, 212,
   October 10, 1896.
Dial (Chicago),XII, 364, February, 1892; XIV, 150–151, March 1, 1893;
   XIV, 244–246, April 16, 1893.
Journal of Speculative Philosophy, XIV, 421–454, October, 1880.
Lakeside Monthly, VIII, 331–339, November, 1872.
Literary World, X, 52, February 15, 1879; XI, 296, August 28, 1880; XI,
   314, September 11, 1880; XIV, 47, February 10, 1883; XIV, 103–104,
   April 17, 1883; XVII, 49, February 6, 1886; XVIII, 19–20, January
   27, 1887; XIX, 70, March 5, 1888; XXII, 95, March 14, 1891; XXIII,
   246, July, 1892; XXIV, 75–76, March 11, 1893; XXIV, 69–70, March
   11, 1895; XXVI, 300, September 21, 1895.
Magazine of Art, XXV, 492–495, 1900.
Methodist Review, LIV, 574–583, July–August, 1894.
Nation, The, XXVII, 401–412, December 26, 1878; XXVIII, 30–31, January
   9, 1879; XXXVII, 100–101, August 2, 1883; XLIV, 146–147, February
   17, 1887; XLVIII, 113–116, February 9, 1889; LVI, 68–70, January
   26, 1893; LVI, 87–88, February 2, 1893; LXIII, 36, July 9, 1896.
New Englander and Yale Review, XVI n.s., 138–146, February, 1891.
New Princeton Review, IV, 289–305, November, 1887.
North American Review, CLIX, 108, 240, 353, July, August, September,
   1894.
Poet-Lore, I, 592, 1890; II, 107, 131, 225–235, 1891; III, 155, 1892; IV, 135–
   144, 289–304, 315–318, 397–408, 527, 1892; V, 578, 1893; VII, 483, 1895;
   VIII, 332–342, 406–420, 1896; IX, 585–606, 1897.
Sewanee Review, VII, 335–341, July, 1899.
Universalist Quarterly and General Review, I, 80–93, January, 1864.
Western, a Journal of Literature, Education, and Art, (St. Louis), II,
   129–161, March, 1876.

C. SINCE 1900

BEACH, JOSEPH WARREN, "Latter-Day Critics of Shelley," *Yale Review,*
   XI n.s., 718–731, April, 1921.
CAIRNS, W. B., "Some Notes on Poe's 'Al Aaraaf'," *Modern Philology,*
   XIII, 33–44, May, 1915.
COBB, PALMER, "Influence of E. T. A. Hoffmann in the Tales of Edgar Allan
   Poe," *Studies in Philology,* III, 1–104, 1908.
MARSH, GEORGE W., "The Early Reviews of Shelley," *Modern Philology,*
   XXVII, 73–95, August, 1929.
SICKELS, ELEANOR, "Shelley and Charles Brockden Brown," *Publications
   of the Modern Language Association,* XLV, 1116–1128, September,
   1930.
STROUT, ALAN L., "Maga, Champion of Shelley," *Studies in Philology,*
   XXIX, 95–119, January, 1932.
WOODBERRY, GEORGE E., "The Poe-Chivers Papers," *Century,* LXV, 435–
   447, 545–558, January, February, 1903.

II. Selected List

(Before 1900)

(Anonymous), "The Shelley Papers," *American Quarterly Review*, XIX, 257–287, June, 1836.

(Anonymous), "Death Verses, or a stroll through the valley of the shadow of death with Tennyson, in company with Shelley, Milton, Blair, Swift, Coleridge, Moore, and Others," *American Whig Review*, XIII, 534–544, June, 1851.

(Anonymous), "Some Remarks on Shelley's Life;" a review of Dowden's *Life of Shelley*, *Atlantic Monthly*, LIX, 559–567, April, 1887.

(Anonymous). "Poetical Works of Percy Bysshe Shelley, " *Boston Quarterly Review*, IV, 393–436, October, 1841.

(Anonymous), "Shelley and Tennyson" *Democratic Review*, XXVII n.s., 49–54, January, 1854.

(Anonymous), a review of the *Poetical Works of Percy Bysshe Shelley*, edited by G. G. Foster, *Harbinger*, 74–75, January 3, 1846.

(Anonymous), "Criticism. Percy Bysshe Shelley," *New York Literary Gazette and Phi Beta Kappa Repository*, I, 53–54, September, 1825–March, 1826.

(Anonymous), "Shelley," *The Lakeside Monthly*, VIII, 331–339, November, 1872.

(Anonymous), "Shelley," *Southern Literary Messenger*, XII, 737–742, December, 1846.

(Anonymous), "Shelley," *Yale Literary Magazine*, V, 183–189, 1839–1840.

ALGER, C. W., "In Memoriam, Shelley," *Poet-Lore*, IV, 315–318, 1892.

ANDERSON, MELVILLE, "The Centenary Edition of Shelley," *Dial*, XIV, 244–246, April 16, 1893.

AXSON, STOCKTON, "Shelley's 'The Triumph of Life.' " *The Citizen*, I, 209–212, November, 1895.

BARRETT, JOSEPH HARTWELL, "Character of Shelley," *American Whig Review*, V, 534–547, May, 1847.

BOWEN, FRANCIS, "The Poets and Poetry of Europe, by Henry Wadsworth Longfellow," *North American Review*, LXI, 199–231, July, 1845.

BOWEN, GEORGE SPENCER, "The Philosophical Element in Shelley," *Journal of Speculative Philosophy*, XIV, 421–454, October, 1880.

CHIVERS, THOMAS HOLLY, "Shelley," An extract from a lecture on the "Genius of Shelley." *Southern Literary Messenger*, X, 104–106, February, 1844.

CLARKE, HELEN A., "A Sketch of the Promethean Myth in Poetry," *Poet-Lore*, IV, 135–144, 1892.

CLARKE, JAMES FREEMAN, A letter in reply to Andrews Norton, *Boston Daily Advertiser*, September 28, 1838.

CLARKE, JAMES FREEMAN, "The New School in Literature and Religion," *Western Messenger*, November, 1838, VI–VII, 42–47.

CURRY, OTWAY, "Percy Bysshe Shelley," *The Hesperian*, II, 440–447, April, 1839.

CURTIS, G. W., "Southern Italy, "*Sartain's Union Magazine*, III–IV, 22–26, July, 1848.

"D. L.," "Shelley and Pollok," *Western Messenger*, II and III, 474–478, February, 1837.

DOWE, W., "More Words about Shelley," *Atlantic Monthly*, III, 59–66, July, 1860.

"EGERIA," "Character and Writing of Shelley," *Literary Journal and Weekly Register of Science and the Arts*, I, 252–253, January 11, 1834. (Providence, R. I.).

GODWIN, PARKE, "Percy Bysshe Shelley," *Democratic Review*, III n.s., 602–623, December, 1843. (Also published in *Out of the Past*, 111–145, by Parke Godwin).

GULLIVER, JULIA H., "Shelley—the Poet," *New Englander and Yale Review*, XIV n.s., 138–146, February, 1890.

HARRISON, JAMES A., "Two Views of Shelley;" "A Few Words about Shelley," *The Critic*, IV, 97–98, August 29, 1885; VII, 73, February, 1890.

HOLLAND, R. A., "The Soul of Shelley," *The Western, a Journal of Literature, Education, and Art*, II, 129–161, March, 1876.

HUNT, THORNTON, "Shelley. By One Who Knew Him," *Atlantic Monthly*, XI, 184–204, February, 1863.

MACKIE, JOHN M., "Shelley," *The Dial*, I, 470–493, April, 1841.

MALONE, JOHN, "A Search for Shelley's American Ancestor," *Century Magazine*, XXII n.s., 634–636, August, 1892.

NORTON, ANDREWS, "Shelley and the *Western Messenger*," *Boston Daily Advertiser*, October 5, 1838.

PARKES, KINETON, "Shelley's Faith: I. Its Development and Relativity; II. Its Prophecy." *Poet-Lore*, IV, 289–304, 397–408, 1892.

PEABODY, WILLIAM BROWNE OLIVER, "The Decline of Poetry," *North American Review*, XXVIII, 1–18, January, 1829.

PLATT, ISAAC HULL, "Shelley and Whitman: A Comparison and a Contrast," *Poet-Lore*, VIII, 332–343, 1896.

"P. P.," "Percy Bysshe Shelley," *Philadelphia Monthly Magazine*, II, 245–247, July, 1828.

REED, P. FISHE, "Principles of Poetry—No. 111," *The Genius of the West*, 268–270, September, 1855.

SCUDDER, VIDA D., "The *Prometheus Unbound* of Shelley." In three parts. I. The Drama and the Time. II. The Myth of the Drama. III. The Drama as a Work of Art. *Atlantic Monthly*, LXX, 106, 261, 391, July, August, September, 1892.

SMITH, MRS. SEBA, "Shelley," *Southern Literary Messenger*, VI, 717–720, November, 1840.

TUCKERMAN, HENRY T., "Some Remarks on Shelley," *Southern Literary Messenger*, VI, 393–396, June, 1840.

TUCKERMAN, HENRY T., "Shelley," *Southern Literary Messenger*, VII, 28–29, January, 1841.

TWAIN, MARK, "In Defense of Harriet Shelley," *North American Review*, CLIX, 108, 240, 353, July, August, September, 1894.

WARNER, CHARLES DUDLEY, "Shelley," *The New Princeton Review*, IV, 289–305, November, 1887.

WHIPPLE, EDWIN P., "The Complete Poetical Works of William Wordsworth," *North American Review*, LIX, 352–383.

WHIPPLE, EDWIN P., "The British Critics," *North American Review*, LXI, 468–497, October, 1845.

WHIPPLE, EDWIN P., "The Poets and Poetry of England," *American Whig Review*, II, 30–58, July, 1845.

WHITTIER, JOHN GREENLEAF, "Infidelity—No. II," *Essex Gazette*, (Haverhill, Mass.), February 6, 1830.

WHITTIER, JOHN GREENLEAF, "Percy B. Shelley," *Essex Gazette*, February 27, 1830.

WILSON, ALICE, "Shelley and Verlaine," *Poet-Lore*, VIII, 406–420, 1896.

WOODBERRY, GEORGE E., "Shelley's Work," *Century Magazine*, XLIV, 622–629, August, 1892.

INDEX

223